OSTAR

The full story of The Observer single-handed transatlantic
and the two-handed round Britain races

What if some little paine the passage have,
That makes fraile flesh to feare the bitter wave?
Is not short paine well borne, that brings long ease,
And layes the soul to sleep in quiet grave?
Sleep after toyle, port after stormie seas,
Ease after warre, death after life does greatly
please.

EDMUND SPENCER (1552?-1599)

OSTAR

The full story of The Observer single-handed transatlantic and the two-handed round Britain races

Lloyd Foster

Foulis

Haynes

A FOULIS Boating Book

First published 1989
© Lloyd Foster 1989

Published by:
Haynes Publishing Group
Sparkford, Near Yeovil, Somerset
BA22 7JJ, England

Haynes Publications Inc.
861 Lawrence Drive, Newbury Park, California
91320, USA

**British Library Cataloguing in Publication
Data**
Foster, Lloyd
  OSTAR: Observer Single – handed Transatlantic
Race.
  1. Atlantic. North Atlantic Ocean. Yachts.
Racing. Races. Observer Singlehanded
Transatlantic Race, history
  I. Title
  797.1`4'091631
ISBN 0 85429 730 8

Library of Congress Catalog Card Number
89-84711

Editor: Peter Johnson
Page Layout: Syd Guppy

Printed in England by:
J.H. Haynes & Co. Ltd.

Contents

Acknowledgements

The author is very grateful to the following who are among many who have contributed in a variety of ways: Mrs Elizabeth Balcon *(The Observer)*, Dr Glin Bennett, Rear Admiral R.M. Burgoyne (Royal Institute of Navigation), Robin Duchesne (Royal Yachting Association), Commander Dick Edwards, Crispin Gill, Mrs Bridget Hasler, Jack Hemming *(Multihull International)*, Cathy Hawkins, The Highlands and Islands Development Board, Dame Naomi James, Henk Jukkema, Roy Kingon, *The Lancet*, Jock McCleod, Captain Colin McMullen, Alan Miller, Dick Newick, *The Observer*, Lt.Cdr. Peter Odling-Smee, David Palmer, Michael Richey, Anthony Rowe, The Royal Western Yacht Club of England, Patrick Searle Prints, Major Ewen Southby-Tailyour, Dr Claudio Stampi, The United States Coast Guard, Mrs Edna Wallis, Henk van der Weg, *The Western Morning News*, Witze der Zee.

Photo Credits

(by page number)

Tony Bullimore	*119, 123 (top), 130*
Roel Engels	*135*
Dave Evans	*28 (bottom)*
Crispin Gill	*16, 17*
Fritz Henle	*27*
J. Hodder/The Observer	*90*
Roger Lean-Varcoe	*118 (top), 125*
Alex Macdonald-Smith	*86*
Eamon McCabe/The Observer	*96 (top), 102, 110 (bottom)*
Jock McCleod/Yachting World	*42*
Tony McGrath/The Observer	*33*
Multihull International	*37, 41, 49, 78, 79, 83, 124, 128*
The Observer	*19, 28 (top right), 29 (top left), 38, 39, 46 (bottom), 58, 62, 66, 67, 68, 69, 70, 71, 72, 89, 91 (bottom left), 91, (bottom right), 95, 96 (bottom), 97, 109, 110 (top), 111, 112, 113, 114, 115, 116, 117, 118, 120, 123 (bottom), 129, 132, 133 (top), 138*

C.C.O'Hanlon	*104*
Patrick Searle Prints	*frontispiece*
Pendella Studios	*61*
J.H. Peterson	*99, 100*
Photo Bateau	*56, 57*
Phoenix Photos	*105*
Pickthall Picture Library	*cover*
Royal Air Force	*22, 106*
Royal Navy	*81, 87*
Chris Smith/The Observer	*28 (top left), 29 (bottom), 30, 48, 60, 64, 65*
Newell Smith/The Observer	*32*
South African Navy	*29 (top right)*
Edna Wallis	*80, 91 (top left & right)*
John Wanstell/The Observer	*49*
Western Morning News	*10, 11, 18*

Introduction

The idea of this book came from members of the Royal Western Yacht Club and competitors in the races concerned, several of whom had said that, after eleven years in the secretarial chair, I should commit some memories to paper.

The book traces the development of a whole new form of ocean racing which sprang from Blondie Hasler's original brain child, the Single-handed Transatlantic Race. I have called the Round Britain Race a child of the single-handed race, which I think it was; Blondie thought of it and, if it had been sensible to do so, would no doubt have suggested it be single-handed. It was not sensible to race around the British Isles single-handed so the two-handed concept was originated.

Unlike other books written about the races, this one is written from the point of view of the organizers and takes the reader behind the scenes to give some idea of the factors which have affected theevolution of the rules, not all having always been universally understood. It may not be widely appreciated just how many people are involved in staging one of these events. As many as 100 club members may be involved in any one race. They include committee members, scrutineers and race office watchkeepers.

Inevitably, history tends to concentrate on winners but, in the races recorded here, even finishing is a triumph. However, when I say that the book contains the names of over 1800 crews and their yachts, the reader will understand that many will go unmentioned despite the magnitude of their achievement. I hope I have struck a balance between winners and those who did not win, and indeed those who were unfortunate enough not to finish.

Various people have from time to time decried the way the Single-handed Transatlantic Race and its offsprings have developed and suggested that its founder was unhappy about the way things have gone. I have tried to set the record straight by quoting his own words.

For the past fifteen years I have been either the secretary or a member of the race committee of the single-handed race, and I can see no way in which the race could have remained as it started, a nice gentlemanly, amateur affair. Nor do I believe it would have been in anyone's interest that it should. I hope that those who cruise the oceans will reflect that many of the things that make their lives more agreeable were originated by the single-handers, and that their development was often made possible through the help of sponsors.

One of the great merits of the Royal Western's series of races, which have evolved from the first OSTAR, is the freedom the rules have given owners and designers to invent and experiment. The lack of a rule has avoided yachts being built to a rating and if owners wanted to use water ballast they have not needed to indulge in clandestine humping of cans of water from one bunk to another. They have simply said they want to try it and the committee has come up with a broad rule to ensure that it is not overdone.

It was a great sadness to me that, whilst I was still only beginning my work on this book, Jack Odling-Smee died, to be followed all too soon by Blondie Hasler. I hope they would have approved of my version of their story. I am most grateful to Peter Odling-Smee and Bridget Hasler for making Jack's and Blondie's files and records available to me and to Bridget for checking my manuscript where I have made reference to Blondie.

Lloyd Foster

1

Hasler's Amazing Idea

The First Single-handed Transatlantic Race 1960

"Described by one experienced yachtsman as 'the most sporting event of the century', a transatlantic race for single-handed sailing boats will start from the south coast of England on Saturday 11 June 1960 and will finish off Sheepshead Bay, in the approaches to New York, at least a month later".

So ran a press release issued in November 1959, and in the following month, Lieutenant Colonel H.G. Hasler, D.S.O., O.B.E., Royal Marines, better known as "Blondie" Hasler, wrote to the Vice-Commodore of the Royal Western Yacht Club of England, (the Commodore at that time was Sir Winston Churchill), as follows:

Dear Lord Morley,

You may have noticed a recent announcement in the press about the single-handed transatlantic race, which will start from the south coast of England on Saturday 11 June 1960, but in case you missed it I enclose two copies of our press release.

As chairman of the committee of prospective competitors, I am looking for a club on the south coast that would be prepared to handle the British end of the race, and from which the race could be started. The race rules have already been drawn up and will shortly be duplicated in an agreed form.

My purpose in writing is to ask whether it is possible that the Royal Western would be prepared to act as the organizing club?

If you do not reject the idea out of hand, Francis Chichester and I would very much welcome the opportunity of explaining the project to you in more detail, either in London or anywhere else that you wish.

Yours sincerely

Signed H.G. Hasler

Meanwhile Francis Chichester had written to the Secretary of the Royal Western, George Everitt, strongly urging the Club to take it on. How then did all this start?

Blondie Hasler first had the idea back in 1956 and had aroused the interest of the Slocum Society who agreed to organize and sponsor the race. In January 1957 Blondie wrote to the Editor of *The Observer*, David Astor, to ask if his paper would sponsor the race. In his letter he suggested that "all entries would first have to qualify, by sailing a fairly stiff course, say, Cowes to Bantry and back, non-stop each way. This would weed out unseaworthy entries". He went on to say that "there would, obviously, be some risk to life, but less, in my opinion, than in the Grand National". He also commented that "it would inevitably attract adverse criticism . . ." No one could accuse him of pulling the wool over their eyes, and it was perhaps not surprising that by the end of the month his request had been turned down. Among the reasons given were just the points he had mentioned and which I have quoted. Whilst the

Slocum Society, in the shape of its Secretary, Richard McCloskey, seemed enthusiastic, the fact that McCloskey conducted the society's affairs from the American Embassy in Lima, Peru, was not conducive to rapid progress. Indeed it was this that led them to say quite firmly that they could not put on the race until 1960.

In September 1957 the Slocum Society issued a Notice of Race, with proposed rules, for a race "during the summer of 1960" and, in the same month Blondie asked the Island Sailing Club, in Cowes, of which he was a member, to start it. The Secretary replied that his committee had considered it but "they consider the proposition outside the sphere of the activities of this club". Blondie then wrote to Mr F.G. Mitchell, Commodore of the Royal Corinthian Yacht Club, who replied that the Royal Corinthian Yacht Club at Cowes would be delighted to start the race. It was announced that the Club would not however take any part in the control of the race and all enquiries were to be addressed to the Slocum Society.

Chris Brasher records, in *Singlehanded*, how Francis Chichester, in 1957 spotted a notice of the race in the Royal Ocean Racing Club, London. Chichester was then on his way to hospital and the prognosis was such that he could never have believed that, two years later, on 15 October 1959 he would be able to write to Blondie Hasler saying, "I understand from Mr Somerville, Editor of The Yachtsman, that you are organizing the solo race to New York next year. This seems to be a most sporting event and I am very keen to be a starter. Could you please let me have details."

In July 1958, with nearly two years to go, McCloskey reported having "115 reasonably serious applications" but he guessed, as it turned out accurately, that there would only be four or five at the start. At this time Blondie was not sure that he himself would be able to take part due to his other commitments. Meanwhile McCloskey was having problems with arranging the finish, despite the fact that he was by then in America. He was also much handicapped by ill-health. In May 1959, following a meeting, over dinner, of some of the members of the Slocum Society, they came up with the idea of the race being in two legs via the Azores. This prompted Blondie to come up with a long, forthright, though at the same time tongue-in-cheek, telegram to the Slocum Society which started, "BEWILDERED FATUOUS PROPOSAL TO ROUTE TA RACE VIA AZORES." He went on to say that if they persisted in this notion he would have to withdraw and organise his own race. By this time he was himself a member of the society so felt able to add "IF FREE DINNER HAS THIS EFFECT ON MEMBERS SUGGEST SUCH FUNCTIONS PROHIBITED IN SOCIETY RULES."

To this cable, of which I have only quoted a small part, the Commodore of the Society, Mr John J. Pflieger, replied in amiable terms, but it was clear that the Slocum Society were not going to conduct the race the way Blondie wanted it. He wrote back outlining the course of events so far and said, ruefully, ". . . since then the state of health of my brainchild has been steadily sapped by successive letters from McCloskey". It was apparent that the Slocum Society were moving towards a cruise in company rather than a race.

In July 1959 Blondie approached a contact in the *Daily Express* to see if there was a chance that that paper might sponsor the race and he told the Slocum Society that he was doing so. Whilst he got a negative response from the *Daily Express*, he did get a letter from Chris Brasher, at *The Observer*, who said that he had persuaded the paper to put up a trophy for the race. Meanwhile, over in America, the Slocum Society was apparently trying to accommodate the various ideas of their very cruising orientated and individualistic members, as well as those of various professed potential entries. The result was chaos and decisions notable by their absence until they announced that they were going to run a "Transatlantic Cruising Competition". This prompted Blondie to form his own small committee of possible competitors, of which Francis Chichester became the secretary, and on 28 November 1959 he told the Slocum Society that he had taken over the running of the race. They could run a cruising event alongside it if they wished. They would continue to be responsible for the finishing arrangements of the race. In the event this latter task was to be undertaken by Bruce Robinson and Blondie recorded later that " . . . they [the Slocum Society] were throughout the only people doing anything to organize the finish. They co-opted the Sheepshead Bay Yacht Club, the U.S. Coast Guard and others. Bruce did the whole of this organization personally."

It now became important to find a club in England who would take on the job of organizing the start and other preparation. A positive response came from the Rear-Commodore of the Royal Western Yacht Club of England, Jack

The Founder Fathers – Blondie Hasler, Francis Chichester & Jack Odling-Smee.

Odling-Smee who was to watch over the single-handed Transatlantic Race for the next 20 years.

Odling-Smee formed a sub-committee, of which he was the chairman, and other members were, Commander Robin Gardiner, Commander Philip Yonge (Queen's Harbour Master, Plymouth) Mr Cecil Roberts and Dr Neil Beaton.

Having found himself a yacht club of repute to take on the organization, Blondie's next encouragement was to be offered sponsorship by *The Observer*. Until then their commitment had only been to provide a trophy. This started a long and amicable association between the Royal Western YC and *The Observer* which was to continue until 1986. From this combination came the short title by which the race was generally known, OSTAR. Short titles are not popular with sponsors, but few people are prepared, constantly, to get their tongues around the race names which result from sponsorship. The titles of the chapters in this book give the correct titles of the various races and I think the reader will appreciate that short titles have some merit.

Although there were eight entries for the first race, only four came to the line on 11 June 1960, thereby fulfilling the prophesy of Richard McCloskey two years earlier. Jean Lacombe started three days later and took 74 days to complete the course. An interesting feature of the first race was the widely divergent routes chosen by the competitors. These are shown on track chart 1. Blondie was convinced that the northern route would give the highest proportion of favourable winds, on the supposition that the depressions would be to the south of him. He had been reading the North Atlantic Directory and the following quote is actually taken from his telegram to the

Slocum Society, mentioned earlier, on the subject of the Azores. "By Captain Boid RN – I scarcely know of any group of islands more liable to sudden squalls, storms and changes of weather than the neighbourhood of these. No continuous fine weather may be expected at these islands until May or even later from summer solstice to the autumnal equinox between which periods frequent long calms prevail or light baffling airs. The climate of Flores and Corvo is delightful but violent storms and sudden squalls are experienced in their vicinity at all seasons." Clearly *Jester* was not going to go that way!

In the event Francis Chichester's route, which approximated to the Great Circle, took him to the finish in 40 days, 8 days ahead of Blondie, to win the race. This first race was the only one in which there were no multihulled yachts. No one knew where anyone was during the first race, although each yacht had been issued with a radio transmitter. Blondie Hasler always hated radios in yachts and, after the first race, he wrote to the

Francis Chichester's Gipsy Moth III. *The mizzen mast carried self-steering gear which he called Miranda.*

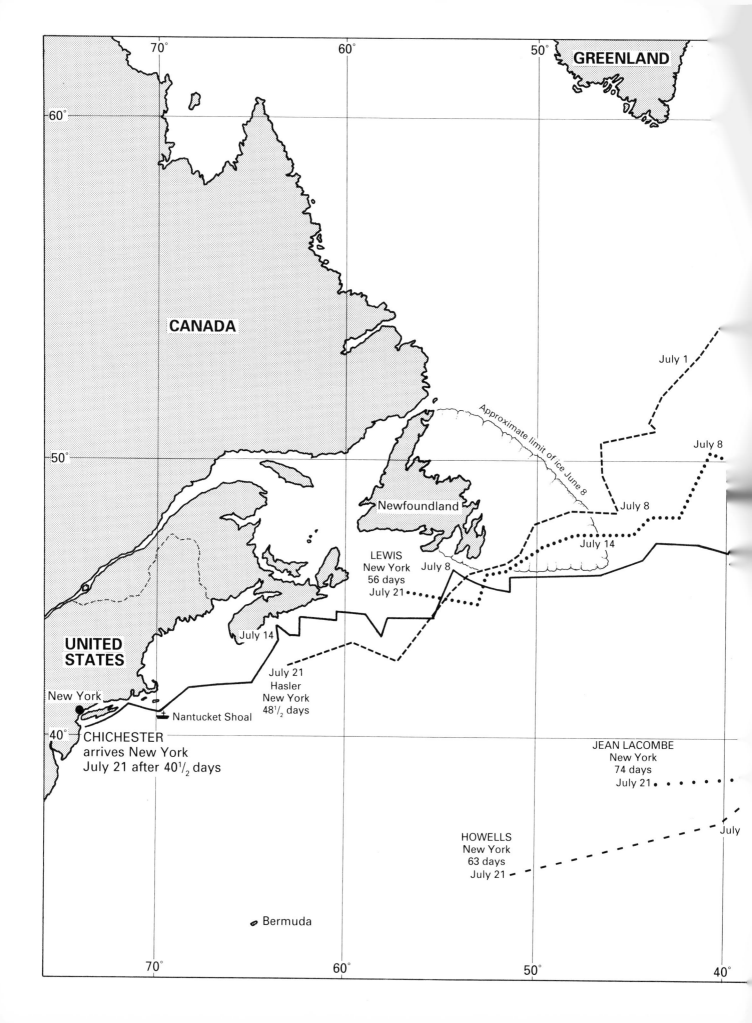

GREENLAND

70°

60°

50°

CANADA

July 1

60°

July 8

50°

Approximate limit of ice June 8

July 8

Newfoundland

July 8

July 14

LEWIS
New York
56 days
July 21

UNITED
STATES

July 14

July 21
Hasler
New York
48½ days

New York

Nantucket Shoal

40°

CHICHESTER
arrives New York
July 21 after 40½ days

JEAN LACOMBE
New York
74 days
July 21

July

HOWELLS
New York
63 days
July 21

Bermuda

70°

60°

50°

40°

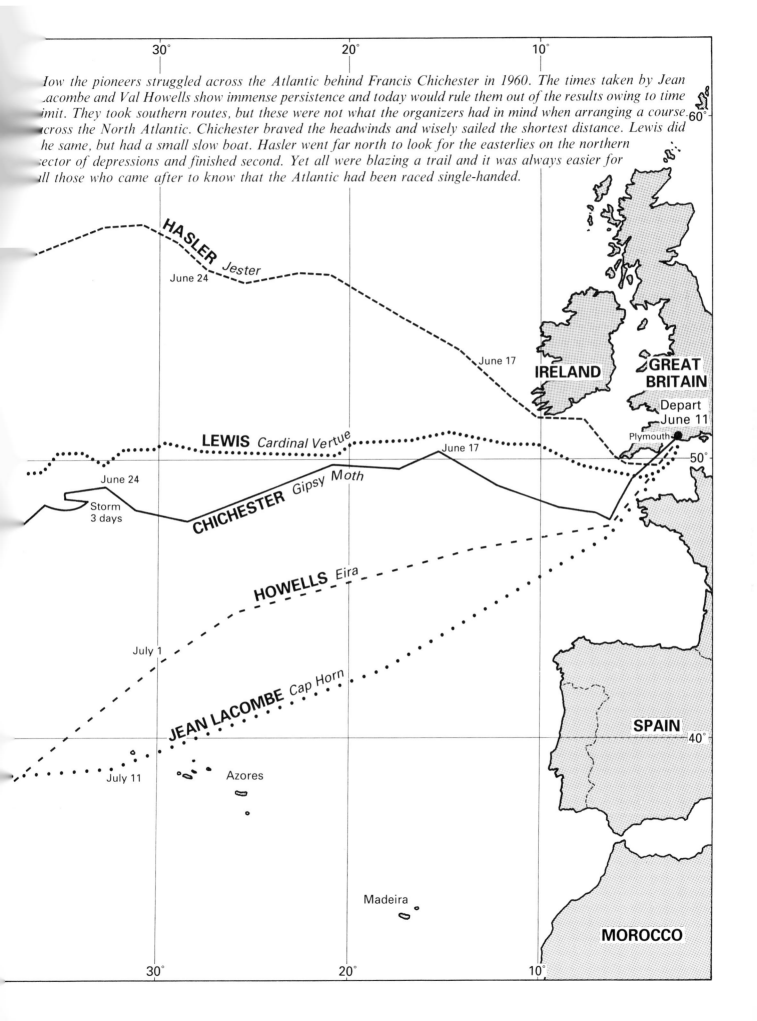

How the pioneers struggled across the Atlantic behind Francis Chichester in 1960. The times taken by Jean Lacombe and Val Howells show immense persistence and today would rule them out of the results owing to time limit. They took southern routes, but these were not what the organizers had in mind when arranging a course across the North Atlantic. Chichester braved the headwinds and wisely sailed the shortest distance. Lewis did the same, but had a small slow boat. Hasler went far north to look for the easterlies on the northern sector of depressions and finished second. Yet all were blazing a trail and it was always easier for all those who came after to know that the Atlantic had been raced single-handed.

Secretary of the Royal Western, about the race, and one of the things he said was, "This race amply confirmed my previous views on wireless transmitters! Please don't ever do anything to make these damned things compulsory!".

In order to try to find out what is going on, and how people are doing, the organizers of almost all big events have tried making radio reporting a requirement under the rules, and it has generally been a headache for one reason or another. For a start, electricity and lots of salt water are not good companions and inevitably there are sets which go wrong. The problem arises in sorting out whose set went wrong and who did not report as he was told to for one reason or another. Then there are those perverse characters who report, but give the wrong position to fool their fellow competitors.

One of the reasons Blondie was against yachts having radios was that he feared that, if they got into difficulties, they would send out distress signals and cause a lot of trouble! He said, "It would be more seemly for the entrant to drown like a gentleman". In the event of course, there would have been many more fatalities in the race if they had not been able to call for help. No race organizer today could even think of denying the competitors the wherewithal to summon help, although there is an argument that yachts would be more seaworthy if they were unable to do so.

After the 1960 race there was, of course, a wash-up to see what needed changing in any future event. The main alteration decided upon was that the finish be moved to Newport, Rhode Island. This would enable yachts to stay clear of shipping, often in fog, approaching New York. There are also regulations governing the navigation of vessels within these areas where there are separation zones, and these are not helpful to racing yachtsmen. The New York Yacht Club was in favour of moving the finish to Newport and was prepared to help through its station the Ida Lewis Yacht Club. This brought about the continued involvement of the latter club which formed a committee under the chairmanship of Mr Bill Thomas to make arrangements for the finish of the 1964 race.

A trimaran had been accepted for the first race but had not started. When it came to writing the rules for the second race, the committee was by no means sure that it liked the idea of multihulls in the race and felt it needed to find out more about the capabilities of these craft. The sailing secretary, by then Captain Terence Shaw, was instructed to write to the yachting press calling for accounts of various voyages, by multihulled yachts, which would justify their inclusion in a future race. He was soon deluged with correspondence from multihull folk, quite astonished that there should be any question as to their suitability. However one well known designer of cruising catamarans said firmly that, "Any catamaran that carries more than 150 square feet of sail per ton of displacement is OUT for seawork". He also added that "any catamaran that lifts a hull in inshore racing is out for seawork".

For 1964 the committee allowed in multihulls but, reserved the right to refuse any yacht they thought unsuitable. The committee always valued the opinions, fed in from time to time, by Blondie Hasler, and, on the question of multihulls in the race, he wrote, in August 1963"; "I would agree with anyone who said that multihulled yachts have not yet proved that they can be driven to windward across the North Atlantic, whether single-handed or not.

Nevertheless, the lesson of history is that boats which are considered unseaworthy by the 'expert' of today will be proved seaworthy, or will be developed into something seaworthy, tomorrow. Conversely, many craft thought to be seaworthy in the past would, rightly, be thought unseaworthy today." In January 1964 he wrote to *Yachts and Yachting*: "All who are interested in the development of new types of sailing yacht will welcome the decision of the RWYC to accept multihulled craft as entrants in the single-handed transatlantic race. I now hope that one or two modern cruising catamarans and trimarans will accept the challenge, if only in order to silence those critics who believe that such craft are incapable of making an efficient passage *to windward* across the North Atlantic."

2

Tabarly Beats the English

The Second Single-handed Transatlantic Race 1964

For 1964 the rules of the race were almost the same as for the first one. One change was the introduction of a handicap prize which was based on waterline length and worked for monohulls, but not for multis. Later a handicap system was devised for both types but like many handicap systems the only really satisfied competitor was the winner. There was also a strong feeling that this was a race in which boat sailed against boat and this led later on to the dropping of handicaps and simple subdivision into more classes. The 1964 race produced the first problem entry. A prospective entrant declared that he wished to sail a boat 12 feet (3.6 m) overall. This he insisted was within the rules and the committee should accept him. However it did not question the fact that the boat might have been able to complete the course, but it felt it was too small to arrive in a reasonable time. In future there were to be lower limits on length imposed.

For 1964, a 44 foot (13.4 m) ketch, *Penduick II*, was purpose-built. A French Navy lieutenant, Eric Tabarly, was given time off together with support and encouragement by his government.

All those who sailed in the first race were back again, though only Francis Chichester and Blondie Hasler were sailing the same boats. Val Howells sailed a 35 foot (10.7 m) steel cutter, *Akka*, which was a production yacht on delivery to America.

David Lewis had switched to a multihull in the shape of a catamaran named *Rehu Moana*. She was built for cruising and after the race he went on to sail her round the world. The fifth founder member, Jean Lacombe had moved from his 21 foot (6.4 m) *Cap Horn* to his new 22 foot (6.7 m) glass fibre sloop *Golif*. All five dramatically improved their previous times: *Gipsy Moth III* came down from 40 to 29 days, *Jester* from 48 to 37 and, after changing boats, the other three managed better times: Val Howells came down from 63 to 32 days, David Lewis 65 to 38 and Jean Lacombe from 74 to 46. There were 15 starters of whom one, *Marco Polo*, started three days late. All finished with the exception of *Tammie Norie*, who returned to Plymouth and later completed the crossing to America independently.

In looking at the results, the fortunes of individual competitors need to be taken into account. As often happens in yacht racing, the winner carried a breeze through to the finish, while those behind were left with none for a time. Derek Kelsall, in his Piver designed trimaran *Folatre*, which he built himself, hit something which he thought might have been a whale. It demolished his rudder. He did a temporary repair and returned over 500 miles to Plymouth. He then re-started and made the passage to Newport in 34 days, although his official time for the race was 61 days. Mike

Bill Howell hanks on the jib on his 30 foot cutter Stardrift.

the same. Although he lost his self steering gear about a third of the way across, Eric Tabarly managed to finish first in 27 days and 3 hours. This was probably the most important thing that happened in any OSTAR, apart from the successful completion of the first one. A Frenchman in Newport at the time prophesied that the effect on young Frenchmen would be sensational. He was absolutely right. The effect on President de Gaulle was equally sensational and he made Eric Tabarly a Chevalier of the Legion of Honour at once and he was accorded a hero's welcome in Paris. Those who cruised in French waters in the fifties and early sixties could hardly have imagined the transformation which was to take place in the next few years. In popular cruising, and racing which has stemmed from short-handed racing, French sailors have surged ahead with successes and innovations.

After the 1964 race, Blondie wrote a retrospective piece about the race which illustrates very clearly what he thought were the important facets. Fundamental to his thinking was the principle that competitors should be able to look after themselves and be self sufficient to the extent that at no stage should they require outside

Ellison had been lent the 36 foot junk rigged schooner *Ilala,* a re-rigged Nicholson 36. Her two masts, because of the junk rig, were unstayed and with 1500 miles still to go, the foremast fell over the side. Due to halyard problems Mike was only able to set reduced sail on the mainmast. He finally made Newport in 46 days. Bob Bunker, in his traditionally clinker built Folkboat, fell from aloft and broke a wrist, a painful and severe handicap.

As always the choice of route varied enormously. Blondie Hasler chose the northern route and was rewarded with some good following winds. If the depressions follow their normal tracks it is possible to take advantage of the easterly winds to the north of them while those to the south are butting into westerlies. Mike Butterfield, in *Misty Miller,* took the southern route and nipped into Flores, in the Azores, for some minor repairs before continuing. Geoffrey Chaffey, in *Ericht,* did

Val Howells combined the race with the delivery of the yacht Akka.

Chichester sails Gipsy Moth III *through the lee of Mike Ellison in his junk-rigged schooner* Ilala *as they leave Plymouth.*

assistance let alone rescue. It was this philosophy that led to the inclusion of the rule which read "Yachts must be fully independent and capable of carrying out their own repairs at sea. Crews have no right to expect, or demand rescue operations to be launched on their behalf".

In his summary of the 1964 race Hasler wrote: "Now that it's over, and we are returning to the more complex stresses of communal life, we can look back on the second Single-handed Transatlantic Race and see what we learned. Once again every competitor proved well able to look after himself, even those who had to put back into harbour for repairs. One boat gave up after an honourable attempt: all thirteen others arrived at Newport, Rhode Island, a long way inside the time limit. This was doubly impressive since several of the new competitors were relatively inexperienced, and there were three multihulled boats (two

catamarans and a trimaran) which were, I think, competing for the honour of being the first such craft to cross the Atlantic from East to West. The trimaran *Folatre,* though last of the three to finish, finally sailed direct from Plymouth to Newport in under 35 days, which would have given her fourth place if she had been able to do it first time.

Many people (including me, dash it) may still doubt the ability of the mutihuller to cope with the ultimate (and very rare) hazard, in which a rogue wave picks you up to a great height and then crashes bodily, throwing the boat, perhaps upside-down, into a trough of water that feels like concrete. I have only once met such a wave, and then not in the Atlantic but 20 miles off Aberdeen. It nearly sank *Jester,* and I still don't know whether any multihuller would have survived, but at least we know that three different types have now completed this race at speeds which are not much

Blondie Hasler and Jester *are surrounded by spectator boats at the start.*

slower than those of good single-hulled boats of comparable size. With further development, a multihuller may possibly be able to win, although my own guess is that the singlehuller, given comparable development, will always do better in hard going and rough water.

The race was remarkable, particularly for those of us who chose a northern route, in the high proportion of following winds, and I think nearly all boats may be said to have had unusually good luck with their weather.

Eric Tabarly's win in the lovely *Pen-duick II* delighted me for two reasons: he was a foreign entrant in a British event, and his boat was the first ever to have been designed specifically for the race. This is exactly what I had hoped would happen when we first planned the thing. I have since heard some sour British criticism of the "fuss" made in France over his success, but it is perhaps easier to recognise chauvinism in others than in ourselves. The fact is that the boat was designed and built on a very small budget, and Eric's performance in getting her to the Brenton Reef in 27 days, in spite

of an unserviceable vane steering gear, must rank very near the summit of single-handed sailing.

In second place, Francis Chichester again improved on his previous record time, and continued to give us an example of a well prepared and efficient ocean racer expertly sailed and navigated.

We were all surprised, if not dismayed, by the size and erratic behaviour of the spectator fleet that turned out for the start, and *Akka's* infuriating collision may at least underline the need for some spectator control in the future. It will not be easy, but to the combination of the Royal Western and the Royal Navy, all things are possible. The fact that Val Howells was able to finish third after this episode, and after later having to put back into Baltimore with a faulty halyard block, shows how hard he was sailing this steel-built family cruising boat. Without mishaps, he might have been second.

As to the future, there are signs that the race may begin to attract a type of competitor who regards it (quite wrongly) as a test of courage

Eric Tabarly, the first Frenchman to win the OSTAR and also to win it twice.

nothing else, this might reduce the number of gear failures during the race, but it should also relieve the club of much of their responsibility for assessing the competence of the crews.

Original rules, drafted in 1957, laid down that any yacht using wireless transmission would thereby be disqualified. I felt that the essence of the race was independence, and that if some boats made routine transmissions and some didn't, and if some wireless transmitters broke down, the general picture received at home would be confused, and would cause unnecessary anxiety. This may still be true. It is, I think, the British press that has pushed its selected champions into using wireless transmitters, and some of this press participation seems to be becoming altogether too feverish, and may be having a bad effect both on the competitors and on the prestige of the race amongst serious sailing people. The British yachting press reports the race factually and in perspective.

If we can keep everything on the rails, I think the Single-handed Transatlantic Race will develop into a legitimate and respected branch of yacht racing, and some of the technical lessons learnt from it will soon begin to benefit cruising and ocean racing yachtsman everywhere. For example, wind vane steergears, which were a novelty in 1960, and now so firmly established in this country that we may already have forgotten that it was the first single-handed race that gave them their main boost."

rather than skill, and it may be that the qualification for entry should now be stiffened, perhaps back to the original idea whereby each entrant and his boat first had to qualify by making a long single-handed passage together. If it did

3

Two on Board

The First Round Britain Sailing Race 1966

In November 1964 Blondie Hasler proposed to the Royal Western Yacht Club that there should be a race around the British Isles for yachts manned by only two persons and so a race committee was formed under the chairmanship of Lt. Col. Jack Odling-Smee with members Commanders Dick Edwards and Robin Gardiner, Mr Henry Williams, who became Rear Commodore of the Club in 1966 and later Commodore, and Captain Terence Shaw, the sailing secretary of the club. The race would be jointly sponsored by *The Observer* and the *Daily Express.*

The course, of nearly 2000 miles, would include stopovers, of 48 hours each, in four ports. It would circumnavigate the British Isles, except the Channel Islands and Rockall. Otherwise all islands and off-lying rocks were to be left to starboard. After careful consideration, and some reconnaissance, it was decided that the stopover ports would be Crosshaven, in southern Ireland, Castle Bay, Barra, in the Outer Hebrides, Lerwick in Shetland, and Harwich. After the first race Harwich was replaced by Lowestoft as the east coast port. It was agreed that the Round Britain Race would, like the OSTAR, be a four yearly event. The first race was set for 1966. The character of the event was set by the rule which said:— 'The race is a sporting event to encourage the development of suitable boats, gear, supplies and

techniques for efficient short-handed cruising under sail, and also to test the speed and seaworthiness of widely different types of boats by enabling them to race against each other on equal terms.'

Critics might say that a race of this nature is no place in which to find out if a boat is seaworthy or not. But again Blondie Hasler spoke, "The only reliable judge of seaworthiness is the sea itself, and the seaworthiness of an individual boat depends to a large extent on how she is handled. Many popular features in the design of modern racers

Opposite page:
The stopping points in the Round Britain and Ireland race have remained the same, dividing the 1850-mile course only into very approximate equal legs. The first leg to the yachting port of Crosshaven is appropriately the shortest. Then follow two Atlantic passages broken by the stopover at Castlebay, where yachts use their own anchors in poor holding ground, a circumstance which has caused problems in the past. The longest leg, from Lerwick to Lowestoft, passes through the oil and gas wells and rigs of the North Sea, before the final stretch across the Thames Estuary with its lights and buoys and down Channel to a line off the Royal Western Yacht Club at Plymouth.

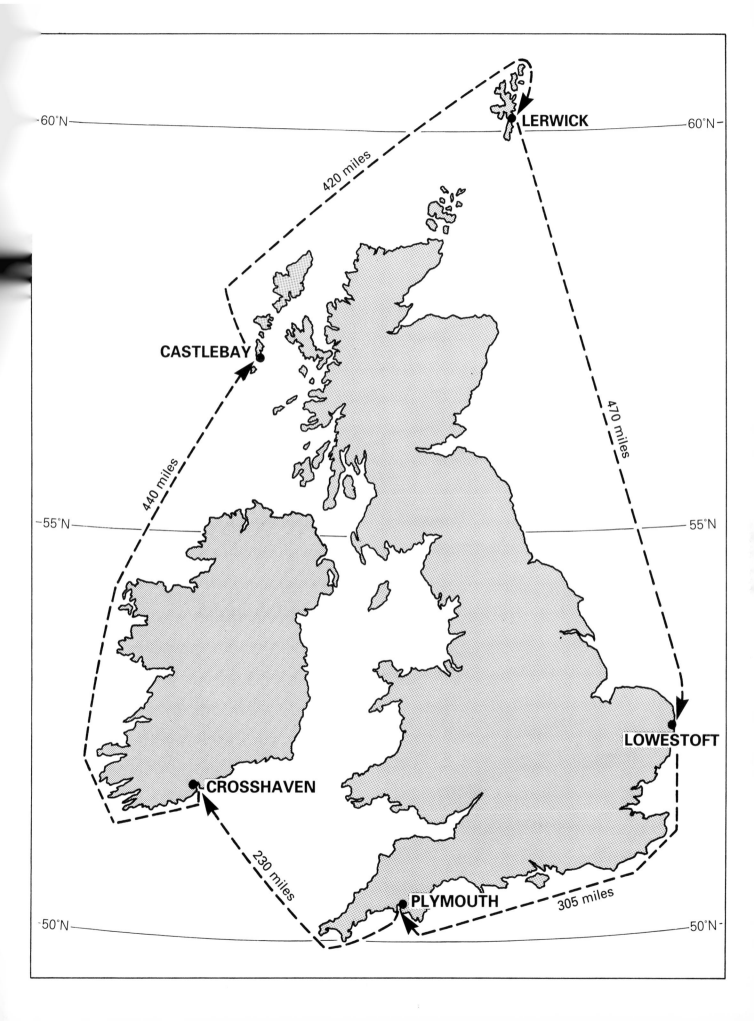

LERWICK

420 miles

CASTLEBAY

440 miles

470 miles

LOWESTOFT

CROSSHAVEN

230 miles

PLYMOUTH

305 miles

60°N

55°N

50°N

Derek Kelsall's Toria *(14) was altogether too quick for her rivals* Severn *(23) and* Mabel Amelia *(2243), seen here at the start of the first Round Britain Race.*

would have been thought quite unseaworthy forty years ago. It is reasonable for inspection teams to reject anything that is in bad condition, but very difficult to reject a hull or rig as being inherently unseaworthy, particularly when the skipper is at least as experienced as the inspector . . . . To exclude a boat on a questionable point of opinion is not usual in yacht racing, creates instant bad feeling, and leaves the opinion unproven. To allow the sea to eliminate a design feature is fair, unanswerable, and a useful contribution to the science of seafaring. One of the main points of our two races is to allow experimenters a free rein and to learn something from the results."

The Round Britain Race has certainly produced an amazing assortment of yachts. We have seen the 70 foot (21.3 m) purpose-built racing yachts, both monohulled and multihulled, along with family cruising boats of all shapes and sizes. We have seen young, athletic crews sitting out quarter-tonners (26 footers, 7.9 m) for long periods while others have chosen to go round comfortably in a 47 ft (14.3 m) cruising boat with a junk rig which they could handle almost completely from inside. As time has gone on the size of the fleet has grown and this has made it more and more possible for those of a size to sort themselves out, find out who are their direct competitors and enjoy racing against them at sea and meeting them in each port. To add to the interest, a handicap system was devised but the important thing has always been the boat for boat competition. Handicapping was not universally approved of by the competitors and in one race the only entry on one, daily, page of a yacht's log read 'wind northerly (from ahead) force 9 HOPE THE HANDICAPPER DROPS DEAD!' In latter years the handicapping was, as in the OSTAR, replaced by the sub-division of the fleet into a number of classes in which all yachts race "boat for boat."

Although the 48 hour stopovers are intended for rest, replenishment and repair, they are very much enjoyed as occasions for socializing. A tremendous spirit builds up amongst the crews of yachts of like speed as they meet each other in successive ports. The short-handed races attract some real characters and I know of no other race in which there is so much evident enjoyment on the part of the competitors. Much of the success of the race has been due to the enthusiastic help given, both to the Royal Western Yacht Club and to the competitors, by those in the ports at which the yachts call. In the early days there was no Royal Western presence in the stopover ports and all the work fell on the local volunteers. As the race has grown so has the number of Royal Western committee members deployed around the course.

In the first port, Crosshaven, the host Club is the Royal Cork Yacht Club (Incorporating the Royal Munster Yacht Club). Established in 1720, the Royal Cork Yacht Club is generally recognized as the oldest yacht club in the world. It is used to hosting many yachting events and this, coupled with the traditional Irish hospitality, makes the first stopover a memorable, if not always restful, one. One year, servicemen in the crews were not allowed ashore during their stay in Crosshaven but the Royal Cork Yacht Club and the Royal Naval Sailing Association's Local Officer, John Minchin, saw to it that they were not forgotten. In a letter afterwards the Vice Admiral of the Club wrote: 'The highlight of the week was a separate cocktail party, given by some of our members on their rafted up yachts at moorings, for those poor souls who were regrettably confined to boats – it was a most enjoyable affair and we didn't lose a man!'

In the next port of call, Castle Bay, Barra, there is no yacht club but things were in the hands of the Postmaster, Mr Hugh Morrison, OBE, who was also the Secretary and Treasurer of the Lifeboat, and Mr John McNeil who was coxswain/mechanic of the Lifeboat. John McNeil spent much of the time sorting out yachts who had anchored in one of the many places where the holding ground is bad. He also repaired engines and put right defects of all kinds in the yachts. His efforts were truly prodigious.

At the next stop, the Lerwick Boating Club organize host families for the yachts, who look after their every need including baths, washing and drying wet gear. By the time they reach Lerwick the crews need some domestic support. Originally the Lerwick Boating Club's premises were very small and it was a matter of continual amazement how many people they could get into their tiny bar when the race competitors were there. They have since moved to more palatial premises but the hospitality has in no way diminished. In the first place, our man in Lerwick was Mr Mallace, but he was relieved in 1974 by Mr George Burgess, who together with Captain & Mrs Shaw, from the Royal Western, became familiar to all Round Britain sailors for their work during the time the yachts are there.

In Lowestoft the Royal Norfolk and Suffolk Yacht Club are hosts from their handsome club house overlooking the harbour entrance. Their members turn out at all hours to tow yachts in and look after their needs. As always, in a port which is not only commercial but fishing as well, much tactful liaison is necessary with other interests when inflicting a fleet of racing yachts on the port, and the Royal Norfolk and Suffolk have always managed to keep everyone as happy as such a mixture can be.

The first race, in 1966, was blessed with predominantly fair winds and the result was interesting in that out of 16 starters the first 6 to finish were multihulled and the next 4 monohulled. They were the only finishers with 5 retirements and 1 disqualification. Derek Kelsall entered a brand new boat of his own design, a 42 foot (12.8 m) trimaran called *Toria*. The crew was putting the finishing touches to her right up to the starting gun. She then went out in front and stayed there throughout the race. Her time of 19 days 17 hours was not beaten until 1974. *Snow Goose,* owned and skippered by Don Robertson, was a ten year old, Prout designed cruising catamaran of 36½ feet (11.1 m). She had been consistently well sailed over the years and finished only 15 hours behind the winner. Her crew was David Cooksey. Next came *Iroquois,* sailed by Mike and Peter Ellison. She was a production cruising catamaran of 30 feet, (9.1 m) designed by Rod Macalpine-Downie. She was however specially prepared for the race and could not be said to have been in her normal cruising mode. *Iroquois* came only 15 hours behind *Snow Goose* and won the Genesta Trophy for the first yacht on handicap. The fourth to finish was *Startled Faun*, an Arthur Piver designed trimaran of 33 feet (10 m). She was sailed by Eric Willis and crewed by Tony Smith. After her came the 40 foot (12.2 m) catamaran *Mirrorcat,* designed by Rod Macalpine-Downie and sailed by Stephen Fearon-Wilson with the designer as crew. She was another new boat and suffered from insufficient trial time before the race. She damaged her mast on the way to the start and was delayed 8 hours in Plymouth. The sixth multihull to finish was *Victress,* a 40 foot (2.2 m) trimaran designed by Arthur Piver and owned and sailed by Commander Nigel Tetley who had used her as his floating home for three years before the race. She was ketch rigged and sailed the race in her normal cruising trim.

The first monohull to finish was *Severn*, at $47^{1}/_{2}$ feet (14.5 m) the largest of the fleet. She was a William Fife designed 8 metre and at the time of the race was 36 years old. She was sailed by her owner, Tony Wheeler, and crewed by Major Angus Buchan. In the early days of short-handed sailing races, $47^{1}/_{2}$ feet was considered 'a very large yacht for two people to race hard over such a long course'. In the next race we were to see a 71 footer and, in the one after that, a yacht of 80 feet, and finally the 236 foot monster which Alain Colas sailed single-handed in the 1976 OSTAR. I don't think anyone would advocate these very large yachts as being "suitable for short-handed cruising" but certainly, with modern systems designed for short-handing, the size of yacht which can comfortably be handled by two people has increased enormously. Leslie Williams sailed *Blue Saluki* in the first race. She was $36^{1}/_{2}$ feet (11.1 m) and his crew was D.D. Mathews. They finshed 8th. 9th came *Dinah* a 33 foot (10 m) sloop which had been virtually salvaged by her owner, Alex Smith, and re-rigged as a Bermudian sloop. Last to finish was a new $41^{1}/_{2}$ foot (12.6 m) Class II ocean racer designed by Kim Holman and built by A.H.

Moody. She was skippered by her owner, Bernard McManus and crewed by J.A. Macadam. Amongst those who did not finish, there were three fairly revolutionary boats. Blondie Hasler entered a very radical flat bottomed, slab sided $45^{1}/_{2}$ footer, (13.9 m) to designs produced in association with a model yacht designer. She was called *Sumner*, and with his wife Bridget, they were doing well until shortly after leaving Barra she suffered a damaged rudder and was forced to retire to Castle Bay. *Matamona* was a swingfloat trimaran designed by John Westell and sailed by Gilbert Turner and George Langwell, but after reaching Lerwick the crew had to return home so she retired. The trimaran *TAO* finished the course, but with only one person on board, so suffered automatic disqualification. It seems there was some disagreement which resulted in one of the two stepping ashore. This problem was to recur in a later race.

This first Round Britain Race was enormously encouraging for multihullers, who had been largely ostracized by the rest of the racing fraternity, and for whom there were very few ocean racing opportunities. It showed everyone what multihulled yachts could do.

4

A Heavy Weather Race

The Third Single-handed Transatlantic Race 1968

There had been no great dramas or problems in the last race, so it seems the committee felt that the rules needed little amendment, although a qualifying cruise of 500 miles was added as a requirement. For 1968, a proa, that is an assymetric multihull which can only take the wind on one side, was proposed for entry. She was called *Cheers* and was designed by Dick Newick, who formed a three man team called "Project Cheers". He was the designer; Tom Follet was the skipper and Jim Morris the backer. All were from the USA. By July 1967 they were in a position to submit their entry for the race. They sent full details of the yacht and these were duly circulated to the race committee members. At a meeting of the committee on 2 October it was decided that *Cheers* could not be accepted even as a provisional entry and Tom Follett was told this. The Project Cheers team was not to be put off, and work went on until *Cheers* was launched on 12 December 1967. Then followed an intense period of trials and modifications. Finally Tom Follet took off for a trial cruise which took him from St Croix, in the Virgin Islands, to Martinique and back, but not without incident. In the lee of Guadeloupe he capsized while he was asleep (he assumed he was taken aback and caught with the wind on the wrong side). The possibility of this happening to single-handed proas had always been the

committee argument against entry. With the aid of a passing ship *Cheers* was sorted out and sailed back to St Croix where a sponson was fitted which would ensure that, in the event of a capsize, the masts would remain clear of the water. Various sheet tripping devices were also fitted. A report of the trial cruise, including an account of the capsize and what was being done to prevent a recurrence, was sent to the Royal Western who remained unreceptive to *Cheers'* entry.

Still full of confidence the *Cheers* team continued the preparation of the boat for her single-handed voyage to England and Tom Follet recounts that "the next day I loaded stores and took care of last minute odds and ends and was ready to leave on 31 March. Took a short sail out of harbour in the afternoon to see if everything was still O.K. and it was and *Cheers* and I were ready to hit the trail. Dashed off a letter to the yacht club in England telling them I was on the way and would see them in about a month for a chat about entering the race." True to his word Tom arrived in England on 29th April to be told that he had been accepted as a provisional entry in the race. In due course Tom and *Cheers* were welcomed in Plymouth as fully fledged entrants. The committee had no need to regret their change of heart and Tom has always been very understanding about their reluctance to have him in the first place. In the event of course they had a very well designed and built yacht, very well prepared, tried and presented for the race by an expert team and with a first class seaman to sail her. Tom finished the race in 27 days, beaten only by Geoffrey Williams in his 57 foot, (17.4 m), *Sir Thomas Lipton,* and Bruce Dalling in his 50 foot (15.2 m) *Voortrekker,* both monohulls. He was therefore not only third overall but first multihull to finish.

There have been several other attempts over the years to emulate Tom's achievement but no other proa has ever managed to finish and indeed the committee subsequently said quite firmly, 'no proas'. Dick Newick always wanted to get another proa in the race and I remember him putting part of the argument for so doing very succinctly when he said, "well, if you're looking to save weight, it sure helps to leave one hull 'home!' "

Of the 35 yachts which started the 1968 OSTAR, only 19 finished and of the 16 who did not make it, 5 were the subject of rescues of one sort or another. Of these Joan de Kat's was the most dramatic. He abandoned his trimaran when she started to break up and spent over two days in his liferaft. *The Times* of June 25th 1968 carried a full account by de Kat of his ordeal and if any race competitor now feels that he is being made to carry too many distress flares he should get a back copy and read de Kat's account. He was spotted after many hours of searching by an R.A.F. maritime aircraft and duly picked up by a ship. Edith Bauman was taken off her trimaran *Koala III,* some 300 miles from the Azores after sending out a distress call. Eric Willis was taken ill when some 300 miles from Cape Cod and, after two paramedics had been dropped to him, he was taken off by a U.S. Coast Guard cutter and his yacht towed to port.

These dramas aroused the attentions of the 'It's dangerous it should be stopped' and 'who is paying for all these searches and rescues?' brigades. To the first, one can only say 'of course it's dangerous, that's why they do it' and the others are well covered by the answer given by Air Vice Marshall Johnstone after the de Kat rescue: 'Can you equate a human life against pounds, shillings and pence ? besides its jolly good practice for us'. I was frequently had at on this point when being interviewed by the media and on one occasion I recalled the time when I was captain of a frigate off Iceland one dark winter's night when we were called to assist a trawler, one of many fishing there. As I stood by the plotting table evaluating the

Tom Follett's proa Cheers. *Note the sponson on the main hull, fitted following the capsize during early trials.*

numerous plotted positions of the trawlers, and trying to find the one in trouble, one of the sailors doing the plotting suddenly turned to me and said 'this is far better than all those bloody NATO exercises, this is real people'. I have spent many hours in rescues at sea and although sometimes they are extremely tedious, and one often knows unlikely to be successful, they are always worthwhile and, when successful, incredibly rewarding. Furthermore, in many cases, as far as the armed forces are concerned, they provide good training value with the best of all prizes at the end, a human life.

Returning to Joan de Kat however, it has to be said that he should not have been allowed to sail and Jack Odling-Smee used to say that that really was one fish who should not have got through the net. The boat simply was not good enough. As years went by there were to be other combinations of skippers and boats who caused the committee much agonising before they either let them go or turned them down. Ever since its inception, the committee has striven to make the race as safe as

The 25 foot (7.6m) trimaran Amistad *sailed by Bernard Rodriguez had won the New York – Bermuda Multihull Race the previous year. She finished the 1986 OSTAR in 47 days.*

Leslie Williams stands beneath Spirit of Cutty Sark *just before her launch.*

Competitors pose in front of the Royal Western Yacht Club in Plymouth.
Back row *L to R Bill Howell. Bruce Dalling. Bernard Rodriguez. Tom Follett. David Pyle. Mike Richey. Geoffrey Williams. William Wallin. Edith Bauman. Mike Pulsford. Les Williams. Eric Willis. Egon Heinemann. Claus Hehner. Eric Tabarly. Lionel Paillard. Bernard Waquet. Sandy Munro. Andre Foezon*
Middle row *Jean de Kat. Nigel Burgess. Stephen Packenham. Noel Bevan. Martin Minter-Kemp. B de Castelbajac. Alex Carrozzo. Bertil Embom. Colin Forbes. Robert Wingate. Brian Cooke. Alain Gliksman. M. Cuiklinski*
Front row *Yves Terlain. Ake Matteson. Guy Piazzini*

Nigel Burgess sailed in the 1968 race and then again 20 years later.

Brian Cooke sailed a sturdy monohull, Opus, *in this race but later turned to multihulls. He was lost at sea on his way to attempting a long distance speed record.*

Voortrekker, *sailed by Bruce Dalling to second place in 1968, was still going strong in 1988.*

any hazardous undertaking can be. I well recall Jack Odling-Smee describing it in just those terms to the skippers assembled for their pre-race briefing. Therein lies one of the race's great attractions and, when it has been accomplished, its satisfaction.

Geoffrey Williams's win in 1968 was not without contention. The first problem concerned the final part of the course and an error in the printed sailing instructions. Whereas it was intended that yachts should round the Nantucket Light, the instructions omitted the word 'light'. This error was pointed out to competitors at the pre-race briefing, which Williams attended, but claimed he had been out of the room, called to the telephone when this amendment was dealt with. He passed between the light and Nantucket Island on his way to the finishing line.

29

*Tom Follett (*Cheers*), Geoffrey Williams* (Sir Thomas Lipton) *and Bruce Dalling* (Voortrekker) *after the finish of the 1968 race.*

In answer to a query about this, many years later, Jack Odling-Smee said, amongst other things, "Later that evening, Geoffrey Williams radioed the Coastguards giving his position and ETA from which it was obvious he had no intention of rounding the Nantucket Light Vessel. Further messages were relayed to and from me by telephone. On being informed of his error he assured me that he had written instructions onboard which made no mention of Nantucket Light Vessel. Would he be disqualified if he followed these directions? Bearing in mind that he was in a dangerous position amid the Nantucket shoals with a fresh to strong easterly wind, I did not like to order him to beat back to get into a position to round the light, but I did say that his position in the race could be the subject of a protest which would have to be decided by the committee. I explained this again when I met him on the finishing line. Bruce Dalling arrived next day in *Voortrekker* and I explained the situation to him and asked him if he would like to put in a formal protest. He was adamant that he would not. He was very tired and obviously disappointed not to have come in first. I did not pursue the matter further at that stage. Later, when he had had a good sleep, and a meal, I tried to persuade him that he should put in a protest but he continued to reject the idea completely. Clearly, Geoffrey Williams would have had a case against the Royal Western Yacht Club for not ensuring that his sailing instructions were correct, had he been disqualified. While Bruce Dalling would have a strong case for a protest in that, in fact, Geoffrey Williams had not sailed the whole course. Since no protest had been put in and my committee and I could have been said to have been negligent, we had no option but to declare Geoffrey Williams to be the winner."

Bruce Dalling's sponsors made a protest some 48 hours after he had finished but, as the protest was not from a competitor, it was invalid. Geoffrey Williams had incurred a penalty for not presenting his yacht for pre-race inspection as the rules demanded but that did not affect the race result. The other contentious point was that, during the race, Williams had been receiving advice from England which helped him to steer the most favourable course as far as the developing weather patterns were concerned. This of course constituted outside assistance. There was nothing in the rules which specifically forbade this, but it was felt to be against the spirit of the rules.

Pundits at home started quoting the IYRU racing rules about outside assistance but failed to appreciate that the OSTAR has never been sailed under these conventional rules of yacht racing.

The sailing instructions for the race always state, quite categorically, that "The race will be sailed under the special rules of the Royal Western Yacht Club. Throughout the race, including the start and the finish, the International Rules for the Prevention of Collisions at Sea will apply". The committee subsequently agreed that they did not approve of the sort of assistance that Williams had had and, for the following race a new rule was added which prohibited 'pre-arranged transmissions for the use of individual competitors". However by the 1980s the rule was abandoned because of the advance of yacht electronics.

5

A Two-handed in a Big One

The Second Round Britain Sailing Race 1970

The second Round Britain Sailing Race was again sponsored by *The Observer* and the *Daily Express*. The fleet had grown to 25 starters and of these 20 finished. For the first time there was an overseas entry, in the shape of Philip Weld from the U.S.A., in his Kelsall designed *Trumpeter,* a 44 foot (13.4 m) trimaran. There were 13 multihulls and 12 monohulls. *Toria* was back, re-named *Gancia Girl,* and Derek Kelsall entered a brand new $51^1/2$ foot (15.7 m) proa of his own design, called *Sidewinder.*

A feature of the entry list was the strong Naval and Royal Marine component. *Ocean Spirit,* at 71 feet (21.6 m), the longest yacht in the race, was sailed by Lieutenant Leslie Williams, RN and Lieutenant Robin Knox-Johnston RNR, *Gancia Girl* had a mixed RN/RM crew with Chief Petty Officer Dave Butcher and Lieutenant Mike Shuttleworth RM. *Speedwell* was sailed by two Royal Marine Officers, Captain Ewen Southby-Tailyour and Lieutenant Roger Dillon. Commander John Lawson skippered *Rinaldo* and Lieutenant Guy Hornett crewed for Mike Perry in *Blue Smoke.* Lieutenants Mike McMullen and Martin Read, both Royal Marines, sailed *Binkie,* the smallest boat in the race, and two Chief Petty Officers, Mike Wigston and Bill Davies sailed the 36 foot (11.0 m) *Electron of Portsea. Snow Goose* was back again, still with Don Robertson and David Cooksey, and amongst the monohulls was a

dark horse in the shape of Michael Pipe's 48 foot (14.6 m) *Slithy Tove,* a yacht with narrow beam designed, among other things, for building on a slim budget.

The yachts started from Plymouth in quiet conditions and they ran out of wind and into fog off the Lizard. The leaders found better visibility, and a gentle south westerly breeze, after rounding the Bishop Rock lighthouse, off the Scillies, and these gentle conditions prevailed till Crosshaven. *Trumpeter,* Philip Weld, led the fleet into Crosshaven, with a time of 1 day 19 hours, *Ocean Spirit* followed only 15 minutes later. From then on *Ocean Spirit* was to keep ahead of the fleet until the finish, although, on the Lerwick to Lowestoft leg both *Snow Goose* and *Minnetaree* achieved better times.

On the first leg the back half of the fleet were left at sea in calms whilst the clock had, so to speak, stopped for the leaders who were enjoying their 48 hour stop-over in Crosshaven. *Speedwell,* who had not so long ago overtaken *Binkie,* was overtaken by her, rowing towards the finishing line, which she crossed ahead of *Speedwell.* (This was not against the rules but $25^1/2$ feet (7.8 m) is easier to row than 49!) (15.0 m).

After Crosshaven the weather deteriorated for the leading boats and, whilst *Tehini* found it too much for her and retired, *Trixia* was almost

Ocean Spirit *setting out to win the 1970 Round Britain Race.*

dismasted when her weather backstay parted and she narrowly avoided losing her mast. She retired to her home port. The leading boats went on to have some very hard weather up the west coast and again in the Channel on the last leg, whereas *Speedwell's* log records only two days above force 6 and nothing above force 7, the latter being on the Crosshaven to Barra leg. *Ocean Spirit* arrived first in Castle Bay followed by *Slithy Tove* and then came the first multihull, *Apache Sundancer.* Despite the rough weather, *Minnetaree* managed the fastest time for the leg, except for *Ocean Spirit,* and this brought her up to 6th place at Castle Bay. *Snow Goose* lost a rudder in the gale off the west coast of Ireland and this proved a particular handicap as she approached Castle Bay, where she, *Trumpeter* and *Minnetaree* found themselves cross tacking after some 700 miles of sailing since the start.

Writing after the race, Mike McMullen said:

"The leg from Crosshaven to Barra was, certainly for *Binkie,* the most alarming. Once round the south west corner of Eire a westerly gale blew up which lasted the whole way up to the Hebrides. In winds gusting to force 8 we ran up the Atlantic coast of Ireland before frighteningly large seas at a very high speed. At one stage we were knocked flat by a sea which gave us both unfavourable impressions of the whole proceedings and in a moment of weakness I almost (not quite) wished I was with 45 (Commando) over in Belfast 130 miles away.

"Added to rotten weather was the dangerous factor of very poor visibility and distinctly inhospitable shore under our lee. It was with distinct feelings of relief that we came alongside our comfortable RFA [Royal Fleet Auxiliary], *Speedwell* in the pleasant, land-locked harbour of Castle Bay, Barra. She had had an eventful passage

32

too and her self steering gear had been smashed by a heavy sea. Fortunately this proved repairable and worked well for the rest of the race.

"It was the luckless *Gancia Girl* who had really suffered on this leg. First, her self steering broke irreparably, followed shortly by the teleflex cable connecting the wheel to the rudder. Mike and Dave were then steering her with the emergency tiller (a very arduous business on a trimaran) when two of the three pintles (hinges connecting the rudder to the main hull) sheared. This meant that the yacht was very nearly unsteerable and, with the rocks of Barra Head getting closer, about a mile at this stage in thick fog and gusting force 9, prospects could hardly be deemed encouraging. It was with the greatest of skill and good seamanship they weathered the headland and coaxed her into harbour, still wearing the Mae Wests they had put on in preparation for shipwreck. This damage cost

them four days in port and spoilt any chance they might have had of winning."

On the next leg, from Barra to Lerwick, Mike remarked on the bird life: "One of the most enchanting things during this phase was the bird life. St Kilda is the largest gannetry in the world and the sight of these beautiful birds diving, in their thousands, is simple unforgettable. Puffins abound and create great amusement by their pathetic efforts to take off. Panic-stricken by the sight of the yacht bearing down on them, and bloated with fish, they flop along the surface only to get "goffered" by the breaking crest. We also saw Fulmars, Skuas, Guilemots, Shags, Cormorants, Kittiwakes, Storm Petrels and a very large shark. Porpoises abounded."

Approaching Muckle Flugga they were not too busy bird watching to steal a march on some of their rivals. Whereas they had given the outer rocks

Robin Knox-Johnston and Leslie Williams kept Ocean Spirit *at the head of the fleet after the first leg.*

a wide berth to avoid the tidal race, Mike McMullen and Martin Read cut in close to the Out Stack, the most northerly piece of land of the British Isles and inside the tidal race, thereby gaining themselves four hours. The principal lighthouse keeper, Mr Tulloch, was so impressed by this tactic that he rushed to hoist, and dip, his ensign in tribute. He said later, "It was a grand piece of sailing: I had to admire those lads for their daring".

The leading boats found the wind still at gale force, and from the north west, when they came to re-start on the leg to Lerwick. *Slithy Tove* sprang a leak and was forced to go into Stornoway, on the Isle of Lewis, for repairs. This was of course allowed by the rules but she was never able to make up the time she lost. When they reached Lerwick they had dropped from 2nd to 19th place. The order at Lerwick was *Ocean Spirit, Apache Sundancer, Trumpeter* and *Snow Goose*.

After the 1966 race the east coast port was changed from Harwich to Lowestoft, so it was to Lowestoft that *Ocean Spirit* later set off with a gaggle of multihulls in hot pursuit. *Trumpeter* had to return to Lerwick for further repairs to her leaking floats which had been a constant problem since leaving Plymouth. However *Sundancer* and *Snow Goose* kept on, sometimes in sight of one another and sometimes not. *Snow Goose* beat *Sundancer* into Lowestoft by three hours, but neither had caught up with *Ocean Spirit*. The last leg could be expected to be a beat to windward, but the leaders had another gale and the later boats had calms. By the time *Snow Goose* had reached the Isle of Wight, the sea was very rough and the wind rising to force 9. Don Robertson and David Cooksey decided to duck in under the lee of the island, and came to anchor off Shanklin Pier where they were able to enjoy six hours well deserved sleep. *Trumpeter* and *Minnetaree* were not far away doing the same thing.

Sundancer, however, not knowing that her immediate adversaries were sheltering, pressed on hard until, when they were about 8 miles southeast of Ventnor, Isle of Wight, disaster struck. They went up the side of a very steep wave and became airborne at the top. By the time they landed back in the water they were already over to about 45 degrees. The boat never recovered an even keel and they went on into a capsize which laid them over with the mast flat on the water, held from going further by the masthead float. The float became detached but not, mercifully, before Peter Ellison,

who had been asleep in the cabin, was able to get out and join Mike Butterfield. Together they managed to get the life-raft launched and boarded it. Some hours later a passing ship saw their flares and rescued them. Meanwhile *Snow Goose* had got under way again, although the wind and sea had not abated. They fought their way westward for some 36 hours before reaching Plymouth to be second yacht to finish.

The gale in the English Channel had deprived the multihulls of any chance of catching *Ocean Spirit* who powered her way through the gale to finish nearly two days ahead and thus amply save her penalty of 12 hours which she carried, like a millstone round her neck, all the way round Britain. It would be ungenerous, and indeed foolish, to attribute her win entirely to the size of the yacht. It was a tremendous achievement for two men to sail a boat that size around that course in that weather. There must have been many times when they were approaching exhaustion, handling gear that size in those conditions.

Bob Harris, Phil Weld's crewman, said ruefully in defending the performance of the multihulls in the race, "Sure, a monohull was first to finish, but she had to be 71 feet of the latest and best design, crewed by two supermen". He went on to remind us that *Snowgose* who came second was "a 36 foot, ten year old, Prout catamaran". He could have added "sailed by a 62 year old skipper". Anyway his comment was, in passing, a very valid tribute to Leslie Williams and Robin Knox-Johnston and to Don Robertson and David Cooksey.

Behind *Snow Goose* came *Trumpeter* who had managed to claw her way back up the fleet after having to return to Lerwick for repairs. This was a tremendous achievement and shows that, had she not had all the troubles she had with her leaking floats, she would have been a very real threat to *Ocean Spirit,* gales or no gales. Only four hours after *Trumpeter,* came *Minnetaree* to win the prize for the first under 35 foot yacht. A prize she richly deserved. The leaders having had a gale to contend with on the last lap, the tail enders had the opposite and Mike McMullen and Martin Read rowed from the time they were off Salcombe until they arrived in Plymouth. (This Mike later described as "Readpower"). They were rewarded by winning the *Daily Express* Trophy for the first yacht on corrected time (handicap), a surprise in the circumstances of the weather pattern.

All the other competitors who made it to

Plymouth could, in a sense, be declared winners. They had beaten the course and all the weather which had been thrown at them. The race was a particular triumph for the multihulls because at that time they were considered quite unsuitable for ocean racing, indeed that opinion is still widely held even today. But they had shown that they could keep going, and going to windward, in very severe conditions, and see off monohulls of similar length or bigger. Certainly *Sundancer's* capsize was picked on as evidence that multihulls are unstable, but it could be argued that, some years later a top flight, fully manned, ocean racer, *Morning Cloud,* was lost in the same place in much the same conditions, and she wasn't racing.

The race organizers came in for a word of praise in an article in Multihull International written by the owner of *Snow Goose* when he said: "I do not think it has been appreciated how much we yachtsmen owe to the flag officers of the Royal Western Yacht Club of England. This must be one of the oldest and most respected and, one might expect, most conservative of clubs, but they had the courage and foresight to give their support and to organize two of the greatest events in the yachting calendar, the transatlantic and round Britian and Ireland races."

6

First, Second and Third for France

The Fourth Observer Single-handed Transatlantic Race 1972

By 1971 it seemed that there would need to be a numerical limit placed on entries, and various ways of doing this were discussed, as they were to be in later years, but in the event no limit was needed and the final entry stood at 59 of whom 55 started and 43 finished, although three of these were outside the time allowed for the race.

Rule changes since the last race, in 1968, included a prize for the first yacht under 35 feet, and separate handicap prizes for monohulls and multihulls. For the first time a rule covered sponsorship and it read: 'Entries may be sponsored and/or financed by another person, body or organization. The RWYC of E are not averse to the sponsoring of entries and are indeed glad of the help that has been given to the competitors in the previous races, which undoubtedly added to the interest in them. Nevertheless they are concerned that this race should remain a sporting event and reserve the right to refuse an entry if it appears that the primary object of it is to promote a commercial project not connected with the object of the race. In particular a yacht owned or sponsored wholly or partly by a group or organization may not display any emblem or wording that relates specifically to such sponsor other than a house flag whose largest dimension must not be more than 5% of the yacht's overall length and whose design may not incorporate any wording.'

It will be seen that the yacht's name could not reflect the sponsorship, though in the event one or two did. Here was the beginning of the trend to the outright advertising on hulls and sails seen in this and other races today. There was also legislation to prohibit the use of radar, hyperbolic position fixing aids such as Loran, and pre-arranged radio transmissions for the benefit of individual competitors. It was this form of assistance which was used by Geoffrey Williams in 1968. Also introduced was a rule which allowed the use of electricity to power self steering devices but only if the power was generated by the use of wind or water flow. This late amendment to the rules was drafted by Blondie Hasler and promulgated on 15 May 1972. It was to remain a rule, with the later addition of the sun's rays as a means of generating power, until 1984 when any means could be used for charging batteries. The reasons for introducing this rule were stated in the notice accompanying the amendment: "The objects of these rules are: 1. To allow experiments in generating electricity from wind and/or water flow in so far as these could be of value to cruising yachtsmen. 2. To encourage the development of electrically operated self-steering gears powered by wind or water flow. 3. To prohibit powered hauling devices, even if powered from wind or water flow, since these would permit a single-hander to manage a larger yacht than

Pen Duick IV, *here sailing under her later name,* Manureva, *was sailed by Alain Colas to the second French OSTAR win.*

would otherwise be possible. Reliance on such devices would be unseamanlike and give a large boat an unfair advantage in this race." Here emphasis was being put on practical developments of value to the ordinary cruising yacht owner. The dominance of sponsored hi-tech boats was yet to arrive.

The first evidence of governmental interest in the race came in April 1972 when the British Department of Trade and Industry said that the rules for the fourth OSTAR had come to their notice and that they were "pleased to note the provision for safety equipment at item 30". However they went on to say that they would prefer, even the most obvious, items to be listed and drew attention to their leaflet on the subject, (which was already held by the race committee). Over the years the amount of detail in the list of required items has increased with the aim of trying to avoid competitors leaving behind important items in the interest of saving weight, or expense.

In 1972 there were signs that the nature of

OSTAR was changing with an increase in the extent of sponsorship and the advent of professional skippers. In particular there was an attempt to win the race by the sheer size of the yacht and *Vendredi Treize*, at 128 feet (39.0 m) was the first example of this. She was rigged as a threemasted staysail schooner with the simplest possible rig, just three boomed staysails, one on each mast, which were self tacking. She was designed by Dick Carter, of the United States, and owned by the film director Claude Lelouch. Jean Yves Terlain masterminded the project and was her skipper. He had set his sights on a time of 20 days, and also intended this to be the winning time. In the event she was beaten into second place by Alain Colas sailing his 70 foot (21.3 m) trimaran *Pen Duick IV* in a time of 20½ days. *Vendredi* missed her 20 day target and finished in 21 days and 5 hours.

The fleet was, as usual a very varied one from the 128 footer down to *Willing Griffin*, 19 feet (58 m). Martin Minter-Kemp sailed a 65 foot

Pen Duick IV *comes in to berth in darkness at* *Newport.*

Alain Colas, the 1972 winner.

Bill Howell sailing his third OSTAR in 1972 had to retire after being in collision, but was back again for the next race.

Peter Crowther sailed the "gaffer" Golden Vanity in 1972 and finished after 88 days!

Jean Yves Terlain sailed his 128 foot (39m) schooner Vendredi Treize *into second place.*

Vendredi Treize *is taken in tow by the U.S. Coast Guard after finishing.*

(19.8 m) monohull, *Strongbow* designed by Paul Weychan and Brian Cooke had the 59 foot (18.0 m) *British Steel*, originally sailed by Chay Blyth, designed by Robert Clarke. Among multihulls in addition to *Penduick IV*, (later to be known as *Manureva* and from which Alain was to be tragically lost in the 1978 Route du Rhum Race,) were Cap 33, 53 feet (16.1 m), sailed by Jean-Marie Vidal, *Three Cheers*, 46 feet (4.0 m) sailed by Tom Follet, and *Trumpeter* 44 feet (13.4 m), sailed by Philip Weld.

Other interesting boats included *Jester*, in her fourth race and sailed by Mike Richey, and *Gipsy Moth V*, sailed by Sir Francis Chichester. Perhaps the most unlikely boat of all was the old 38 foot (11.6 m) gaff cutter, *Golden Vanity*, built in 1908, and sailed by Peter Crowther and his pet cat. It was as well he had company because he took 88 days to reach Newport! David Blagden managed to get his tiny *Willing Griffin* in within the time limit for the race, taking 52 days. Monohulls predominated and there were only 7 multis to the monos 48. There were 11 retirements and one yacht had to be abandoned. However the race went fairly smoothly and the French scooped all the prizes except the monohull handicap award which went to *Blue Smoke*, sailed by Guy Hornett. The first British yacht to finish was Brian Cooke's *British Steel*. Martin Minter-Kemp brought in *Strongbow* in 7th place.

Three days separated the second and third boats while down at the bottom end of the fleet, no less than nine boats took over 50 days, three of them failing to finish within the 60 days time limit. Among these was *Nike*, sailed by Richard Konkolski, the Czech, who was dismasted and restarted 12 days later. Richard managed to extricate himself from Czechoslovakia quite regularly for these races and one morning he came bounding into my office with an enormous grin on his face saying that he had sailed away from Poland, where he kept his yacht, with all the family to make a new life in America, where he now lives.

An early drama in the race concerned Sir Francis Chichester, co-founder of the race who had come first in the first race and second in the second one. Since then he had completed his famous circumnavigation and made several transatlantic voyages. Sir Francis was by now 70 years old and his fitness to undertake another race was, to say the least, questionable. Not so questionable was his determination to sail. On the Thursday evening before the Saturday start, he presided, as Commodore of the Royal Western Yacht Club, over the pre-race dinner at the Holiday Inn in Plymouth. Those who saw him start on the following Saturday were concerned by the way that he handled *Gypsy Moth V*, at 57 feet (17.4 m) a handful enough for a young man, let alone a man of 70 whose health was rapidly deteriorating.

A week later he decided to return to Plymouth. This must have been an agonizing decision for him to take. His ship to shore radio was out of action and the lack of the reports he had undertaken to make was causing concern. Messages sent back through ships and aircraft led to a confused situation in which a rescue operation was put in motion. A French weather ship, in trying to help him, damaged his mizzen. Finally *H.M.S. Salisbury* to which Giles Chichester had been flown out by helicopter, made a rendezvous

Ill health forced Sir Francis Chichester to turn for home in his Gipsy Moth V.

Jock McCleod's 47 foot (14.3m) Ron Glas, *built for comfort and easy handling, finished in 38¹/2 days.*

with the yacht. Giles was transferred and later joined by Lieutenant Commander Peter Martin and two of the *Salisbury's* ship's company to help sail *Gipsy Moth V* back to Plymouth. Sir Francis was a sick man and was destined never to sail again. He died later that year.

On the other side of the Atlantic, and a bit later on, Bill Howell was doing well in his 43 foot catamaran *Tahiti Bill,* only about 100 miles from the finish, when he was in collision with a Russian trawler in thick fog. A fleet of these Russian ships was operating right across the approaches to Nantucket Lightship, adding an additional and unexpected hazard. *Tahiti Bill* was later taken in tow by a Russian support ship and then handed over to a United States Coastguard vessel for the final 50 miles into Newport. Despite his misfortune on this occasion Bill always asked to retain his race number, 13, for subsequent races.

The only yacht to be lost in the race was that of a band leader, Bob Miller, *Mersea Pearl,* a 43 foot sloop. She was dismasted some 500 miles southeast of St John's, Newfoundland. He managed to get a signal through to Portishead Radio and, as a result, was taken in tow by the Norwegian ship *Hoegh Minerva,* 16,000 tons. However the ship was not prepared to slow down to accommodate the tow and when the tow parted *Mersea Pearl* was left adrift. She was later found and recovered by the US Navy.

7

Multihull Success and Lots of Wind

The Third Royal Western/Observer Round Britain Race 1974

The Round Britain Race achieved in 1974 61 starters from six different nations, three times the number in the previous race.

The formidable combination of Robin Knox-Johnston and Leslie Williams, who had driven *Ocean Spirit* to victory in 1970, separated, to other boats. Robin Knox-Johnston teamed up with Gerald Boxall to sail the 70 foot (21.3 m) catamaran *British Oxygen* while Leslie Williams and Peter Blake sailed the 80 foot (24.4 m) *Burton Cutter*, a yacht normally with a crew of fifteen. She had competed in the 1973 Whitbread Round the World Race and had the fastest time on the Portsmouth to Cape Town leg of that race. Philip Weld was back with a new 60 foot trimaran, *Gulf Streamer*, and Alain Colas entered the 70 foot trimaran *Manureva*, built by Eric Tabarly for the 1968 OSTAR, as *Penduick IV*, and sailed to victory in the 1972 OSTAR by Colas. After that race Alain Colas took her on a record-breaking round the world voyage with only one stop in which he covered 29,600 miles in 168 days. He pointed out that the yacht was a direct result of the Round Britain Race because Tabarly, having seen what *Toria* could do in the 1966 Round Britain, ordered her for the 1968 OSTAR in preference to a monohull. He went on to say "these two races have done everything for the development of multihulls". Mike McMullen entered his Newick

designed *Three Cheers*, which Tom Follet had sailed so successfully in the 1972 OSTAR, and there was a new Kelsall designed 35 foot (10.7 m) trimaran called *F.T.* sailed by David Palmer (then news editor of *The Financial Times*). This boat was built not only for this race but with the 1976 OSTAR in mind in which David had his sights on the Jester Trophy. Nick Keig had a new Kelsall designed trimaran called *Three Legs of Mann* which he had built himself. Also in the fleet were the old faithfuls *Snow Goose*, this time sailed by John Hart and John Bennett, and *Toria*, now *Gancia Girl*, sailed by Tony Bullimore and Arthur Ellis.

Of great interest to everyone was the entry of Donald Parr's *Quailo III*, a thoroughbred Class I ocean racer which had been in the 1973 Admiral's Cup team and in the highly successful British team for the Southern Cross Cup in Australia. Here was a chance to see how a top flight conventional ocean racer would fare against her miscellaneous competitors, albeit only two-handed. It was also of interest to have a dedicated RORC ocean racing skipper wanting to try another form of the sport when many of the yacht racing "establishment" were scornfully describing these sort of races as "stunt races". The chairman of the Racing Rules Committee of the International Yacht Racing Union (IYRU) spoke of the rules being "bent if not blatantly disregarded". So blinkered was the vision of some sections of the establishment, that they could not conceive of any sailing race being conducted other than in accordance with the IRYU rules. The chairman went on to recommend that clubs who organized events, such as the Whitbread Round the World Race, should be refused affiliation by their national authorities. Fortunately for sailing, this suggestion did not find widespread support.

There were other conventional ocean racers in the fleet: Robin Aisher lent his *Frigate* to John Holmes, one of Donald Parr's regular crew, and Alan Goodfellow entered his *Hippokampus*. Among small boats were a 25 foot (7.6 m) Folkboat sailed by Richard and Edmund Gatehouse, Richard Clifford's Contessa 26, *Shamaal II*, the Royal Engineers Yacht Club's Contessa 26 *Contessa Caroline*, sailed by Roger Justice and Chris Haskell, the Tankard 24 *Windsor Life*, sailed by Royal Marines Sergeant Gerry Norman, Ewen Southby-Tailyour's Hurley 24, *Black Velvet* and Rod White's Halcyon 24 *Bluff*.

Richard Clifford did well to bring *Shamaal II* home in 24th place overall but perhaps the most remarkable feat was that of the two Swiss boys, Beat Guttinger and Albert Schiess, who sailed their 24 foot (7.3 m) Quarter Tonner *Petit Suisse* into 20th place. Their handling of their tiny boat in a succession of gales and very heavy seas won everyone's admiration. A film made about the race had some remarkable shots of them sailing *Petit Suisse*, dinghy fashion, around Muckle Flugga, the northernmost point of the course. Colin Forbes, who made the film must have been delighted to be rewarded with these shots, having humped his gear over hill and bog to be there at the time.

The first leg of the race was sailed as usual in quiet conditions with the main problems being fog and light winds. This proved to be the undoing of Alain Colas who only managed 10th place, nearly ten hours behind the leader, *British Oxygen*. He subsequently admitted that he had seriously underestimated his competitors and should have removed a lot of the heavy radio equiment, and stocks of spare parts he had onboard for his circumnavigation. Multihulls lead the fleet into Crosshaven and *Quailo III* was the first monohull, in 8th place, followed by *Slithy Tove* 9th, and *Burton Cutter* 11th. On the second leg, to Barra, the four leaders, *British Oxygen*, *Three Cheers*, *Triple Arrow* and *Gulf Streamer*, maintained their positions but Mike McMullen brought his *Three Cheers* in only

Robin Knox-Johnston and Gerry Boxall had British Oxygen *out in front most of the time to win the 1974 Round Britain Race in 18 days.*

just over an hour behind *British Oxygen*. This was the leg which took the greatest toll of the yachts: *Battle Royal*, *Mantis*, *Tane Nui* and *Tehini* all retired in, or just after leaving, Crosshaven and several other boats sought refuge in ports and anchorages up the Irish coast and in the Scottish islands. Once again the Wharram polynesian catamarans had failed to get further than Crosshaven. *Black Velvet*, having battled up the Irish coast almost to Barra, turned and headed south because it was evident his crew would not go beyond Barra, he had had enough. It was said that whereas Ewen could keep going on a diet of sardines and whisky, his crew couldn't! Ewen took *Black Velvet* all the way back to Plymouth, mostly singlehanded, changed crew and then sailed up the Channel to Lowestoft to do the last leg of the race as an honorary competitor. Jeremy Hurlbatt and Malcolm Bird retired into Oban and then took *Fidget* through the Caledonian Canal, into the North Sea, and thence home via Lowestoft.

A fascinating race within the race took place, on the second leg, between *F.T.* and *Quailo*. David Palmer describes it in his book The Atlantic Challenge: "In mid-afternoon, *Quailo III,* the only real thoroughbred ocean racer in the whole fleet of 61 boats, heaves into view, half a mile away from us on our port beam. It is the beginning of a race that lasts for the next 36 hours. Every time the wind goes a little ahead of the beam, *Quailo,* with her 39$\frac{1}{2}$ feet waterline and heavy displacement, inches ahead. Whenever the wind backs to abaft the beam, *F.T.* slides past *Quailo*. At dusk, *Quailo* is pulling away from us as the wind moves slightly north of east. But the following day, having cleared Black Rock and Eagle Island in the small hours of the morning, we overhaul *Quailo* again, and again start racing each other, changing positions all day. With sunset approaching, the dark and brooding shape of Barra Head comes up ahead of us. As it does so, the wind begins to die, and backs through 10 degrees and we start edging away from *Quailo*. Darkness sets in and *Quailo's* lights recede behind us, until we can no longer see them. Our little race is won – at least for this leg.

As we approach the entrance to Castle Bay Harbour, we pass too close to a mass of rock known as Muldoanich and lose our wind. We drift past Muldoanich, and beat towards the finishing line. The wind is all over the place, and I make two bad tacks. With 50 yards to go I look over my shoulder. *Quailo's* lights are moving fast up behind me. She has held her speed past Muldoanich, and is pointing high towards the finishing line. I tack on to starboard, and force her to tack too. I try and hold her on past the line, so that I can tack onto port and cross ahead of her. But she points too high, she just steers across my bow. Two more tacks, faultlessly executed, and *Quailo* crosses the line 15 seconds ahead of us. Where else in the world would two boats as totally different as *Quailo,* the thoroughbred ocean racer, and *F.T.* the brash little trimaran, have a race like this – for 36 hours we have been within a few miles of each other."

There were various dramas on the leg to

Lerwick and the committee allowed a degree of indulgence to some competitors which was appreciated by those concerned, but considered over the odds by those who were not. Basically the concept was that following a mishap – even including a capsize – the competitor was allowed to sail back to the point where he had received assistance and then pick up the race again from there. The elasticity in the rules was not repeated in subsequent races. The chief beneficiary of this liberalism was Brian Cooke, who, when approaching Lerwick, was lying becalmed and virtually still in the water, when a terrific gust came down from the high cliff to the north of him, and simply flipped *Triple Arrow* over before anything could be done. Fortunately the capsize was seen by Mrs Angela Hawkins who was watching through binoculars. She immediately alerted the Coastguards. Eric Jensen the crew was soon on the upturned bottom of the yacht but Brian was trapped under the netting which joins the hulls. However he was finally extricated with a cut eye. The yacht was salvaged and, as soon as the repairs were sufficiently advanced, Brian and Eric sailed out to the position of the capsize, under jury rig, and back to complete the leg. Then started their compulsory 48 hour stopover during which repairs were completed. She resumed the race and managed to climb back up the fleet to finish in Plymouth in 8th place overall.

Croda Way was dismasted off Barra, managed to get back in there and, with virtually no local resources, repaired the mast and rejoined the race – a remarkable feat. Probably most disappointed of all those who were forced to retire were Michael Pipe and Ian Porter in *Slithy Tove,* a revolutionary designed monohull of 48 feet. They had managed to get one place ahead of the Nicholson 55, *Quailo,* by Barra, and were then forced to retire and take a short cut into Lerwick with rigging problems. An unusual casualty on the third leg was *Tower Casper*. The owner and skipper, Martin Wills, was, in his working life, mate of a small merchant ship, belonging to Tower Shipping Line, whose Master was Colin Hoare, now his crew. As the only two officers in the ship one would have expected that they knew each other fairly well, and that they would be able to face life at sea together with equanimity. However, maybe the boot being on the other foot, so to speak, had something to do with the fundamental disagreement which arose after they left Barra, in stinking awful weather, to sail to Lerwick.

Nick Keig and his brother Peter took Three Legs of Mann, *35 feet (10.6m) round to finish in 5th place.*

Martin Wills whose crew decided enough was enough after Castle Bay.

Somewhere near St Kilda, not the most hospitable place in the best of weather, Colin Hoare decided that they were mad to be at sea in such weather in *Tower Casper* and said he would like to be put ashore. They therefore returned to Barra and he disembarked. Martin sailed again, on his own, for Lerwick. There was some surprise when he arrived in Lerwick with no crew, and of course, he had, by sailing without a crew, disqualified himself from the race.

Martin is one of the characters that short handed racing has discovered – after, I think it was an OSTAR start, I went back to the club after the start and found Martin sitting happily on a stool at the bar. What, I asked, are you doing there? "Oh," says he, "I didn't feel like starting today, I think I'll go tomorrow" – and he did! *British Oxygen* was going well, as they approached Lerwick, but, when the time came to get down their huge genoa, it stuck fast. As a result the boat suffered considerable damage and they came third over the line at the end of that leg. *Three Cheers* was in first, followed by *Gulf Streamer*. The repairing of *British Oxygen* caused some controversy because, during the race, yachts may only make use of such facilities as they find in the ports and which are available to everyone. It was held, by some, that a "works team" had worked on *British Oxygen* in contravention of this rule. However, the works team image was created by the many volunteers involved being issued with British Oxygen T Shirts and finally it was agreed that the rule had not been infringed and the protests, which had been pending, were withdrawn. *British Oxygen* was ready to sail on time in her pursuit of the leaders, *Three Cheers* and *Gulf Steamer*.

As *British Oxygen* left Lerwick, *F.T.* appeared after having had a wretched passage from Barra. They had suffered problems with their main beams and with leaks, and the weather had been awful, they had spent some hours hove-to and were just beginning to think things were getting better when the bottom hinge fitting of the rudder broke. This had happened on the first leg but they thought the repair, done in Crosshaven would have solved the problem. They were some 130 miles south-west of Muckle Flugga at the time, a bad place in which to have steering failure.

They decided that they must ship the spare rudder they had brought with them and started to do this. In removing the old one it slipped and drifted away. They shipped the outboard motor and tried to get back to it but a sea broke the engine bracket and the engine was swamped. Abandoning the old rudder, they set about fitting the spare one, not an easy thing to do in the open, heaving ocean and as they struggled they fractured the top hinge fitting. Mercifully it did not break completely and after two and a half hours they were able to get under way again, nursing the boat along, under reduced sail, in order to impose the minimum strain on the rudder fittings.

Leslie Dyball, whose 67 years made him the oldest competitor in the race, arrived in good shape with fly fishing rods, with which to enjoy his visit to Shetland. By Lerwick he was well placed in the handicap order and on the next leg, to Lowestoft he improved his position so much that on arrival in Plymouth he was first on handicap. There is a tendency to think of the course from Lerwick as being all downhill, if only because it looks that way on the chart. True the most northerly and exposed part of the course is behind, but the North Sea can be very violent. On the passage south, to Lowestoft, John Westell and Bill Cherry, in their trimaran *John Willie* suddenly found that their boat had become a proa! One float had broken off. Unlike other proas however, they could not go about and they felt there was no future for them on the one tack they could sail. They therefore sent out a distress call which was soon answered by the German Trawler *Junger Pioneer*. They abandoned the yacht and were taken in to Lerwick. The main hull, and its one float, was towed in to an east coast port and a call some days later to the Royal

Western Yacht Club by the Coastguards, gave news that the other float was being towed into Stavanger, in Norway.

Disaster very nearly struck Mike McMullen on the leg south. He went forward in *Three Cheers* to change headsails, in a fresh wind and rough sea, and was simply bounced overboard from the heaving deck. The boat was moving fast and, although he managed to grasp a lifeline, he could not hold on to it as he was dragged through the water. He let go and the yacht went over him almost breaking one of his legs as she did so. He surfaced some 50 yards from the yacht. Fully clothed, with foul weather gear complete with seaboots, he soon became waterlogged. Meanwhile Martin Read had luffed the boat up into the wind and she drifted back towards Mike who was able to grab hold of the yacht, though maintaining his grip with great difficulty. To enable him to do this Martin had to get all the sail off the boat. Mike was quite unable to hoist himself back on board, nor could this be achieved with Martin's help. Martin therefore grabbed a halyard, attached it to Mike and winched him aboard. History does not recall how long this episode took, from the moment they were sailing until they were able to proceed, but when one considers that *Three Cheers* finished only an hour and eleven minutes after *British Oxygen,* in Plymouth, one is bound to ask who would have been the winner if it had not happened.

British Oxygen was the leader into Lowestoft by a little over 9 hours and this coupled with the fact that she had the tides right for her departure, put her in a very strong position. Lowestoft, as a stopover port in this race, can be extremely frustrating. Many is the time when a yacht has reached within spitting distance of the finishing line there only to have the wind fail and the tidal stream turn against them. Or conversely when it is their time to go out to restart a rushing northerly stream and a light wind make it impossible to make any progress. One gets becalmed in a foul tide in lots of other places, but do so at, or near a finishing line is frustrating if handicapping is in use. By Lowestoft, *Burton Cutter* had worked out a lead of 8 hours over *Quailo* and they were 6th and 7th respectively. After Lowestoft there was no change in the positions of the first ten yachts. Robin Knox-Johnston and Gerry Boxall brought *British Oxygen* in to Plymouth a few minutes before 4.00 p.m. on 24 July with an elapsed time of 18 days 4 hours 26 minutes, which knocked a day and a half off *Toria's* 1966 record time.

Clare Francis (right) and Eve Bonham sailed Cherry Blossom.

Philip Weld and David Cooksey could only manage third in Gulf Streamer.

Before the race Philip Weld had been up to a bit of predicting, and had reckoned that *Gulf Streamer* would need 254 hours sailing to complete the course and that she would be beaten by *Manureva* who would need 240 hours. In the event the winner was not *Manureva* but *British Oxygen* who actually took 244^1/4 hours (only 4^1/2 hours different to Philip Weld's predicted winner's time), and he himself in *Gulf Streamer* bettered his predicted time by 6^1/2 hours – remarkably accurate. It must have been a great disappointment for Phil Weld to come third again but there was a marvellous quote from him after the race which gave an insight of what a sportsman he was. He said "It has been such terrific fun; the point of the whole thing is the marvellous people you meet, the other contestants, the camp followers and the locals in each port. The Round Britain is a wonderful race."

Due to the yachts concerned being in different weather patterns, there were some interesting comparisons to be made between the elapsed time for different yachts on the last leg. The fastest time was put up by *Croda Way* who did it in 1 day 21^3/4 hours, against the winner's time of 2 days 9^1/4 hours. On the last leg *Manureva* very nearly came to grief when a Greek merchant ship hit her, causing damage which, though she was able to finish the race, was, structurally serious. Any account of a race inevitably highlights the winners

and the disasters, but in a race like the Round Britain, and particularly when the weather is as bad as it was in 1974, at least for most of the competitors, all those who finish have, in a sense, won. Those who study the tables of results will pick out the ones they think did particularly well. Leslie Dyball and Larry Pardey sailed consistently well to be worthy winners on handicap, and 13th overall. *Petit Suisse* was a popular taker of the second place on handicap. Clare Francis and Eve Bonham in *Cherry Blossom* showed us how far we had come from the days when clubs sailed "Ladies races" over shortened courses and only on fine days! After a slow first leg in light winds they clawed their way up the fleet, doing particularly well between Barra and Lerwick to finish 22nd overall, and 3rd on handicap. Richard Clifford demonstrated how one can lose a place in a race whilst standing in the bar afterwards. Re-living the final moments of the race, he disclosed that he had entered Plymouth through the eastern entrance. Quite understandably, he had failed to check this final detail in the sailing instructions which directed that yachts should use the western entrance when coming in to finish. This, slightly pedantic, detail of the course instructions was subsequently dropped lest others should be caught in the same way. Richard suffered a one hour penalty which affected his handicap, but not overall, place.

8

OSTAR in Controversy

In the autumn of 1972 there was much discussion, within the race committee, about the rules for the 1976 race. In particular, following the entry of *Vendredi 13* in the race earlier that year, there was concern at to whether or how to control the size of the yachts for 1976.

A suggestion came from Brian Cooke, who had sailed *British Steel* in 1972, that a time penalty should be applied to all yachts over 50 feet (15.2 m) in length on the basis of so much for each foot over 50. This idea was embodied in a first draft of the rules for 1976 as a penalty, but for yachts over 65 feet (19.8 m). This would have meant that one part of the fleet would be sailing boat-for-boat and those at the top end under a very arbitrary handicap system. Blondie Hasler came out strongly against this scheme and favoured a straight upper size limit of 65 feet (19.8 m). In the end, all ideas of placing an upper limit on yachts was discarded together with any form of penalty for size. The result of these descisions was, as we shall see, to be spectacular.

There were to be three classes: *Jester Class* for less than 38 ft (11.5 m) overall and less than 28 ft (8.5 m) waterline; *Gipsy Moth Class* for less than 65 ft (19.8 m) overall and less than 46 ft (14.0 m) waterline; *Penduick Class* Yachts bigger than these. Other rule changes included a slight relaxation in the limitations on sponsors' names appearing on the yachts. For the first time the yacht's name could reflect the name of the sponsor, but the way it was displayed was limited to "either bow and the stern, in each case within an area not exceeding six feet (1.8 m) by six inches (0.15 m), and the name may not contain more than 20 letters . . . ."

The time limit for the race was cut to 50 days and the course altered so that yachts could pass between the Nantucket Light Vessel and Nantucket Island. This was done to keep yachts clear of the main shipping channel leading to New York and the traffic separation lanes in that area. In the spring of 1975 word came that the finish of the OSTAR was going to co-incide with a major assembly of Tall Ships in Newport and that the port would not be able to cope with both events. I think this was little more than bar gossip, but it sparked off a suggestion from Philip Weld and Dick Newick that we should move the finish of our race to Gloucester, where Philip lived. The reaction of competitors, and others who were consulted, varied from very enthusiastic to the competitor who wrote "someone must be out of his cotton-picking mind!" He took four more pages to tell the committee why the race must stay in Newport. The powers that be in Newport got to hear of the proposal to shift the finish and came up strongly, saying that of course they could cope with both events. However, the research that went into the possible move was interesting and convinced the committee that Newport was the best place, Tall Ships or no Tall Ships. As Mike McMullen pointed out, moving the finishing end of the course changes the factors affecting the competitor's choice of route from Plymouth. A shift to the north favours the northern route and one to the south, the southern route. Leaving it at Newport leaves competitors with the dilemma they have had since 1960. So after all the finish remained at Newport.

The years leading up to the 1976 OSTAR were years of crisis, as far as the race was concerned and there were many who thought that it had got out of control. In the 1972 race French competitors had done well. A trimaran had won, but a big monohull was second; there were those who believed that this concept, of an easily handled big monohull, with a long waterline length, was a good one. Thus two, quite different, lines of design vessels would be pursued over the next four years. It was interesting that the man who won in a trimaran in 1972 should be the one to pursue the monohull line and the one who came second in a monohull should go for a multihull in 1976. How they fared was to be even more interesting.

There seemed, at this time, to be hundreds of people, in many countries, who had become convinced that sailing in the OSTAR was something they must do. Over 600 people applied for the rules and conditions for the race and word got around that the race was out of hand. Certainly the organizers became concerned at the prospect of controlling the entry list, although such an eventuality had been allowed for in the drafting of the rules which had been available to prospective entrants late in 1972, three and a half years before the race. It has always seemed surprising that some prospective entrants will launch a hugely expensive campaign and, much later, when fully committed, apply to enter the race. This was the case in 1975 when, in July the committee announced that no more entries could be accepted. The plan was to stop at 100. The reaction to this announcement was spectacular in its widespread and international extent. Indignation, anger and despair were all featured in the letters and telegrams which quickly arrived on the Secretary's desk. Amongst them it was sad to see so many old friends, who should have known better, and there were so many of them it would have been worth someone putting together another race to absorb the surplus.

A month later, a notice was sent out, containing something of a rebuke to those who

hadn't done their planning properly, and saying: "Since our notice of 30 July, in which it was announced that the entry list for the 1976 Royal Western Observer Single-handed Race must be closed, was issued it has been clear that many prospective entrants have committed themselves to expensive, and time consuming projects without having taken advantage of the rule which allowed them to reserve a place in the race. Others have not even obtained copies of the rules. To avoid disappointing those who were so placed, the committee has reviewed the question of closing the list now. It has decided that entries can now be accepted but that all applicants must have either qualified and entered, or paid a deposit under Rule 6.8 by 31 December 1975. FROM THIS DATE NO FURTHER APPLICATIONS WILL BE CONSIDERED. The committee has further decided that it may have to start the race in two sections with the Penduick and Gipsy Moth classes starting 24 hours before the Jester class. This would have the effect of reducing the congestion of yachts in the approaches to the Channel in the first few days of the race."

The last paragraph of that notice stirred up another flurry of correspondence, largely expressing the disgust of the Jester class at being left 24 hours behind. Clare Francis argued cogently on their behalf and it was finally agreed to start the three classes at half hourly intervals. Whilst the problem of the number of entries was worrying the committee another worry, emanating from France, was causing concern. Some time, I think in 1974, Jack Odling-Smee told me that Alain Colas had been on the telephone to ask if the rules were right when they said there was no upper size limit. Jack had replied, jocularly, that, if he could get his boat into Millbay Docks for the inspections, it would be all right. He had no idea what Colas had in mind. In Febraury 1975 he was sent a press cutting, from *Nice Matin*, which disclosed the plans for a boat to be called *Manureva* (later named *Club Méditerranée*). She was to be a four masted yacht of 236 feet overall length (71.9 m).

In March the committee met to discuss Colas' proposed entry, although at this time Colas had said nothing to the Royal Western about his new boat. It was agreed that, if it was as the paper had reported, it should be turned down. Jack Odling-Smee wrote to Colas to inform him of this decision. On 2 April, Colas appeared before the committee to present his case for the entry being allowed. This he did with great competence and charm. He gave details of a number of "passive" devices which would be fitted to give warning of approaching vessels and ice. He described how, by means of a number of remote controls, he could control the yacht from a number of different positions. He emphasized that the sail plan had been so designed that no single sail would be any larger that the sails he had successfully handled in his trimaran *Penduick IV* (in which he had won the 1972 race). With Mike McMullen, himself a competitor, abstaining, the committee voted by a majority to allow the entry, and on 8 April the chairman wrote to Colas to tell him. This letter, which was also to be used as a press release is worth including here because, later, the question of what electronic aids he should be allowed became a contentious issue between Colas and the committee and was much discussed in the press. The letter said: "The RWYC committee, having given careful consideration to your proposed entry and the explanations you gave regarding it, are prepared to accept it as a provisional entry and also to the completion of adequate sea trials in addition to the qualifying cruise. The committee will want to be kept informed of the progress of these trials and, because of the exceptional size of the vessel, consider they may well have to give you special instructions regarding the inspection and the start of the race. Regarding other matters which you mentioned at our meeting, such as radar and weather facsimile, the committee have, and will continue to keep these matters under review but are not prepared to alter the existing rules. The idea of the race was that the entry should rely on his own seamanship and prudent judgment, with as little as possible aid from the shore or other vessels. While radio receivers, transmitters and direction finding are allowed, the above policy has been maintained as it is considered to be fairer to all competitors. However equipment designed to avoid more immediate dangers, such as collisions with icebergs or other vessels, will normally be allowed provided it does not give an unfair advantage in the prosecution of the race. Radar could clearly give considerable advantage, to those possessing it, in the closing stage of the race and is therefore not allowed. Moreover its value, as a safety precaution for a tired lone mariner can be over estimated and there is plenty of evidence to show that reliance on radar can be the cause of accidents".

In the following month, May 1975, Alain Colas suffered a serious setback to his plans. Whilst coming in to anchor in his 70 foot (21.3 m) trimaran *Manureva* his leg became entangled in the anchor warp, which virtually stripped the foot from his right leg. He literally held on to his foot and would not let it be amputated. Nothing daunted he continued to direct his project from his hospital bed. His room was hung about with the plans and schedules, and in July he wrote to say, "Surgeons have done wonders and I shall be able to join the party next June for the race to Newport. The four masted fellow is well under way . . . and incorporating new safety features prompted by what had been said when the committee agreed to know about the scheme". He apologised for his writing explaining that he was "pinned down in a funny position". In October 1975 Jack Odling-Smee wrote to Alain Colas expressing concern that, after his accident, he might not be able to sail the yacht, and explained that we were in no way bound to accept another skipper. (This we had maintained all along). This was a very sympathetically worded letter and expressed the hope that he would be sufficiently recovered to sail.

In February 1976 the Chairman wrote again expressing the Committee's concern both as regards Colas' physical condition and also the fact that the yacht's programme was running late. He invited Alain to come over to meet the committee again. So, on 29 February 1976 they assembled, augmented by a doctor member of the club who was a yachtsman with a circumnavigation to his credit. As Alain came in, and walked the length of the ante-room of the Club, all eyes were, as he must have expected, upon him, to see how well he could walk. He did it bravely, but, as the doctor said afterwards, for all the good his foot was to him he might just as well have been without it. The meeting went on for some time, as he was questioned about the yacht and himself. He was reminded that originally he had said that he would sail the yacht, crewed, to America and then sail back single-handed, and that would be his qualifying cruise. There was now no time for this, but Alain claimed that the America and back trip was never a binding condition of his entry. In this I think he was technically correct, but it had been an undertaking which had influenced the committee when they originally agreed to his entry being accepted. Colas complained that we were making special rules for him, but it was explained to him that this was necessary in view of the unusually large size of his yacht. Before withdrawing, Colas listed a number of safety features that were being incorporated in the yacht.

Members of the Committee must have been swayed, to a greater or lesser extent, by Alain's courage and determination after his accident, and of course they were remembering that he had won the last race. Of his seamanlike qualities no one had any doubt at all, and so it was a very exceptional man we were dealing with.

Finally a letter was typed which gave the Committee's decision and which imposed certain conditions. Alain signed, as agreeing, and was gone. The letter read: "The Committee having heard from you an up to date report on progress and having seen your medical certificate, has decided as follows: 1. That the conditions under which you were provisionally accepted have not been met in that the yacht's programme and sea trials have not followed the plan you outlined to us, i.e., a trip across the Atlantic with a work-up crew and a return passage, single-handed, during the winter.

2. Since you were provisionally accepted you have had a serious accident. The committee accepted your provisional entry only with yourself, an exceptionally experienced seaman, as crew. As you have already been advised, there can be no question of any reserve crew being accepted.

3. The Committee has noted the enormous amount of original thinking and effort in the furtherance of safety at sea which has already been devoted to the enterprise.

The Committee has therefore decided that your provisional entry should stand, subject to the following conditions: a. The qualifying cruise must be completed in accordance with Rule 8. b. As previously indicated, and particulary in view of your injury, further sea trials will be required as follows: 1. A single-handed cruise in the North Atlantic must be competed, by yourself, over a distance, between not more than four points, of 1500 miles. 2. This cruise to be successfully completed by 15 May 1976. 3. Evidence of this trial must be sent to the Committee in the same way as that for the qualifying cruise. The reservations as regards pre-race inspection and the start, mentioned in our letter of 8 April remain."

Late in January 1976 the Council of the RYA expressed concern about the number and size of the yachts taking part in the OSTAR. As a result the Royal Western Yacht Club was asked to meet the RYA in London on 2 March to talk about the race. I accompanied Jack Odling-Smee to that meeting at which we explained the arrangements being made for the race and, in particular, special

measures on account of the size of the fleet and some of the competing yachts. The RYA appeared to be satisfied that all that could be done was being done but asked that competitors be instructed to carry the shapes and lights to indicate "not under command" for use when they were sleeping or not able to keep a look-out. This idea started a whole other controversy which we need not pursue here. It was fortuitous that at this time the Deputy Chairman of the RYA was David Edwards, who had been Commodore of the Royal Ocean Racing Club. Not only was he a very experienced ocean racing skipper, but also a solicitor. This combination of a wealth of experience and an ability to argue a case made him an excellent mediator. On 20 May 1976 a meeting was held in London between representatives of the Marine Division of the Department of Trade and the RYA, to discuss the arrangements which had been made by the Royal Western Yacht Club for the OSTAR "in the interests of marine safety". The DOT were worried by a number of aspects including the number of entries, the size of some of them and the inability of the skippers to maintain a constant look-out. Apart from the matter of the race about to be held, the question of future events was also discussed and the RYA asked to give its views. The RYA were in favour of restricting numbers and sizes of entries and of discouraging multihulled yachts "which lack fundamental stability" however they felt that they should defend the right of sensible single-handed yachtsmen to participate subject to reasonable rules to control such events. The committee, and certainly the competitors, were unaware that these eleventh hour deliberations on the future of the race were taking place. Perhaps it was just as well.

This is perhaps a good point at which to consider some of the rules which the committee has evolved, over the years, directed at making the race as safe as possible as well as reducing the number of retirements after the start.

In the first place one needs to be sure that those who are occupying places in a limited entry race are bone fide competitors and not there to impress their friends for a while before fading out before the start. On the other hand there are those, over the years, who have genuinely intended to take part but, having no previous experience of long distance single-handed sailing, did not know that it was not really their scene. The qualifying cruise was designed to sort these sort of people out.

One day a girl arrived in my office, saying that

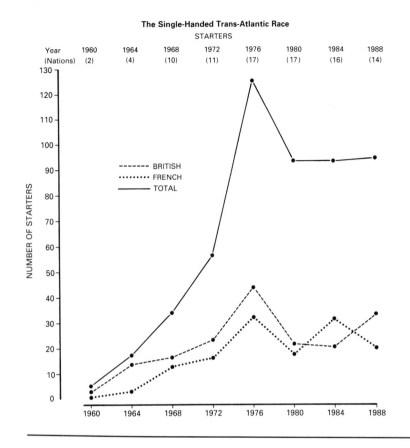

The Single-Handed Trans-Atlantic Race

The number of starters in each year of OSTAR. It will be remembered that after 1976, there was an extensive debate about both the size of yachts and the numbers taking part. After that numbers of entries were limited and although the number of starters each time was smaller than the entry, it has remained very consistent and is acknowledged as convenient. Numbers of British and French starters show no special trends, but French support and success remain strong, while the British, as might be expected form about one third of the entries.

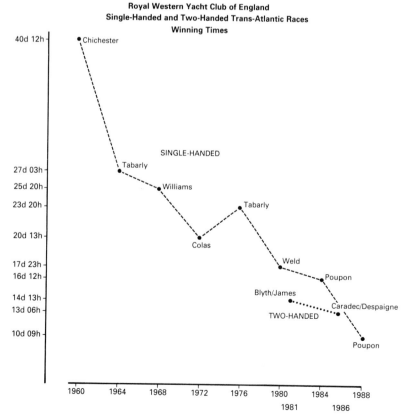

Royal Western Yacht Club of England
Single-Handed and Two-Handed Trans-Atlantic Races
Winning Times

The almost steady increase in the speed of the winners of OSTAR is seen in these elapsed times over the course. The first drastic reduction in time was by Eric Tabarly in Pen Duick in 1964, making Chichester's pioneering effort look more of a cruise. However it must be remembered that in general the boats have increased in size. There must be some limit to the speed of a 60ft sailing boat; yet who is to say that this has yet been reached. Faster speeds have been put up on almost the same course with fully crewed multihulls sailing eastward, so certainly better times may be seen. The two-handed race records may have faster potential.

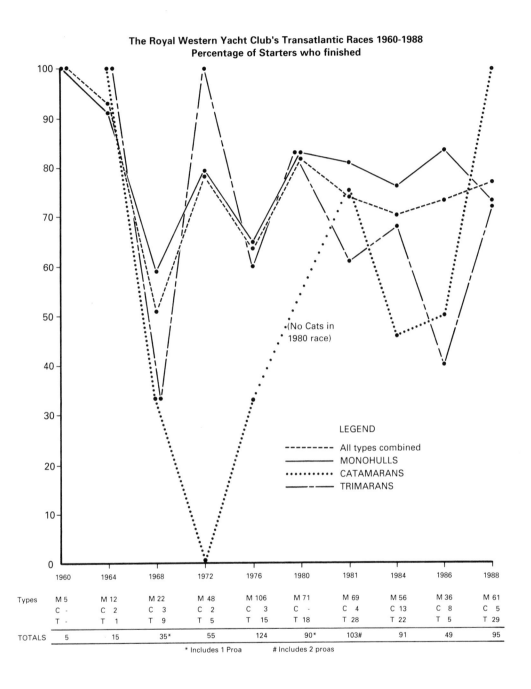

The Royal Western Yacht Club's Transatlantic Races 1960-1988
Percentage of Starters who finished

(No Cats in 1980 race)

LEGEND
- - - - - - All types combined
———— MONOHULLS
············ CATAMARANS
— - — - TRIMARANS

	1960	1964	1968	1972	1976	1980	1981	1984	1986	1988
Types	M 5	M 12	M 22	M 48	M 106	M 71	M 69	M 56	M 36	M 61
	C -	C 2	C 3	C 2	C 3	C -	C 4	C 13	C 8	C 5
	T -	T 1	T 9	T 5	T 15	T 18	T 28	T 22	T 5	T 29
TOTALS	5	15	35*	55	124	90*	103#	91	49	95

* Includes 1 Proa   # Includes 2 proas

The Atlantic weather on each OSTAR obviously plays a major part in determining the number of finishers in the race. 1968 and 1978 as is recounted in the text were years when conditions took a heavy toll. There is a slight sign from 1984 onwards that the boats are becoming a little more reliable. The big catamarans have certainly come to the fore and through this graph does not show, that is also where the winners came from in later years.

As the big multis "get there", one can expect to see multihulls showing a higher return in future years, with monohulls as smaller and more "amateur". However, historically monohulls have the edge in reliability.

she had come to Plymouth in a yacht she was borrowing for the race and was about to go out to do her 500 mile qualifying cruise. The next day she was back saying that she had returned in order to sort out a problem with the boat. For the second time she set out only to return with another problem, Finally after the third attempt she came to see me and as I talked to her I knew exactly what the problem was. "Look, I said," the qualifying cruise is devised to help competitors as well as the organizers. For many people it is the first real experience of sailing offshore alone and some people find it is just not for them. I don't think you really want to go ahead with it and there is absolutely nothing to be ashamed of – much better to make a sensible decision now not to go."

She seemed much relieved at this suggestion. Now all she had to do was agree, which she did and sailed happily away to enjoy sailing in the congenial company of others, which is, after all, what most people prefer. To cheer her up, I had told her about a certain doctor who arrived one day in a very handsome, well found yacht and picked up a mooring off the club. He came ashore and told me he was about to sail to do his 500 mile cruise, and, later in the day sailed out. His yacht was quite large but very much a cruising boat so I was surprised to see him back on the mooring some 36 hours later. That was quick, I said as he came, beaming, into my office. Thirty six hours of my own company is quite enough to persuade me that single-handing is not for me, he replied and we

Club Mediterranée was launched upside down and ...

went through to the bar to celebrate his return into society.

These are two experiences I know about because they happened in Plymouth, but there must have been many others elsewhere. How much better to give up gracefully and quietly at that stage than to give up after the start. There are of course two elements being tested during a qualifying cruise, the skipper and his boat, as well as the combination of the two. One might think anyone about to start a single-handed transatlantic voyage, particularly going westward and to windward, would make quite sure that his or her boat was fully tried and tested before starting. Despite the rules we have devised there are always some who slip through insufficiently prepared.

Alain Colas' failure to win the 1976 OSTAR could be attributed to lack of sea trials despite all the efforts of the committee, who actually made him do more than the rules demanded. The great *Club Mediterranée,* which cost a fortune to build and was full of the most sophisticated equipment that ever went to sea in a yacht, failed to win because, one after the other, the halyards failed. More sea time before the race would have pin-pointed this weakness. The French girl skipper Florence Arthaud was persuaded at the last minute that her rigging needed renewal or adjustment. So, the evening before the start, work was going on to this end. Next morning, on her way to the start, her mast fell over the side, and that was her out of the race. There is always something to be said for

... then righted by hawsers attached to the hull.

Georgi Georgiev, the first Bulgarian entry, went on to complete a circumnavigation after the race. He was later lost at sea.

Bob Lenguel, big ship radio man and small boat single-hander, met his first Plymouth girl by boarding the lifeboat at sea.

having had to come a long way for the race and in this respect entries from the United States have benefited from the long passage to Plymouth. Philip Weld, who won the 1980 race, always seemed to arrive in a state of complete preparedness, and an aura of calm surrounded his boat when all about him were engaged in frantic last minute preparations. Too often have we seen a yacht with a man up the mast in a bosun's chair on the morning of the start.

For 1976 Clare Francis entered a boat called *Robertsons Golly* in deference to the firm who sponsored her, and this caused some concern to a lady in Bermuda. She wrote to say that everyone knows "we don't talk about a Golly these days. The club must stop her calling her boat that". In reply I pointed out that the Gollywog was the trade mark of her sponsors and there was nothing we could do about that. With my tongue in my cheek I went on to say that the last time Clare sailed in one of our races she sailed a boat called *Cherry Blossom* and on that occasion she had a little bunch of cherries on the back of her white trousers and I couldn't promise there wouldn't be a Golly there this time. Neither Clare nor the Royal Western had any more complaints.

One of the Bulgarian entries arrived in Plymouth and was instantly arrested. Georgi

Georgiev left Bulgaria with his yacht in a merchant ship which it was planned should enter Plymouth and discharge Georgi and the yacht. However, when the ship arrived off Plymouth there was a thick fog and she decided not to come in. They lowered the yacht over the side, put Georgi in her and told him the course for Plymouth. In the fullness of time and still in thick fog Georgi sailed right in to the basin in front of the Club. I took him at once to Millbay Docks to clear customs, where he was promptly arrested. He had no visa and had broken the law by disembarking himself and his boat without the proper formalities. He remained under boat arrest for several days until, following intercessions on his behalf by the editor of *The Observer* to the Home Office, Dr Shirley Summerskill, the Parliamentary Under Secretary of State at the Home Office, authorized his release and wrote to say that this must not happen again!

One of those who did not get to the start was the unfortunate Philip Weld whose trimaran *Gulf Streamer* was capsized by a rogue wave on his way across. He and his crew spent four and a half days living in the upturned hull before being rescued by a ship. The yacht was later picked up by a Russian ship and has subsequently been seen sailing in the Baltic. Chay Blyth also came unstuck in his attempt to win the race with the 80 foot (24.4 m) trimaran *Great Britain III*. He had just completed his mileage and was approaching Dartmouth from Start Point when, whilst he was below getting ready to enter harbour, he was struck by a merchant ship. The ship did not stop nor apparently was she aware that she had been in collision. Chay tried to make Salcombe but, with one float very badly damaged, the yacht capsized, watched by an Auxiliary Coastguard at Prawle Point. There was a rough sea and Chay was in the water for some time before being rescued by a trawler, who later towed the trimaran into Plymouth. She could not be repaired in time for the race. The outcry which followed Chay's accident was not directed at the ship, who in good visibility, had run down an 80 foot sailing vessel, but at Chay for being singlehanded!

At the bottom end of the 1976 fleet there was a little boat called *Prodigal*, owned and skippered by an American, Bob Lenguel. He was, when not sailing, a radio officer in a large merchant ship and so it was not surprising he had effective radio in his yacht. He and I had been in correspondence for some time before he finally left the USA to sail to Plymouth and as he came he kept me informed of his position and ETA. One morning he radioed to

say that he was becalmed near the Eddystone lighthouse ten miles south of Plymouth. We were in the middle of a very calm spell of weather and the prospects for him looked unpromising if he was to complete his passage under sail. I therefore set off in the club launch to offer him a tow in, but when I found him, as he had said, near the Eddystone, "like hell was he going to accept a tow after coming all that way", so I passed him his mail and returned to Plymouth. Later a breeze sprang up and, as he was approaching Plymouth he was spotted by the Plymouth lifeboat which was at sea on some trial or other. The coxswain went over to see *Prodigal* and, as he came close to her Bob spotted that there was a girl onboard the lifeboat, whereupon he ran up alongside the lifeboat exclaiming "God dammit, a woman" and leapt onboard leaving *Prodigal* to cannon off the lifeboat's rubbing strake and sail away. The lifeboat coxswain, John Dear, expressed concern that he had left his boat sailing unmanned but Bob replied "Thats O.K. she's on auto". The lifeboat duly replaced Bob onboard and I met him inside the harbour where the wind had gone very light again. I finally presuaded him to take a tow but not before he had set up a loudspeaker on his foredeck through which he transmitted the strains of *Rule Britannia* alternating with *The Star Spangled Banner*. Bob did the 1976 and 1980 races, retired from the 1984 race and withdrew a few weeks before the 1988 event saying that it had all overtaken him, and was now too big and commercial and not like it used to be.

From her arrival in Plymouth it was clear that the pre-race inspection of *Club Mediterranee* was beyond the expertise of the usual inspection teams. With the aid of the Royal Navy the scope and function of her computerised navigation and other systems were assessed and it was clear that some of them were not allowed by the rules. In 1976 competitors were not allowed radio navigational aids (except DF), radar or weather facimile receivers. Colas had all these and more. The Committee's insistence that some of the computer's functions must be rendered inoperable before the start not only upset Colas but prompted a leading article in The Times. The leader writer thought the Committee were being unreasonable but it would have been quite wrong to allow Colas aids which were specifically denied to the other competitors.

One extra ordinary starter was to be Ambrogio Fogar, from Italy, who had entered a 25 foot (7.62 m) catamaran called *Spirit of Surprise*, a modified Hellcat, which is for afternoon racing in

Ambrogio Fogar's aptly named catamaran caused some surprise when allowed to start. He retired to the Azores when structural failure loomed.

sheltered waters. In Millbay basin the skipper demonstrated his method of righting the cat in the event of a capsize, which seemed fine in a still basin but would be another thing in mid-Atlantic. His accommodation consisted of two slots, one in each hull, down which he could slide his body into a reclining, but not horizontal, position. After a very careful inspection Ambrogrio was given an acceptance certificate and all he then needed was a diving suit and sandwiches for thirty days! He took

The Lizzie McMullen Trophy, presented by competitors, together with the Royal Western Yacht Club and The Observer *to commemorate Lizzie's death on the eve of the race.*

the southern route and very nearly got there but just before reaching the point of no return, between the Azores and Newport, he decided that in view of the fact that the boat was showing signs of structural weakness he should retire to the Azores.

On Thursday 3 June, only 48 hours before the start of the race, the whole assembly was shattered to learn the news that Lizzie McMullen had been electrocuted and killed when helping her husband, Mike, to polish the bottom of *Three Cheers*. She had dropped the electric polisher into shallow water and went to pick it up. The sadness of it seemed to be accentuated by the naturally tensed up state of those who were in the final stages of preparing for the great event. Mike was a very

THE LIZZIE McMULLEN TROPHY
for the First Multihull in the Royal Western/Observer Singlehanded Transatlantic Race
Presented in her memory by the Competitors in the 1976 Race
The Royal Western Yacht Club of England. The Observer and Other Friends.

1976 THIRD TURTLE M.BIRCH
1980 MOXIE PHILIP WELD
1984 FLEURY MICHON PHILIPPE POUPON

popular figure and the loss he suddenly had to bear was keenly felt by all those connected with the race. Within hours of Lizzie's death, the suggestion was made that a trophy should be created in her memory. I think the suggestion came from Stuart Woods, but it was so unanimously agreed that it is hard to attribute it to any one in particular. The Royal Western Yacht Club and *The Observer* immediately agreed to this new trophy and made substantial donations towards it.

As I moved about the club and in Millbay Docks seeing to the last minute arrangements for the race, my pockets filled up with donations pressed into my hand by competitors also concerned with their last minute preparations, but anxious to be associated with the trophy. So was

born the Lizzie McMullen Memorial Trophy, a handsome silver-plated model of *Three Cheers* which has ever since, been awarded to the first multihulled yacht to finish.

The funeral took place the following day, Friday, and Mike bravely decided that he would start with the rest the next day. He and Lizzie had worked together to prepare *Three Cheers* and he felt it would be her wish that he went through with it. For Mike, who he, as well as many others, thought had a very good chance of winning, there could have been no worse prelude to the race. He sailed with the others on 5 June, and, apart from being sighted off Galley Head, on the south-west coast of Ireland, on 6 June, he was never seen again.

Mike McMullen

9

Big Boats and Biggest Entry

The Fifth Royal Western/Observer Single-handed Transatlantic Race 1976

In view of the number of yachts, the start of the race was arranged outside Plymouth Sound. The starting line was set on an east/west line across the main, western, approach channel to Plymouth with areas to the north and south of the line marked by buoys and reserved for competing yachts. The areas were patrolled by naval and police launches in an effort to keep them clear. This line had been chosen to take advantage of the lee provided by Rame Head and Penlee point in the event of strong winds between south and north, through west. Despite the division of the fleet into three classes it proved a little cramped and as soon as the big class had started, the spectator boats, until then fairly well under control, swarmed in, oblivious of the fact that there were still two more starts to follow. In later years we started all the yachts together and moved the line further out to give everyone more space. I wondered how many of the competitors, or anyone else for that matter, noticed that there were no guns for the start of the Penduick class. The saluting gun, mounted in the bows of the minesweeper acting as committee boat, had firing pin problems and the gun was replaced by a very down-market sounding klaxon horn. However I was glad to read in the papers next day that "As the gun boomed out for the start of the race . . ."

125 competitors set off accompanied by one unofficial one, Yan Nedellec, who had taken over *Objectiv Sud 2* at the last moment and was not accepted by the committee since he had not qualified in accordance with the rules. He never got to Newport because he capsized three times, lost his mast and was rescued by the Royal Fleet Auxiliary *Olwen* when making for France under jury rig. During his capsizes he had sustained a serious neck injury, due he thought to a battery having struck him, and it was remarkable that he had managed to jury rig his yacht and sail a considerable distance towards France before being rescued. I saw him in the Naval Hospital in Plymouth after he had been X-rayed and the doctor said that he had virtually broken his neck. However he recovered and was to re-appear in the 1981 Two-Handed Transatlantic Race.

The race was characterized by two vigorous depressions which were to make the northern route extremely hazardous. The first casualty to be reported was Guy Cornou, in *Kervilor II,* who radioed on 8 June that he had back trouble. His report was picked up by a French frigate who went to his assistance, directed to his position by an RAF Nimrod aircraft. The frigate then put three officers onboard the yacht and, with Guy still onboard, they sailed to Falmouth where they arrived two days later. Apart from some retirements, unaided, due to gear failure, the next casualty was Tony Bullimore in *Toria*. On 12 June

Vendredi Treize *(3 masts) and* Club Méditerranée *(4 masts) before the start. The tiny* Jester *with her Chinese lug sail is directly above the stern of* Club Med'. *In the foreground,* Spirit of America.

he was forced to abandon his yacht which had caught fire. He was lucky to be picked up very quickly by a passing merchant ship. The same day a report from France said that Dominique Berthier had been picked up by a French trawler at 1800 after having lost her yacht *Saint Milcent* in collision with a merchant ship off Ushant the previous day.

On 11 June the first depression, Low E, then about 984 millibars, was close south east of Newfoundland and, twenty four hours later, it had deepened and moved rapidly to a position some 450 miles South West of Iceland, 976. At the same time another one was brewing up over Sable Island. This was to become Low F. On 13 June Low E was about 200 miles South of Iceland and Low F had moved from Sable Island to a position 200 miles east of Cape Race, Newfoundland. This was another deep, fast moving, depression. By the

following day Low F had deepened to 972 and was right in the middle of the North Atlantic giving storm force contrary winds to all the leading boats on the northern and great circle routes. Just before noon on Monday 14 June the Ocean Weather Ship R reported receiving a distress signal from the yacht *Gauloise,* Pierre Fehlman, which said "ship leaking request immediate assistance". Her approximate position was 49° N 33° W which meant she was 300 miles south east of the centre of Low F and in gale, or more likely, storm force winds. At 1650 Lands Ends Radio reported that there were four ships answering *Gauloise's* call and the nearest was the *Atlantic Conveyor* who made an ETA of 1855. Two others made their ETA's as 2155. At 2000 Lands End Radio reported a message from *Atlantic Conveyor,* relayed by the Royal Fleet Auxiliary *Pear Leaf,* saying that she would attempt to close *Gauloise* in one hour. Half

Opposite page: Jester. *The only yacht to have started in all the OSTARs.*

Martin Read and Mike McMullen sailed the smallest boat in the 1970 Round Britain Race.

Five Frioul 38s were entered for the 1976 OSTAR. Seen here in Millbay Docks they are, from the inside, Pytheas, Objectiv Sud 3, Objectiv Sud 2, Pierre *and* Objectiv Sud 1. *(Courtesy of Henk Jukkema)*

On his way to the start of the 1976 OSTAR Henk Jukkema took this picture of Mike McMullen taking his Three Cheers *out for what was to be their last race. (Courtesy of Henk Jukkema)*

There were 8 Dutch competitors in the 1980 OSTAR. Standing (L to R): Andre de Jong, Piet ter Laag, Henk van de Weg, Kees Roemers, Wytze van der Zee. Sitting: Henk Jukkema. On ground: Burg Veenemans, Jan Verwoerd. (Courtesy of Henk Jukkema)

A clean start to the 1981 TWOSTAR with not a spectator boat in sight. The orange buoy dividing multis from monos is just to the right of the naval patrol vessel which marked the far end of the line. (Courtesy of Eve Foster)

Spaniel II *in which Kazimierz Kaworski won a prize in the 1980 OSTAR for his outstanding performance.* *(Courtesy of Henk Jukkema)*

Thunderer Raoc *inspects the "Committee Boat" while the guns crew insert ear plugs before the start of the* *1981 TWOSTAR. (Courtesy of Eve Foster)*

Marlow Ropes *(Ex* Exmouth Challenge/Umupro Jardin) *was back in the hands of Mark Gatehouse for the 1985 Round Britain. (Courtesy of James Boyd)*

The fleet sleeps peacefully in eary morning sunshine before the 1984 OSTAR.

Alice's Mirror, *first sailed by Adrian Thompson in the 1982 Round Britain, is seen here in the 1988 OSTAR sailed by Jeremy Heal. (Courtesy of Roger Lean-Varcoe)*

an hour later the Rescue Co-ordination Centre (RCC) in Plymouth reported that *Atlantic Conveyor* was homing in on *Gauloise* on 2182 kHz. We later had a report that Pierre Fehlman had been picked up by *Atlantic Conveyor* but that the yacht was in a sinking condition in position 49° 02′ N, 34° 14′ W.

Meanwhile, back at 1655 on 14 June, we heard that Yvon Fauconnier, in *ITT Oceanic* had broken an arm and had torn sails after a force 10 storm. This report was followed at 2035 by one from Land's End Coastguard who said that *ITT's* position was 48° 30′ N, 37° 30′ W and that a French radio station had reported the yacht "lying down – ship *Triton* proceeding ETA 2200". This was followed by a report from Halifax, Nova Scotia, that the yacht was in position 084° True from St John's distant 630 miles. The rescue of Fauconnier and *ITT* culminated with the Russian tug *Besstrashnij* taking her in tow and at the same time going to the rescue of Jean Yves Terlain, whose 70 foot catamaran *Kriter III* (previously named *British Oxygen*) was breaking up. The tug rescued Terlain and towed *ITT* into St John's. *Kriter III* sank.

Also in trouble at this time was Mike Best, in his 35 foot trimaran *Croda Way*. At 2100 on 14th he reported being in 46° 20′ N, 31° 40′ W in a force 8 gale having had "rotten weather" for three days. One float was loose and his mainsail was ripped "otherwise fine". His position could truly be said to be "mid Atlantic" and at 2030 on 15 June his base, the School of Military Engineering, reported that he was heading for Newfoundland to effect repairs. The next day he was reported heading east and the day after that it was confirmed that he was heading for Plymouth. From there Mike nursed his damaged yacht some 1200 miles. Fortunately he had good radio contact and we were able to feed him special weather forecasts and generally monitor his progress. He finally arrived unaided in Plymouth, a fine feat of seamanship in the best traditions of the race.

Some way to the east of where *Gauloise*, *ITT*

Tabarly, with a crew member still on board, before the start with the two monsters he was to beat to Newport.

Mike Best nursed his Croda Way *back to Plymouth with a damaged float.*

Geoff Hales won the monohull handicap award with his 34 foot (10.4m) Wild Rival *after losing his mainsail in a knockdown.*

and *Kriter III* were playing out their dramas, Patrick Szekely's yacht *Nyarlathotep* suffered major structural damage and sank. He was rescued from his liferaft on 17 June by the Spanish trawler *Touro.* Others to have troubles were Geoff Hales whose Rival 34, *Wild Rival,* was knocked down at the cost of his mainsail, and Colin Drummond in *Sleuth Hound* whose retirement questionnaire included the following: Q. What caused you to retire? A. "Knocked down in force 11, thrown overboard, harness held, injured shoulder, torn main, storm jib, main compass broken, all electronic instruments out, batteries lost acid, VHF gone." Q. By whom were you rescued? A. "Made port under own steam." Geoff Hales luckily had a spare, though old mainsail onboard and with it he nursed his boat to Newport to win the handicap award for monohulls with a passage time of 32^1/$_2$ days. Not so lucky was Angus Primrose who, in his Moody 33 *Demon Demo,* was sailing with only a heavily reefed headsail in gale conditions when he was rolled through 360 degrees. Damage to the yacht was surprisingly small but he lost the mast. He rigged a jury mast using a spinnaker pole and sailed over 1000 miles to Plymouth arriving safely without any help.

Club Méditerranée, already beset by halyard problems, ran into the first of the two storms on the night of 11 June, but managed to keep going. By noon that day Colas estimated that he had covered over a third of the distance to Newport and during the gale he managed to make good 176 miles to windward in the 24 hours to noon 12th. But during that time he suffered sail and halyard damage and after only 24 hours respite, the second, and fiercer, storm arrived with winds between 50 and 70 knots. This went on until 15 June. Although Colas started with five halyards on each of his four masts he had, by the 18 June, so few left that he was finding the yacht difficult to manoeuvre through the imbalance of the sails he was able to set. He therefore decided to go into St John's to reeve new halyards and repair his sails. Because of his extreme northerly route this was not all that much out of his way, but he could ill afford the time. Colas later estimated that, on the basis of what he saw on Tabarly's charts, he had been leading Tabarly by some 330 miles when he went in to St John's.

Tabarly was keeping very quiet but on 19 June a report came, allegedly from the Canadian Coast Guard, that he had been seen 93 miles south of Cape Race, with 850 miles to go and estimating arriving Newport 21 or 22 June. In fact on 19, Tabarly still had some 1200 miles to cover to the finish off Brenton Reef Tower. In the early hours of 29 June, 0312 local time, Tabarly crossed the line and sailed his 73 foot (22.2 m) *Penduick VI* all the way in to Goat Island. In the early light of dawn there he was and that was the first anyone knew of his arrival. For the second time therefore Tabarly was the race winner, and this despite his having to sail most of the race without self-steering gear. The next arrival was *Club Mediterranée*, 7¹/₂ hours later. When he left St John's it was noted that Colas had helpers onboard who hoisted his sails and disembarked at sea. The Rules clearly said that, where a yacht put in for repairs, "when actually anchored or moored other people may come on board . . . and repairs effected". In this case the Committee ruled that there had been an infringement of the rules and Colas was awarded a penalty of 58 hours (10% of his elapsed time). This dropped him to 5th place.

The acrimony over the use of his computer and the penalty at the end should not cloud the achievement of Colas in sailing this huge craft single-handed across the Atlantic, in appalling weather and despite his partial disability following his accident the previous year. It was a great feat but not one which anyone should be allowed to repeat.

On the evening of 30 June I was at a party at which the conversation same round to the race and someone asked me how it was going. I remember saying that, because of the atrocious weather there had been in mid-Atlantic, I was worried that one, or perhaps more, of the competitors would be lost. I put my light out about midnight and had just dropped into that deep sleep that starts the night, when my telephone rang. It was the Lands End Coastguard to say that the yacht *Galloping Gael* had been found with no one on board her. The skipper, Mike Flanagan had been lost overboard. Miserably, I drove in to the club to open up the office so that I could inform the next-of-kin before the news broke on radio or in the press. No one will ever know precisely what happened but it seems likely that, to judge by the state of the sails, he was forward, adjusting sails, when he fell overboard. The Canadian Air Force flew a number of searches but it was quite hopeless. Mike Flanagan's liferafts, of which he had two, were both on board when the yacht was found.

Over the next three days concern for *Three Cheers* increased as more, less competitive boats

Angus Primrose lost his mast in a capsize, but sailed back to Plymouth under jury rig.

Mike Flanagan's yacht Galloping Gael *was found without him. Mike was presumed to have fallen overboard.*

than *Three Cheers,* arrived in Newport. People started suggesting air searches for her but it is difficult to explain to those who clamour for searches of one kind or another how big the ocean is in relation to the amount one can search. Without some focal point or datum there is nothing one can sensibly do. In fact in the case of *Three Cheers* a number of assumptions were made which produced a possible datum for a search and, when this has been updated by computer to allow for drift in the intervening period, a search was flown but without result.

Over a year later in July 1977, some wreckage was washed up in Iceland, 4½ miles west of the Thjorsa River. This consisted of part of a trimaran outrigger float together with a part of a sail, with sail number 9, and was positively identified as part of *Three Cheers,* but this was not reported to the UK until October 1980. Another part of *Three Cheers* was found in March 1980 and I will refer to this later.

As the days went by, yachts continued to arrive in Newport with varying tales to tell; fierce storms and emergency repairs and, on the other hand, frustrating calms, depending upon which route they had chosen. With tracks fanned out over more than 20 degrees of latitude there were bound to be widely varying conditions. Those to the south had a less hectic ride but more frustration due to

calms, although approaching the USA from whatever angle involved a fair share of calms.

Down on the southern route an interesting battle was fought out by the 35 foot Derek Kepsall designed trimaran *FT,* sailed by David Palmer and the bigger, 53 foot (16.5 m) trimaran *CAP 33* sailed by Tom Grossman. They followed virtually the same track as far as 28° West (which is the longitude of the Azores) and at this point *FT,* taking advantage of a wind shift altered course to the south for two days to go down to what he considered the Azores route. He had been five days on the wind in a stiff southwesterly. As he tracked south he passed close east of the Chaucer Bank,

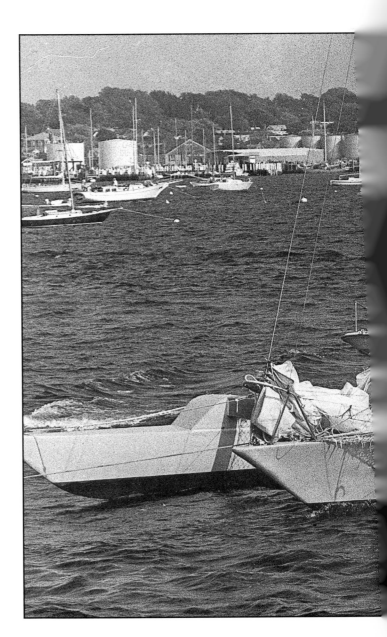

Tom Grossman was the first American to finish in 4th place.

which is an extraordinary mountain ridge coming up from very deep water to within 78 feet of the surface. He was very nearly capsized by a sea which was steepened by the Bank. After passing the Bank he turned westward again for Newport abandoning his plan to follow the more southerly Azores route.

Meanwhile *CAP 33* had continued on a generally south westerly course and had worked out a good lead over *FT*. But on the 18/19 he turned to the southward, crossing ahead of *FT*, until he was south of latitude 40°. Meanwhile *FT* kept north of 40° and by the 29 June was coming up well on *CAP 33* who was having problems to the

south of him. However Tom Grossman managed to get *CAP 33* into Newport almost a day ahead of *FT* to finish 4th overall and 2nd multihull. David Palmer in *FT* finished 7th overall, 3rd multihull and 3rd in the *Jester* Class. He was also the first British skipper to finish. David Palmer reported that the swell when he was in the vicinity of the Chaucer Bank was the biggest he had ever seen. This was due to the storms which were lashing his fellow competitors to the north and holding back *Friends*, the 30 foot (9.1 m) trimaran sailed by Walter Greene, who finished just under three hours after *FT* having at one stage been ahead of her.

David Palmer, here arriving in Newport, sailed his FT *into 7th place to be the first British finisher.*

Dick Newick had reason to be pleased with his *Third Turtle* coming first and *Friends* fourth out of the multihull fleet, a remarkable achievement considering they were only 32 and 30 feet (9.7 and 9.1 m) respectively.

The 1976 OSTAR was the first race in which there was a British lady skipper, Clare Francis, who not only beat the other three girls but also the ladies record for the race. She brought her 38 foot (11.5 m) sloop, *Robertsons' Golly,* into Newport in 13th place overall and 6th in her class. Her elapsed time was 29 days 2 hours. During the race Clare recorded, for BBC Television, her story of the race as she went along. On top of all there was to be done this was a remarkable achievement and, at times a very moving story in which we saw her moments of despondency as well as contentment and triumph. It was later to play an important role in influencing at least one section of the yachting

Mike Birch in his little 32 foot (9.75m) trimaran, The Third Turtle, *took second place.*

The Third Turtle *in Newport.*

Clare Francis, as her T-shirt proclaimed, sailed Robertson's Golly.

Richard Konkolski sailed his little $22^1/2$ foot (6.8m) monohull Nike into 49th place in $39^1/2$ days.

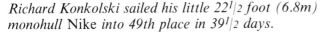

Rodney Kendall's kit-built Achilles 24, Songeur, just made it within the time limit.

Val Howells, veteran of the first two OSTARs, competed this time against his son Philip, but had to retire following a bad fall.

world in the post-race re-appraisal in single-handed sailing. It has always astonished me how many of the girls who go in for singlehanded racing are so slight. On being introduced to a French girl, who had already made a name for herself as a single-hander, I remember saying "Good heavens,

I believe you are even smaller than Clare Francis!" to which she replied "Yes, I think I am." The girls have told me that they get by using their heads, and a lot more patience than the men, and that makes up for the absence of some of the muscle.

Down at the bottom of the fleet, in the 26 foot (7.9 m) and under section, there was a good survival record though only six out of eleven managed to get to Newport within the time limit. Richard Clifford, in his Contessa 26, *Shamaal II*, finished 30th in 33$^1/_2$ days. Next came Richard Konkolski, 49th in his 22$^1/_2$ foot *Nike*, in 39$^1/_2$ days followed by David Sutcliffe, 61st in his Contessa 26, *Lady Anne of St Donats*, in 44 days. Henry Pottle was 66th in his Folkboat *Janina* in 45 days followed by Rodney Kendall in his kit built Achilles 24, *Songeur*, in 49 days and finally, just before the time limit expired came Bob Lenguel in his 25 foot *Prodigal*, in 73rd place in 49$^1/_2$ days. Of the five little boats which did not finish, Chris Smith in *Tumult* 22$^1/_2$ feet, was forced to retire through ill health, Mike Richey decided to take *Jester* on an Irish cruise, Jonathan Virden, in his Folkboat *Sharavoge* ran out of wind and stopped in Bermuda, Simon Hunter took his Contessa 26 into the Azores for the same reason and Rod White completed the course in his Atlanta 26, *Bluff*, but outside the time limit.

Philip Howells finished 35th in 35$^1/_2$ days in his 28 foot (8.5m) Fromstock Filius.

10

Should it be Allowed?

The large sized, heavily sponsored boats of the 1976 race, meant the likelihood of major changes in rules to govern the next event in 1980. For the first time the committee was making rules with the authorities looking on and, at the same time, there were threats, from across the Channel, of other races being organized in which there would be no size limits. There were strong suggestions that the more serious contenders would never scale down the size of their yachts to enter another OSTAR.

Quite apart from the fact that another race including boats like *Club Méditerranée* and *Vendredi 13* would simply not be allowed to happen, the committee, was keen to see the size of yachts brought down to what it considered the right size for single-handed sailing, though what was this?

The first meeting to discuss the new rules was held in September 1976 and certain principles were agreed. For instance, that to have an upper limit might improve rather than spoil the race and that there was no merit in having one length for monohulls and another for multihulls. (This had been suggested because it was thought that, length for length, monohulls were likely to do more damage in the event of a collision than multihulls). The upper size limit would be the same for all types of yacht and it was agreed that this limit would be that of the Gipsy Moth Class in the 1976 race,

namely 65 feet (19.8 m) overall. It was also agreed that the entries should be limited to one hundred on a "first come first served" basis with ten more places to be allocated by the committee.

Following the meeting, the RYA were advised of the overall plans for 1980, including the upper size limit of 65 feet (19.8 m). Their reaction was to suggest that a limit of 45 feet (13.7 m) would be more acceptable! This was put to the OSTAR committee a month later and, after serious consideration a reply to the RYA was agreed, to the effect that a reduction below 55 feet (16.8 m) would be catastrophic for the race and the whole idea of the race. The arguments put to the RYA for a size limit above 45 feet (14 m) were as follows: "1. Yachts over 100 feet (30.5 m) should definitely be excluded. 2. Yachts over 70 feet (21.4 m) are few and far between. They rely on their size for advantage so could equally well be excluded. 3. The same could be said, to a lesser extent, for yachts of 60 foot (18.3 m), so, in the interests of safety, it would no doubt be possible, without destroying the objects of the race, to exclude them too. 4. Among the yachts between 60 and 55 feet (18.3 m and 16.8 m) we find a small number of very interesting, and successful yachts, including Chay Blyth's *British Steel*, Sir Francis Chichester's *Gipsy Moth V*, and *Sir Thomas Lipton*, a light draught, beautiful yacht which inspired the building of the

Ocean Youth Club yachts. It would seem a great pity, and in principle, wrong to exclude such yachts.

"Though it is now almost universally accepted that some upper limit must be imposed, to bring it as low as 45 feet (13.7 m), or even 50 feet (15.2 m), would completely destroy the whole concept of the race. It would so dampen the enthusiasm and imagination of designers and competitors as to reduce the race to an ignominious anti-climax. This is particularly the case as regards multihulls.

"Looking at the 1976 results in isolation it could be concluded that the ideal single-handed ocean cruiser could be one about 40 feet (12.2 m), but taking all the races into account, perhaps the best ones were larger. It is still open to argument whether, for long distance sailing it is better to have a smaller boat, and sail her nearer to maximum potential, or a larger one, sailed less efficiently which gets there quicker and arrives in better shape. But one must here revert to what the race is all about. There must be some latitude left to designers and owners to experiment, outside what might be considered the conventional limits, in order to develop yachts, gear and techniques of a new and interesting design or conception. It is no good "the establishment" just saying it thinks such and such a yacht size is quite big enough for single-handed sailing and leaving it at that. Nor should one, for a specific and infrequent event such

as this, be shackled by bureaucratically tidy mindedness to a figure arrived at for probably quite different reasons. A further reason for resisting any drastic restriction on upper size limits is the fact that many owners and designers build yachts for both the single-handed transatlantic race and the two-handed Round Britain Race and, in their aims these two races are complementary. Indeed we already know of a number of owners who are waiting for our single-handed rules to be published before building for the 1978 Round Britain Race."

Finally agreement was achieved in which there would be an upper *waterline length* of 46 feet (14.0 m) which would, with the overhang limitations imposed by the rules, result in some boats being 55 or 56 feet in length. Thus the class limits for 1980 were set as follows;

	LWL	LOA
JESTER CLASS	26 feet	32 feet
GIPSY MOTH CLASS	36 feet	44 feet
PENDUICK CLASS	46 feet	56 feet

The hulls had to fit in to a "template". See below, and the rules for the 1980 OSTAR went to the printers in December 1976 and so prospective competitors were given plenty of notice about the new size restrictions. There were of course a number of people for whom the new class

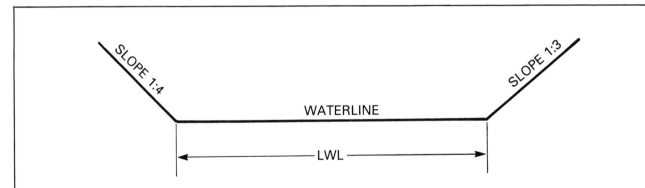

This was the profile which gave limits for the length of competing vessels in the 1980 race. It laid down the waterline for various class limits, but by means of this diagram ensured that the ends of the boat sloped over the sea to give a longer length overall. Subsequently and today there is merely a limit on overall length of hull for the whole race and for classes. Owners and designers can choose their own shape of bow and stern. Before 1980, it was thought that an overall limit would lead to vertical bows: it did, but without ill effects. Anyway a vertical stem is increasingly favoured for all fast boats. The limits by classes for 1980 were set as follows (first figure is LOA in feet, second is waterline): "Pen Duick class" 56/46; "Gipsy Moth class" 44/36; "Jester class" 32/36.

limits were decidedly bad news and one of these was Philip Weld. He had lost *Gulf Streamer* on his way to the 1976 OSTAR and was already into building the replacement, *Rogue Wave*, which at 60 feet (18.3 m) would be ineligible. He was bitterly disappointed with the new size restrictions and so was his designer, Dick Newick.

There were others who were equally upset. It was predicted that French sailors would simply take the race over and, in 1977 it looked as if this was going to happen. In the event they organized several other races: the single-handed Route du Rhum, from St Malo to Guadaloupe and the Transat en Double which went across the Atlantic to Bermuda and back without stopping. Philip Weld entered for the 1978 Route du Rhum with *Rogue Wave* and, in December 1977, when writing to enter for the 1978 Round Britain Race, to my surprise, enclosed an entry form, and entry fee, for the 1980 OSTAR. This last he asked me to say nothing about – "I'd appreciate your keeping as quiet as possible about my foolishness", and he went on to say that if he did not show up for the 1980 race "the entry cheque could remain in the pot to help the RWYC's valiant efforts on behalf of "all types of ocean racing". His plan was to sail the Route du Rhum and, if he did well, that would be it, but if he didn't he would build another boat for the OSTAR.

As it happened Phil had a problem with his mainsail in the Route du Rhum and, once again, he came third. Plan B then swung into action and a new boat, *Moxie* was born, to sail in the 1980 OSTAR. It was to be a decision he did not regret. While the Royal Western was getting its ideas sorted out, the RYA continued to concern itself with ocean single-handed sailing. It so happened that at that time I was a member of the RYA council so, at appropriate moments, I could chip in a few opinions and facts based on personal involvement with the races. The "single-handers" had a certain number of allies and not least of these was John Durie, the General Secretary of the RYA.

At the RYA Council meeting of 27 October 1976, single-handed racing was on the agenda for discussion. The Deputy Chairman, David Edwards, opened the discussion by explaining that the RYA had been brought into it by the Department of Trade and he said the RYA was there to help rather than dictate terms. He said that the Royal Western Yacht Club had produced an excellent report (on the 1976 race) and the only outstanding item at the moment was agreement on an upper size limit for yachts in future races. Until this had been agreed he could not complete his report to the council. It was agreed to defer the debate until his report was complete. John Durie thought that it would be a good thing for members of the Council to see the BBC film, based on Clare Francis's voyage in 1976, and the Chairman, Sir Hugh Forbes, said that the film would provide a valuable background against which to debate the issue.

Before the debate began, we viewed the film which brought into the tranquility of the Royal Thames Yacht Club, where we met, the whole atmosphere of the OSTAR and what it is all about. As she made that film, Clare was not to know that, months later, it would play an important part in a debate in which the whole future of the race was at stake. After seeing it no true yachtsman could be a party to preventing it happening again. Before the council members were the statistics, produced by the Royal Western, of the 1976 race, detailing the casualties and showing what happened to them. In his opening remarks David Edwards drew attention to the report and to the fact that no attempt had been made to hide the fact that there had been three collisions. There had been no damage to other vessels. He said he thought the committee of the Royal Western had acted sensibly and responsibly and that the conditions proposed for the 1980 race were very satisfactory. He hoped his colleagues on the Council would welcome the initiative of the Royal Western. No formal motion was passed at the end of the debate which followed, but the Secretary General was instructed to write to the Royal Western explaining the situation. This of course meant that the race had the tacit approval of the RYA.

In 1977 the International Yacht Racing Union (IYRU) started its own agitation against single-handed racing and it was even suggested that clubs who organized these events should be disowned by their National Authorities and become disaffiliated. Such suggestions were fortunately self-defeating.

Many of the arguments about single-handed sailing are based on misconceptions. For instance there is nothing in the Collision Regulations which says that at least one person must at all times be on deck looking out unceasingly. The rules merely say that a proper look-out must be kept at all times. The frequency with which the horizon needs to be scanned will depend upon many circumstances but there will be times when it will be perfectly possible to go below for a short time and still maintain a proper look-out.

Many of the critics of single-handed sailing are ignorant of the technique employed by experienced single-handers. I doubt if this has anywhere been better summarized than it was in the Journal of the Royal Institute of Navigation by Blondie Hasler, when he wrote:

"In my opinion, the art of single-handing is based, first, on the art of catnapping. I am assisted in this by a kitchen timer which is often set for less than 5 minutes when close to shipping or other hazards. A trained single-hander (it is sometimes overlooked that it does need training) can maintain full mental and physical efficiency for an unlimited number of days without ever sleeping for more than about 20 minutes at a time – often only half a minute – but these catnaps must be taken at frequent intervals throughout the 24 hours, and must be started as soon as he leaves port, long before he begins to feel tired. On the rare occasions when he cannot even lie fully clothed on his bunk for five minutes, the good single-hander learns to nod for a few seconds at a time while actually on watch, and finds that after doing this ten or twenty times he feels less sleepy.

"The second attribute of a good single-hander is the ability to conserve energy by not allowing himself to worry about anything other than an immediate problem, and by not doing unnecessary work unless his situation is so free from problems that boredom sets in, as may well be the case on a long ocean crossing. Unnecessary navigational work is a prime offender, possibly because so many yachtsmen work in offices that it seems natural to work in an office in a single-handed five tonner. Three quarters of the navigational work done by the average yachtsman is unnecessary, and would not have been done by a professional fisherman in the days of sail. Trying to do it all in a small boat bucketing around in the middle of a dirty night is a certain recipe for exhaustion."

11

A Multinational Fleet Round Britain

The Fourth Observer Round Britain Race 1978

Word had got around about the Round Britain Race, and for the first time the list had to be closed. This was done at 120 entries, in the hope that that would produce a final fleet of about 100 boats. Anything more than that would have put too much pressure on the stop-over ports and in particular, Castle Bay, Barra, where the Coxswain of the lifeboat, John McNeil, has his work cut out to fit all the yachts in, because although the bay looks big enough on the chart there are a number of places where the holding is not at all good.

The 120 dropped to 86 and, in the event only 74 yachts came to the line to start. Knowing where to close an entry list is always a problem. Some people enter in case they find they can compete, others have genuine reasons for dropping out, but don't say so in good time, and there are others, one suspects, who send for the rules, and even enter, so that they can chat about it and leave the rule book lying on their coffee table, or in the downstairs W.C., just to impress their friends. Thus 74 crews were hell-bent on getting round and a number hell-bent on winning. It was a fascinating collection of yachts, from the latest in high speed multihulls, to the stately 46 foot (14.0 m) gaff ketch *Melmore*, and the 51 foot (15.5 m) sloop *Elena*, laid down in 1939 by the Berthon Boat Company but not commissioned until 1946. *Melmore* was sailed by her owner, Frank Essen, and *Elena* was lent to

John McKillop, the Kingsbridge sailmaker, and crewed by Charles Steinly, who, sadly, was later lost at sea with his boat. John McKillop's birthday came up when they were at Barra and in deference to the racing he decided to celebrate it a day early. However, it was such a success that they had another one the next day, thereby starting four hours late on the next leg. As there was a south-east gale blowing at the time, presumably any cobwebs were soon blown away.

Chay Blyth was sailing a new Kelsall designed trimaran, *Great Britain IV*, 54 feet. Philip Weld who had lost *Gulf Streamer* on the way to the 1976 OSTAR, had a new Newick designed, 60 foot trimaran which he had named *Rogue Wave*, since that was what had capsized *Gulf Streamer*. Having been third in the last two races he was of course rearing to get to the front of the fleet and, this time, stay there. Robin Knox-Johnston was back with another strong man act, sailing the 77 foot *Great Britain II* with Billy King-Harman. Multihull followers were watching Walter Greene, and his wife Joan, over from America with a boat Walter had designed and built himself, *A Cappella*. She had originally been a bit longer but he trimmed her to just under 35 feet to fit the lower class limit.

Nick Keig had produced a new *Three Legs of Mann*, and there were two of Dick Newick's Val class trimarans, RFD, sailed by Martin Read and

Philip Greig, and *Jan of Santa Cruz*, sailed by Nigel Irens and Mark Pridie. Mike Ellison sailed a production *Comanche* catamaran, of that name, with Reg White to help him. The smallest multihull was *Gazelle*, a 28 foot trimaran and, as her name implied was a most delicately graceful boat, but singularly lacking in creature comforts. Her owner, Charles Dennis planned to sail here with his wife Susan but, by the time it came to the race, a small Dennis had arrived and she was advised not to sail. Julia Awcock took Susan's place at the last minute.

There were a lot of good offshore racing boats who formed themselves into racing groups within the overall race and were very competitive. There were also some which were not quite so competitive. Peter Crowther's *Galway Blazer* and Jock McCleod's *Ròn Glas*, both Chinese lugsail-rigged, were there and Richard Gatehouse

was back in *Skol II*, this time crewed by David Robinson. There were two all girl crews; Stephanie Merry and Katie Clegg sailed the three-quarter tonner *Mezzanine* and Pippa Longley and Katie Clemson sailed *Nikonos III*, a one tonner. Both boats were designed by Ron Holland.

The race went off to a brisk start with westerly winds giving a beat to the Bishop Rock after a reach to the Eddystone, which was the first mark of the course. The wind was westerly force 5 and *Rogue Wave* evidently found this very much to her liking as she was first round the Bishop Rock, after which she was able to lay the course for Crosshaven. The leaders went round the Bishop Rock light house in darkness, but when morning came the keepers warmed to the task of yacht spotting and we were able to get a good idea where a number of yachts were. The race office log

Chay Blyth and Rob James in their Kelsall-designed Great Britain IV *won the 1978 Round Britain in 21 days.*

Philip Weld and David Cooksey repeated their third place in Rogue Wave.

Nigel Irens and Mark Pridie sailed the 31 foot (9.4m) trimaran Jan of Santa Cruz *to 5th place.*

records that a local radio station, who had earlier asked for information was rung up to be given some placings but "a snotty little wench informed me she couldn't care less, and all the reporters had gone home"! The watchkeeper concerned was happier when both the BBC in London and Plymouth rang for the latest news.

In 1978 many lighthouses were still manned, so a lot of information was available from these sources, which we valued very much. I recall a liaison visit to Gwennap Head Coastguard Station, approaching almost on hands and knees in a full gale. This used to be called Lands End Coastguard and was one of the most important in the country. I think the most memorable liaison visit was to the Wolf Rock and Bishop Rock lighthouses, where we were lowered on the wire from a Wessex helicopter. The aim was to wish them, somewhat prematurely, a happy Christmas and to leave them some Christmas fare, including certain beverages which I have since learned are not permitted on lighthouses. However, I hope they enjoyed them and drank the health of passing yachtsmen in Royal Western port.

Second round the Bishop Rock was *Great Britain IV, (GB IV)*. She had hardly settled onto the new course when the fairing on the starboard forward cross beam was damaged and the forward section of the starboard float filled up. The crew hove-to for an hour and a half trying to pump out the float, but to no effect. They then considered where they could best go to carry out repairs and in the end decided to carry on to Crosshaven at slow speed. When they arrived there they were 9 hours behind *Rogue Wave* and in 6th place.

One yacht we always knew about was *Norvantes*, sailed by Peter Jay, at that time British Ambassador in the United States. Presumably his taking part posed something of a security problem which may have accounted for his yacht's excellent communications. His crew was Luke Fitzherbert, who did the 1974 race with David Palmer in *F.T.* He certainly had arranged a more comfortable ride this time, though it did take him a day and a half longer to get round.

After repairs, *G.B.IV* left Crosshaven in pursuit of the leaders. The conditions were light, which favoured her, and half way up the Irish coast they were delighted to see *Rogue Wave* ahead of them, and to be able to overtake her. With 200 miles to go to Barra, the wind headed them and they were on a beat, with a freshening northerly wind. However, in the final stages of the leg they were able to ease sheets and were first into Castle Bay. *Rogue Wave* was second, 4³/₄ hours behind. The light conditions did not suit Robin Knox-Johnston in *G.B.II* and he was 8th into Castle Bay, climbed to 6th by Lowestoft, and then had a slow last lap, when he fell to 12th place at the finish. In the middle of the fleet, a private race was going on with a small group consisting of *Yamaha D'ieteren*, sailed by Yves Anrys, *Mezzanine*, sailed by Stephanie Merry and Katie Clegg, *Attila*, a Nicholson 33 sailed by Jeremy Hurlbatt and Neil MacRae, and the UFO 34, *Jaws*, sailed by Niels Svendsen and Norman Brooks. Also, perhaps surprisingly, mixed up in this little bunch was Tony Bullimore in his 35 foot (10.7 m) trimaran, *Run Around*.

Jeremy Hurlbatt was making up for having had to retire in the last race when he withdrew his yacht *Fidget*, in very bad weather, in deference to her age. He owned her in partnership and she was lost, off the south coast, in the same storm which hit the Fastnet Race in 1979. He was not then sailing her, and the crew were all saved. Tony Bullimore had had to find himself a new yacht because his last one, *Gancia Girl* (ex-*Toria*) had caught fire during the 1976 OSTAR and he had to abandon her. Such pieces as were found later, on the Irish coast, were too small to be reconstituted.

Two boats who would have fared better under the more elastic rules of the 1974 race, were *Hindostan* and *Nikonos III*, both of whom had rigging problems north of Lerwick and used their engines to get in, hoping to be allowed to go back and restart from there. However the rules clearly stated that this was not allowed and they were both

The monohulls jostled at the end of the starting line near the committee boat.

Amongst those in these pictures are: 7 Robertson's Golly, *233* Melmore, *54 (sails Z847)* Petit Suisse, *H 2654* NS44, *1013* Norvantes, *M 35* Lara of Bosham, *3111* Slightly, *88* Ultima Thule, *70* BBC Radio Birmingham.

disqualified. A happier outcome followed the loss, by Tony Smith in *Telstar*, of half his mast, when only 60 miles out of Lerwick. He was left with about 15 foot of mast still standing, but he and his crew, Walter Rietig, from Norway, fixed up a jury rig and sailed the remaining 400 or so miles to Lowestoft. There, within their compulsory 48 hour stop-over period, the mast was repaired and they sailed on. From being 30th at Lerwick and 34th at Lowestoft, they reached Plymouth in 33rd place.

The leading boats after Castle Bay rounded Muckle Flugga, in winds which were very variable with calms, but the last stretch, into Lerwick, was fast and in poor visibility. *G.B.IV* was first in but *Rogue Wave* was only 2 hours behind and *Three Legs* was still in third place. When they left Lerwick they had mostly southerly winds, force 5 up to force 7, so that it was a windward leg. When they got to Lowestoft *Rogue Wave* had worked out a lead of 4 hours and once again *Three Legs* was third.

The leading boats came out of Lowestoft into a south south-westerly wind and, when *G.B.IV* left, a contrary tidal stream. By way of a short cut they lifted the boards and crabbed sideways over the bank into deeper water and less tidal stream. From there they kept hard on the wind, following each shift, until they were close in to the French coast, so close that, as Chay put it, they almost needed passports. Here the wind left them and they anchored between Calais and Cap Blanc Nez where they rode out the foul tide without losing any ground. When the wind came again it was from the south-east but gradually went round to the south-west, so that, from the Owers light ship it was a beat to Plymouth. Rob James reckoned they won the race at anchor, because at that time *Rogue Wave* was going backwards on the tidal stream, on the other side of the Channel.

Quite how Chay and Rob coped with the separation zones in the Straits is not recorded but, since there were no complaints one must assume they either did it right or got away with it! Angus Primrose, who retired at Lowestoft after running out of spare time, was not so lucky as he came south through the Straits. He was caught in the wrong lane and had the doubtful distinction of being the first yachtsman to be prosecuted and fined. *Great Britain IV* finished first at 1224 on 29 July and it later became clear that she was not the only one to have overtaken *Rogue Wave*.

Three Legs finished second at 0059 on 30th, followed 2 hours later by *Rogue Wave*. When we met *Three Legs* as she crossed the line, the first thing Nick Keig said was "I'm sorry about Phil". Four words which said so much, first it showed what sort of a person Nick Keig was, secondly it said what we all thought and thirdly it illustrated the spirit in which the Round Britain has always been sailed. Phil Weld was his usual charming imperturbable self, congratulating winners, and those who came after, all alike. His day was to come, but not in the Round Britain Race, in which he held his own record: three times third.

Walter Greene took his *A Cappella* round just behind the leaders with great consistency, being fourth in every port except Barra, where he dropped to fifth. Considering the three ahead of him were 53, 54 and 60 footers, (16.2 m, 16.4 m and 18.3m) this was a very creditable performance and enormous encouragement for his design and building efforts. Just behind him was Nigel Irens in his Val class Tri. *Jan of Santa Cruz,* whose record ran 7th, 7th, 6th, 7th and finally 6th, though he was promoted to 5th through Dirk Nauta having a time penalty. Immediately behind him was the other Val Tri *RFD* which Martin Read had brought up from 15th in Crosshaven to 7th at the finish. The first monohull to finish was Dirk Nauta's *Tielsa II*, otherwise known as *Bestevaer* and sailed by Gerald Dijkstra, in the 1976 OSTAR. She actually finished 5th overall but had a penalty of 3 hours 15 minutes for late arrival in Plymouth before the start. This placed him 6th, between the two Val class trimarans. $3^{1}/_{2}$ hours after *RFD* came *Slithy Tove* into 8th place, and second monohull to finish. Michael Pipe had come well down the field in the 1970 race after an enforced call at Stornoway to repair a leak, thereby dropping from 2nd to 19th place, and in 1974 he was forced to retire to Lerwick with rigging difficulties, after being 8th into Castle Bay. With him now he had Warren Luhrs, an American, who was very interested in the long and thin concept, which is what *Slithy Tove* was. After the race he went home and the next we knew of him was when he brought his, long thin, *Tuesday's Child* over for the 1980 OSTAR. He was back again in 1981 and again later on with *Thursday's Child*.

Another, not quite so long, but narrow boat was *Kurrewa*, sailed by Fred Dovaston and John Wetherup. She was basically a half scale model of a Twelve Metre class. She came 18th and 3rd in the under 35 Class. *Cherry Valley Duck,* Robert Nickerson's Contessa 35 had a long, and hard fought battle with Beat Guttinger and Albert

Schiess in their new *Petit Suisse,* another Contessa 35. Robert had lead them, sometimes by two places, sometimes by one, all the way round and left Lowestoft 1¹/2 hours ahead at the start of the final leg to Plymouth. When they came to Dungeness they were close, and there was a wind shift. The Swiss were quicker with their sail change and got through into the lead and at Plymouth they were 1¹/4 hours ahead at the finish to take the monohulls under 35 foot prize. Just before *Petit Suisse* were Philip Walwyn and Frances Tate (later Frances Walwyn) in *Whisky Jack* a 34 foot trimaran. They were to become regular entrants in our short-handed races, sailing over from their home in St Kitts to take part and swapping the delights of the Trade Winds for the joys of Muckle Flugga in a force 8.

The little *Gazelle* very nearly came to grief on the last leg. They were in collision with another yacht somewhere off Torbay and one float was damaged. This did not affect them as they came along the coast towards Plymouth, but, as they turned to come in to the finish line the damaged float became the lee float and started to fill up. She came across the harbour getting slower and slower with the lee float sinking deeper and deeper. What an agonizing way to end a two thousand mile race! As we watched from the club launch there was nothing we could do but pray. Gradually she closed the gap to the finish with the top of the float awash, then she was across. She had not only made the finish, but had achieved the best time, for the last leg, in this race, 2d 01h 45m. Immediately we lashed up alongside and helped here in to her berth.

Charles Dennis' crew Julia Awcock had suffered terribly from the wet and cold. The accommodation, if it could be called that, was so restricted that for long periods she was sleeping and sailing in wet clothes without taking off her seaboots and this seriously affected her legs and feet. She was still not back to normal some months after the race. She was a brave girl to keep going until the end.

Not everyone had wind all the way from Lowestoft and, at one point *Great Britain II* and *RFD* were in close company, becalmed, so the crew of *GB II* invited RFDs crew to dinner, during the course of which the two yachts were secured

The little trimaran Gazelle *in which Charles Dennis and Julia Awcock had a fraught finish.*

alongside each other. News of this leaked out to other competitors and, about a month after the race, one of the competitors represented to the committee that there had been too much laxity in the rules, quoting this dinner party as an example, another example referred to the arrival of the girls' in *Mezzanine* in Castle Bay when the, ever chivalrous, crew of *Petit Suisse,* had jumped on board to help the girls anchor. There were other points he raised but, when the committee had considered his letter he was told that although these were technical breaches of the rules " . . . these are typical examples of what makes the spirit of the Round Britain Race different from other events. No one gained an advantage, and much good will was generated. I'm glad no one saw fit to protest."

At this time there was a rule which stipulated that crews must sleep onboard their boats at the stop-over ports, and this was not popular with the crews. It appears that Chay Blyth had said to someone, I'm sure with that impish look he puts on when pulling someone's leg, that he had slept ashore, and this was quoted to the committee. In fact he was quite right, *GB IV* had been dried out ashore for repairs at the time! The rule was originally put in because, like all the other rules, it was in pursuance of an object of the race. After this race the committee agreed to cut out the "living onboard" rule.

12

Weld and America Win

The Sixth Royal Western/Observer Single-handed Transatlantic Race 1980.

Despite the drastic size restrictions for 1980, and the forecasts of an early death for OSTAR, the entry list passed the 100 limit in March 1978, so a waiting list resulted. In the event 90 yachts came to the line for the start.

Considerable feeling was aroused when the Committee refused to allow Marc Pajot to take the place of Eric Tabarly as skipper of *Paul Ricard*. Tabarly was forced to withdraw due to an old skiing injury and Marc Pajot, though he had done a qualifying cruise in *Paul Ricard,* had not completed it by the prescribed time. There was also the problem of Jean-Yves Terlain who had come to Plymouth in his new and unqualified catamaran *Gautier I*. This was a new boat grotesquely resembling two waterborne tanks interconnected by some large drain pipes! In fact she embodied a number of 'state of the art' features. However, since the rules were designed to prevent preliminary sea trials being carried out in mid-Atlantic, under the auspices of the Royal Western's Single-handed Trans-Atlantic Race, it seemed perfectly clear, at least to me, that she should remain precluded.

Without the *Paul Ricard* problem, I don't think there would have been a chance of any rethinking on the *Gautier* issue, but the competitors, led by Philip Weld, launched an appeal for them both to be allowed to sail in the race. In the end a compromise was reached. They could "race" but were not accepted as official entries and therefore were not eligible for any prizes. They were told they must keep clear of other competitors at the start, but took no notice of that instruction! What Philip Weld and his petition signers did not say was what they would have liked to happen if either of the unofficial entries arrived first in Newport. This is of course one very good reason for not bending the rules or making gestures, however sporting, which conflict with the rules by which everyone else is bound.

Jack Knights, writing in *Yachts & Yachting* (July 4th 1980) hoped that if one of them arrived first he would be declared the winner. I doubt if he would have felt that way if he had just sailed the boat which came next and had complied with all the rules and conditions from the outset. (We were to see what happens when someone other than the first to arrive is declared the winner after the 1984 OSTAR.)

In considering the problems of adhering to the rules, one French skipper said that he could quite see why the Royal Western had to make all these rules but he could see no reason why they should enforce them. Those who have had to organize events involving our friends from over La Manche will be familiar with this philosophy! In the event *Gautier* retired with various problems and Marc Pajot arrived fifth, but was not placed.

As the day for the start drew near the Icelanders injected a rather nasty bit of drama by announcing that they had dredged up a piece of yacht, not far south of Iceland, which, because it had instruments on it with serial numbers, had been identified as part of *Three Cheers*. Observing that they had made this discovery in March one might ask why they had not revealed this before. Perhaps they thought they were delivering some sort of message. I don't think it upset any of the competitors but it was not a very kind thing to do.

An innovation in this race was the use of ARGOS, a joint US/French satellite tracking system first used for yacht race tracking in the 1979 Transat en Double race. Each yacht was fitted with a small automatic, self powered transmitter whose signals were received by one or more satellites. The satellite then relayed the signals to earth for interpretation and transmission from the USA to France and onward to the race headquarters in Plymouth. This enabled the race headquarters to monitor the progress of the yachts and in addition provided a safety bonus because each transmitter had a switch which could be operated in emergency to indicate distress. This was in addition to the compulsorily carried EPIRB which when activated transmitted signals which could be picked up by overflying aircraft.

ARGOS was expensive at about £1000 per yacht and this led to the enrolment of Europe 1 as co-sponsors with *The Observer*.

The appearance of ARGOS on the scene meant that yachts had to have a beacon fitted and there was some agonizing as to where the fitters were to be allowed to drill holes for the securing bolts. Over in the Royal Western a good deal of fitting was being done. The computer terminals and all the communications had to be installed in the race office and the large team of members who would be keeping watch during the race had to be briefed. One thing which had to be worked out was the drill to be followed in the event of an emergency. Race organizers always try to inform the relatives of those concerned before they hear it on the radio or read it in the paper. The media are sometimes insensitive about this. With Argos we had a built-in facility for denying anyone else knowledge of an emergency until we gave the all clear for the information to be released.

On the day of the start, dramas started early. The unfortunate Florence Arthaud, who had been persuaded by someone that her rigging needed attention on the previous evening, lost her mast as

Florence Arthaud, who lost her mast on the way to the start.

soon as she was clear of the docks. The problem was caused by inserting a French threaded part into a British threaded part of a bottle screw. She was forced to withdraw from the race. Tom Grossman, in his 56 foot (17.1m) trimaran *Kriter VII*, making his way to the starting area remembered that he had left his stop watch below so went to fetch it. Whilst he was below his yacht rode up on the Spanish yacht *Garuda* and lodged there. *Garuda* suffered surprisingly little damage and was able to proceed, but Tom had to take his yacht to Mashfords yard at Cremyll for repairs to one of his floats. Photographs taken soon after the collision would seem to indicate that Tom was on the starboard tack, and therefore had right of way, but it would have helped if he had been on deck to proclaim this. After some frantic all night work at Mashfords, and I recall ferrying fibreglassing materials over to Cremyll at a late hour, Tom was ready to go the next afternoon and he was logged out at 1535 on 8 June.

A few days into the race ARGOS transmissions began to disappear so either, we were losing boats, or we had problems with system Argos. The first "disappearance" was *Voortrekker*, Bertie Reed. His position came up on 10th June but by 1730 on 11th nothing appeared and the Coastguards were informed. They soon reported that an aircraft not far away would extend its search to see if they could find anything. Then it was noted that *Jeans Foster*, Philip Steggall's 38 foot trimaran, had similarly disappeared from the position reports, and she was added to the list of worries. Aircraft searches went on again the next day and ships had been told to keep a look-out and report. *Chica Boba* was the next to join the list of those whose positions were no longer coming up.

The fact that all three had been lost by Argos but in no case had any one of them used his EPIRB., or made a radio distress signal, made it almost certain that it was an Argos problem. But we had to find out and this was eventually achieved when on 11 *Voortrekker* was sighted and reported by a ship, on 12 *Haute Nendaz* was sighted by an aircraft and the same day *Chica Boba* was heard on radio. Only *Jeans Foster* remained in doubt but, as

the others had been traced and gradually more and more Argos signals ceased, it was assumed that the problem lay with the individual transmitters in the yachts. What had happened, it later transpired, was that a chemical reaction between the setting agent and the resin plastic, from which the casings had been made, rendered them brittle, causing many little cracks to appear which let the water in and put the transmitters out of action. Whilst all that was being sorted out Nicholas Clifton suffered a capsize in his proa *Fleury Michon*, (ex *Merlin*). He was located by an RAF Nimrod aircraft who directed a ship to the scene and Nicholas was picked up.

The start. The whip aerial in the foreground is almost in line with the naval patrol vessel marking the outer limit of the line. Beyond is one of the Brittany Ferries carrying spectators. Identifiable are; 27 Jester, 33 Demon of Hamble, I 46 Chica Boba, 47 Egret, 61 Spaniel, 64 Tuesdays Child, 77 France Loisirs, 79 Ratso II, 82 Victoria, 84 Achillea, 85 Roundabout, 97 Stadt Krefeld.

Meanwhile *Moxie,* clear of such troubles, recorded 116 miles in the first twelve hours of the race. Once clear of the Sole Bank conditions were even better and on 11 June, four days after the start, *Moxie's* noon to noon distance run was only two miles short of 300, with an average speed since starting of over 9 knots. During this period of the race the problem was just how hard they should drive their boats. There was a long way to go and too much greed for speed had to be resisted and a fine balance struck, if boats and gear were to hold together until Newport. In earlier transatlantic races, fully crewed from west to east, the course had included an invisible mark called 'Point Alpha', south of which yachts had to pass. This was to keep them clear of the worst of the fog and ice, and the fishing fleets in the area. For this race, Philip Weld had established his own, private, Point Alpha which was 43° N, 50° W, roughly the Tail of the Bank. He had also, after studying a long succession of weather maps, concluded that he should be south of 45° N before reaching longitude 35° W if he was to avoid the probability of being stopped in his tracks by gales. This and his experience in the 1972 race, when he went too far south and suffered calms, influenced the selection of his route in 1980. In fact when he reached 35° W he was about 50 miles north of his first target and some 80 miles north of his Point Alpha at the Tail of the Bank. After being north at the first position he tried to get down to the south, but was forced north again over the dreaded Newfoundland Bank.

One has to remember that in this race competitors were still not allowed weather facsimile receivers, an aid which Philip particularly advocated, nor was he receiving weather and route information from shore, except in such broadcasts as were available. As they set off across the Atlantic, Philip Steggall in *Jeans Foster,* and Nick Keig in *Three Legs of Mann,* followed the same route as *Moxie,* with *Paul Ricard* away to the north and *Olympus Photo* down to the south. These two "wingers" were to converge on *Moxie's* track by the time they reached 45° W.

While the leaders, at least, were enjoying the good conditions, one competitor was enduring the horrors of severe sickness alone at sea. On the day before the start Henk van de Weg bought a chicken which he cooked, eating half that day and the other half the day of the start. This was very nearly fatal. After four days he became very ill and his condition deteriorated over the next few days. He tried to get medical advice over the radio from passing ships but was always frustrated by language difficulties and achieved nothing. He felt he was so ill that he could die and so he turned his boat towards Europe under only a storm jib and lay on the floor of his cabin and drifted into unconsciousness for a time. After another three days he felt better and wanted to drink. He consumed a quantity of fruit juice and felt so much better that he turned the boat's head again towards Newport. About a week later he had further problems when his yacht, *Tjisje,* hit something which Henk assumed was drifting wood, and the hull was split, amidships. Water was coming in at the rate of some 500 litres a day until he effected some repairs which almost halved the rate of inflow. He must, after his illness, have been very weak but pressed on, the only concession he made was to adjust his course to close Newfoundland so that should his leak get worse he could go in there.

He could have activated his EPIRB or the emergency signal on his Argos transmitter, either of which would have brought him assistance. Yet he showed remarkable fortitude and determination, finishing the race in just under 37 days.

Another example of self reliance and good seamanship followed the dismasting of *Edith,* sailed by Bill Doelger. She was a Val class trimaran and it became clear that something was wrong because she was not making the progress she should have been in the weather around her. The Argos positions alerted the race office and, through Lands End Coastguards, their opposite numbers in Halifax, Nova Scotia, were asked to investigate. Within a matter of hours a ship had found her and reported that she had been dismasted, but was not in need of assistance. She was proceeding to Newport under what was described as jury rig. In fact the mast had been scarcely damaged in this dismanting and Bill Doelger had managed to re-step it under way using his boom and spinnaker pole to get it up. He finished in just over 28 days in 30th position overall, and was awarded one of the two special prizes given by the Royal Western Yacht Club for outstanding performances during the race. The other special prize went to Kazimierz Jaworski for his outstanding performance in *Spaniel II,* a 56 foot (17.2 m) monohull. He finished in 19 days 13 hours, a day inside the previous record. He was in sixth place overall, but the first monohull to finish.

With all the yachts having ARGOS it had been expected that everyone would know exactly where everyone was but, with so many transmitters

Kazimierz Jaworski in Spaniel II *was the first monohull.*

out of action the same old doubts as before shrouded the final outcome of the race. Weld knew he had two or three boats breathing down his neck and, from snatches he caught over the VHF radio he knew they were not far away. He was particularly worried, as the wind went lighter, about Nick Keig, whose *Three Legs of Mann* would almost certainly be gaining in the light weather. Philip Steggall with his ARGOS out of action, was an unknown quantity both to the followers of the race and to himself until a light aircraft spotted him. This sighting was reported by the BBC and Steggall suddenly heard himself being reported as lying second to Phil Weld. One can imagine Steggall's reaction to that news. Imagine also his feelings when, some hours later, he heard a splintering noise beneath the boat as he was hit by a squall. Rushing below he found that his centre board had sheared off. It had evidently been weakened in collision with a whale earlier in the race and the pressure exerted upon it in that sudden squall caused it finally to give up. Had there been a following wind it would not have been too serious, but even as it happened he was being headed and having to beat. Without the centreboard he was making tremendous leeway and going about was a nightmare. When he still had 40 miles to go to the finish he heard the report that Phil Weld had finished in first place. Seven and a half hours later he crossed the line in third place, 41 minutes after

Three Legs so that he was third overall and first in the Gipsy Moth Class.

Phil Weld did not know until the very end that he was about to win, thereby fulfilling his own prophecy that the winner would finish in under 18 days (he had just 48 minutes in hand!) At that time he predicted that the winner would be followed within 24 hours by six other boats. In the event only five made it, but if *Spaniel II* hadn't been delayed by rudder problems that prediction too would have been fulfilled. It was a great day for the Americans and of course for Philip Weld who must have been the most popular winner ever, not only among his fellow countrymen, but by all those who had followed this many attempts in OSTAR and Round Britain races. Even Nick Keig, just after finishing seecond, said "I'm so glad Phil made it". Phil Weld had sailed 3102 miles at an average speed of 7.19 knots. His best daily run had been 245 miles at an average speed of 10.21 knots.

Later the Americans were to be further delighted when Jerry Cartwright arrived to be declared the winner of the Jester Class. Several months later his disqualification had to be announced.

1980 was not a good year for the girls. There were only three of them in the race since Florence Arthaud had lost her mast on the way to the start. Judith Lawson was dismasted to the south east of Sable Island. However Naomi James in her 53 foot monohull *Kriter Lady* made it in good time but not good enough to beat her husband Rob who, in his 31 foot trimaran *Boatfile* had arrived a little less than three days earlier.

Philip Weld, popular winner of the 1980 OSTAR.

Philip Weld sails Moxie *out to the start.*

Anyway of the small boats, all ten of the 28 foot, and under, yachts finished, although *Jester,* having had to put back to Plymouth to restart on 18 June, was outside the time limit. She also made a stop in the Azores on the way. Of all the performances in the small boats, Chris Smith's effort in *Sadler Bluejacket* must stand out. A flip through the results tables at the end of the book will put his performance in perspective. Chris was

awarded the Royal Naval Sailing Association's OSTAR Challenge Trophy for this race. From time to time over the years there have been suggestions that the lower size limit for yachts in the race should be raised. The main argument, it has to be admitted, has been that they take too long and prolong the period during which the organizers and sponsors have to maintain a presence in Newport. However the 1980 race more than justified their being allowed to race. With the exception of *Jester,* all the small boats made it in 40 days or less.

Naomi James sailed the 53 foot (16.15m) monohull Kriter Lady *competing against her husband Rob.*

Philip Steggall in Jeans Foster *was only just beaten into 3rd place by Nick Keig.*

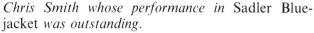

Chris Smith whose performance in Sadler Blue-jacket *was outstanding.*

Walter Greene sailed Chaussettes Olympia *to 5th place.*

Most OSTARs produce their share of hard luck stories and this was no exception. Approaching the finish, the Polish boat *Racynski II,* sailed by Czeslaw Gogolkiewicz, was in collision, in poor visibility, with a fishing boat whose gear swept across the yacht carrying all before it. Goholkiewicz was lucky not to be killed. His yacht was later taken in tow by the US Coast Guard and taken to Point Judith, just south of Newport.

Long after the race was finished, there came a bolt out of the blue in the form of a letter from a Canadian, who said that five months previously he had seen a competitor in the race contravening the rules, and understood that he had not been penalized for so doing. This unfortunate episode was reported in the yachting press at the time, but must be chronicled here, particularly as it resulted in a prizewinner being disqualified. The Canadian's report came from a Cuban fishing vessel. He said that while working on the bridge of the ship he saw a small sailing vessel sending up distress flares to attract attention. On closing the vessel it turned out to be the yacht *Le First* skippered by Jerry Cartwright. He said that Cartwright had asked to be supplied with diesel oil and had been given 20 gallons.

Cartwright's account of what happened was published in the April 1981 edition of *Cruising World* and describes how he had burned up all the lubricating oil in his engine and was therefore unable to charge his batteries. He wanted to get a position report back to race headquarters and to his wife so he asked the fishing boat to report him and also to let him have 3 litres of lubricating oil. In the event he says the Cubans sent a boat over with diesel and lubricating oil in cans which they put aboard his yacht despite his protestations. After the boat had pulled away he ditched the diesel oil and kept the lubricating oil. Cartwright's log recorded the meeting with the Cuban vessel but did not seem to record anything about the transfer, nor did the article Cartwright wrote for *Sail* and which was published in their September 1980 number, although the problem of his lack of lubricating oil is mentioned. After various trans-Atlantic exchanges and Cartwright having admitted receiving a supply of lubricating oil the committee had to conclude that there had been a breach of rules, which read: "Rule 21.1 No physical contact, except for the passing of written messages, may be made with other ships or boats at sea, and no stores may be received from any ship or aircraft during the race. They may, however, be asked for advice or

information and to report the yacht's position and condition. Rule 23.1 Immediately after finishing each crew will be required to sign a declaration that he has sailed the race in accordance with all published rules, or, if any rule has been broken to give a full account of the circumstances, establishing to what, if any, extent the yacht's progress towards the finish was helped by the breach in question.'

Cartwright records in his article how worried his wife must have been, but there was really no reason why anyone should be worried since, at the time, he was breaking the *Jester* record and could in no way be accused of being overdue. True the Royal Western had asked yachts to report when they could, but I am sure no one envisaged a competitor breaking the rules to do so. In any case he was entitled to think that the Cuban fishing boat would relay his position for him. As a result Cartwright was disqualified. I am not going to suggest what the committee might have done if Jerry Cartwright had recorded the transfer on his declaration form, but I would have been surprised if he had been disqualified in that case.

Twenty years after the first OSTAR, Blondie Hasler, in the foreword to Philip Weld's book *Moxie*, gave the answer to those who had been suggesting that he, the founder, disapproved of the way in which the OSTAR had developed. This is what he said:

"Since then the race has been mounted every four years and has developed in a way that has swept aside all previous conceptions of what was possible. The impossible has become reasonable. I am sometimes asked if I approve of what has happened to the race: the huge entry list that has had to be restricted to a manageable number; the strong international rivalry, involving 18 different countries in 1980; the avalanche of commercial sponsorship now enveloping most of the competitors; the emergence of a breed of young semi-professional sailors who are largely supported by these sponsors; the frenzied interest of the press, leading up to the compulsory fitting of Argos transmitters, and the increasing dominance of multihullers in all but the smallest class.

"The quick answer is yes. All these problems are the problems of success. There was no way in which the race could have remained in its unpretentious original form, and I admire the way in which the Royal Western's race committee, firmly led by Jack Odling-Smee, has responded to these mounting pressures whilst fending off the brickbats that have been flung at it by national organisations, by the yachting press, and even by the competitors themselves. I have served on this committee, and can assure any competitor that it is harder work and much less fun than sailing the race.

"Certainly in 1956 I could not have foreseen the way things would go. I thought of a new breed of mono-huller, say about 30 feet overall, with automatically-reefing rig and enclosable control position. Very few designers have chosen to follow this path, which is a pity because such boats would still suit a number of serious cruising yachtsmen.

"Nevertheless, I rejoice that the OSTAR has played a major part in the development of fast and seaworthy multi-hullers, simply by allowing them to race on even terms against the monos."

13

Now Transatlantic Two-Handed

The Observer/Europe 1 Transatlantic Race 1981

For every good idea there are always many claims to have been the originator. In the case of the two-handed Trans-Atlantic race, which soon became known as the TWOSTAR, though more properly the Observer/Europe 1 Trans-Atlantic Race, I claim to have given it its initial push.

Early in 1978 it was clear that the 1980 OSTAR was going to be heavily oversubscribed and I was getting letters and telephone calls from all over the world expressing concern and, in some cases, bewilderment that the numerical limit imposed on the OSTAR was going to preclude a number of people from taking part. This was particularly a problem for those who had already commissioned the building of a boat for the event only to find they could not get in. I wanted to be able to tell these people that all was not lost, they could enter for another race, and why not make it a two-handed one to which no one could object. All this came to me in my bath one evening after a day of dealing with frustrated potential OSTAR competitors.

On 23 March 1978, the club announced a new, two-handed, race to be run from Plymouth to Newport in 1981. From then things moved swiftly and by the time the newly formed race committee met on 20 June, under the chairmanship of Commander F. W. B. Edwards, I was able to report that there had already been over 100 applications for the rules of the new race. The number of entries was limited to 135 plus an additional 15 at the discretion of the committee for special reasons. The upper limit was put at 85 feet and the lower limit at 25 feet.

When the race was first announced someone said, in all seriousness, "recipe for murder". He knew that in the Round Britain Races we had had instances of non-compatibility in the two-man crews in which they had parted company during the race. That he said was fine in the Round Britain Race but quite another thing in mid-Atlantic. No-one has pushed his or her fellow crew member overboard yet, but one assumes skippers choose their crews with a degree of regard for the psychological aspect of the venture.

The entry list soon filled and a waiting list came into operation. No amount of guessing or gazing into crystal balls will, it seems, ever achieve the full number of yachts, which the rules permit, on the starting line on the day. In this case, last minute drop-outs, including one abandoned on the way to Plymouth, cut the fleet which finally assembled in Plymouth to 103. Britain's hopes lay, it seemed, with either Robin Knox-Johnston and Billy King-Harman, in *Sea Falcon,* or Chay Blyth and Rob James in *Brittany Ferries GB*. The first a 70 foot (21.3 m) catamaran and the second a 65 foot (19.8 m) trimaran. Chay and Rob had won the

Robin Knox-Johnston's Sea Falcon.

1978 Round Britain Race together. Against them was ranged a strong French challenge, Eric Tabarly with his foiler trimaran *Paul Ricard,* Marc Pajot in *Elf Aquitaine,* Loic Caradec in *Royale* and Oliver de Kersausson in *Jacques Ribourel* at 78 feet (23.8 m) the biggest boat in the race. Also to be contended with were Mike Birch and Walter Greene in *Tele-7-Jours,* a very formidable combination.

As the day of the start drew nearer the weather forecasts seemed to get worse and competitors and organisers alike became apprehensive, though for different reasons. The competitor's problem is obvious, but not everyone appreciated the problem facing the organisers. In the first place we had a hundred yachts either without engines or with immobilized engines, bottled up in Millbay Docks behind lock gates which could only be opened for the two hours preceding high water. The race date was chosen to allow for the gates opening, the yachts being towed out (all in the two hours) and the race starting. Once out of the basin there were

no berths for the hundred boats. The rules provided for a delay of 25 hours (a day plus the difference in high water times) but the forecast for the Sunday was even worse than that for the Saturday. In order to start a race of this kind from

Robin Knox-Johnston and Billy King-Harman are a well-tried team.

Opposite page top:
The 65½ foot (20m) Shuttleworth-designed trimaran Brittany Ferries GB *was sailed by Chay Blyth and Rob James.*

Opposite page bottom:
At 78 feet (23.8m), Jacques Ribourel *was the largest boat in the race but was dismasted on the sixth day of the race.*

Right:
Charles Heidsieck III *(65 feet/19.8m) seen from the air at the start*

Below:
Cetus *was well reefed down at the start, but forestay trouble forced her to retire to Lisbon.*

Liz and Anne Hammick pose for their pictures on the bow of their Freedom 33 Miss Alfred Marks.

Plymouth it is necessary to set up a very big operation involving a lot of people, most of them Royal Navy or Royal Marines. Ships have to go out to anchor on the line, buoys have to be laid and a host of patrol craft assembled. Furthermore it is necessary to close the port to shipping for the period between the yachts leaving their berths and starting the race. All these things are possible when arranged at long notice and on a Saturday or a Sunday, but picking a later date at random is a whole other thing.

On this occasion, it was decided that, if we could get the yachts out of the basin with the towing craft available, we would go ahead with the start. Early on Saturday morning, 6 June, the decision was made to go ahead. When I reached the bridge of the Royal Fleet Auxiliary *Resource,* the starting ship, the wind was varying between 30 and 40 knots, that is to say force 7 gusting to 8. Fortunately, by the time the yachts came out it had settled down a bit and was nearer 30 knots at the start. Even so conditions were by no means ideal.

The evacuation of the dock went smoothly but dramas ensued when it came to the start and there were some collisions. The trimaran *D'Aucy* (Alain Labbe) and the proa *Sudinox* (Guy Delage) were in collision and *D'Aucy* was dismasted and *Sudinox* holed. Both had to retire from the race. Marc Pajot in *Elf Aquitaine* was in collision with Martin Minter-Kemp in *Exchange Travel,* which left *Elf* with a leak which required regular pumping and caused Martin Minter-Kemp to go into Fowey 20 miles along the course for repairs before continuing the race. The starting line was 8^1/$_2$ cables long with a marker buoy at its mid-point. Multihulls had to start over one half of the line and monohulls over the other. This separation had been arranged to allow for the very different speeds and accelerations of multis and monos. However the two types mingled in the area to the rear of the start line. The fact that a proa was involved in the most serious of the collisions could be due to that disarming habit they have of suddenly deciding that the stern should become the bow and vice versa. The speed at which this decision can be translated into reality can be startling. Add to this the amazing acceleration of all multihulls, and there is plenty of scope for confusion.

Going straight out into bad weather is always unpleasant. Most people need a period in which to get their sea legs again, and everyone needs a period in which to settle down to the routine of being at sea. A gale at the outset makes all this more difficult and generally leads to a crop of early problems and retirements. In this case *Sudinox* and *D'Aucy* were hardly berthed back in Plymouth after their collision when *Royale* was on her way to join them having been dismasted only a few miles from the start. At the end of the first week, 16 yachts had either retired or been abandoned with problems ranging from acute seasickness to dismasting. Robin Knox-Johnston's *Sea Falcon* thrived on the diet of gales and overtook Chay Blyth before himself being overtaken by Olivier de Kersausson in his big trimaran *Jacques Ribourel*. Robin chose a course nearer to the great circle, and therefore north of Chay, and allowed Chay to slip through into the lead.

A week after the start, gales were still giving the yachts a hard time but Chay Blyth and Rob James, in their immensely strong and well prepared *Brittany Ferries GB,* were tearing along out in front pursued by *Jacques Ribourel, Elf Aquitaine* and *Tele-7-Jours.* Behind these leading multis were *Kriter,* who by 11 June had overtaken Florence

Arthaud in her *Monsieur Meuble,* and they were 9th and 10th respectively. The first few days of rough weather proved too much for Eric Tabarly's *Paul Ricard,* and she was forced to retire with structural damage. Philip Steggall and his crew Thomas Wiggins were rescued on 8 June from their upturned trimaran *Bonifacio* when they were some 350 miles south-west of Lands End. In the early stages of the race they had established an early lead and were sailing fast when, with both of them down below, the yacht simply went over due to a combination of sea and wind.

Nigel Irens and Mark Pridie in their 40 foot (12.2 m) trimaran *Gordano Goose* had decided to lie to a sea anchor when it got really rough. The yacht was alternately straining on the warp of the sea anchor and then surging ahead before falling back again on the warp. These violent movements astern imposed great strain on the rudder and although they had lashed it amidships it became damaged and they were forced to retire to the Scillies. Several of the most experienced skippers said that the conditions were as bad as, if not worse than, they had ever experienced.

With the dismasting and subsequent loss of *Eterna Royal Quartz,* the death knell of proas, as far as this series of races was concerned, was rung. Whether *Eterna* and *Tahiti Douche,* lost on her way to Plymouth, would have been lost had the owners not re-rigged them from their original design, who can tell. And would *Sudinox* have completed the course, but for her collision, again who can tell. Misfortune dogged the big Freedom 70, *Kriter Lady II,* which was to have been sailed by Naomi James and Laurel Holland. At the last moment Naomi had to be admitted to hospital (what a mercy this happened before the start and not after it) and John Oakeley was engaged to sail with Laurel. This late change resulted in the yacht being given a penalty but, as it turned out, this was not to matter. The very heavy weather proved too much for the stepping arrangements of her unstayed masts and she ended up resorting to motor for the last part of the passage to Newport. She was thus obliged to retire.

Mike Birch and Walter Greene, after keeping well up with the leaders, were finally forced to retire when the hull of *Tele-7-Jours* started to

Brittany Ferries GB slips across the line in the dark to win.

Chay, Maureen and Samantha Blyth with Rob James in a shower of champagne.

de-laminate. They finally made it into Liverpool, Nova Scotia, but were not able to continue. Chay Blyth and Rob James brought *Brittany Ferries GB* into Newport in a new record time of 14 days 13 hours and 54 minutes, 140 miles ahead of their nearest rival, Marc Pajot, in *Elf Aquitaine*. Eric Loiseau in *Gauloise IV* was third and Robin Knox-Johnston and Billie King-Harman fourth in *Sea Falcon*. They were followed by the first monohull, Bruno Bacilieri and Marc Vallin in *Faram Serenissima* who managed to beat Florence Arthaud and Francois Boucher, in *Monsieur Meubles* by 2^1/2 hours. No less than 13 boats managed to beat Phil Weld's single-handed record of the year before.

There were some astonishingly close finishes to keep the interest up after the arrival of the winners. *Black Jack*, Rodney Barton and Mike Pocock, appeared in close company with *Poppy II*, John Dean and Richard Reddyhoff, finishing in that order but only separated by eight minutes. Closer still were *F. Magazine*, Claire Marty and Catherine Hermann, and *Festival de Lorient*, Marie Noelle Dedienne and Isabelle Bernadin, who finished only two minutes apart. Later on came *Coathelm, Sherpa Bill* and *Assassin*, all within eight

minutes after 25 days' sailing. The husband and wife team, Philip and Frances Walwyn came well up the list in their 45 foot (13.7 m) catamaran *Skyjack*. Regular competitors in the Royal Western's races, they would appear from St Kitts fully prepared and relaxed. There's nothing like a transatlantic cruise to iron out the wrinkles. During the race they came up with *S. Marine*, Olivier Moussy and Louise Chambaz, in light weather, and the French boat invited them alongside to share a bottle of champagne. This exchange of "stores" did not, fortunately, form the subject of a protest and the Walwyns went on to finish 24 hours ahead of *S. Marine*. The achievements of the smaller boats tend to be overlooked after the excitement of all the big ones. I doubt if any except the really discerning watchers appreciated, for example, the feat of Mark Gatehouse and Patrick Holmes in bringing their 30 foot trimaran *Mark One Toolhire* in in only 22 days and 8 hours to win Class VI. Mark was reported to have said that the only way to sail a boat like that in weather like that was to sail her like a dinghy. Right at the end, came *Yang* sailed by Jean Lacombe, veteran of the first OSTAR, this time with a lady called Tony Austin to help him.

14

A Record Fleet: A Record Time

The Binatone Round Britain and Ireland Race 1982

Since the previous Round Britain and Ireland Race *The Observer* had withdrawn sponsorship of the race for they now had two transatlantic races to cope with. Negotiations to obtain a new sponsor went on for some months and it was not until October 1981 that agreement was reached with Binatone International, makers of CB radio which was coming into vogue in Britain, that they would sponsor the event. By this time it seemed that the race was to be a great deal more international and high powered than previously. The entry list reached its numerical limit and a waiting list was established. A very good selection of the top names in the game appeared on the list.

The situation changed somewhat when the French, who seemed to consider the Round Britain Race as a domestic, British, affair, arranged a race from La Rochelle to New Orleans earlier in the year. Although it was said that yachts would have time to get back for the Round Britain Race, Marc Pajot and Robin Knox-Johnston were two who found there were problems in achieving this. Marc thought his problem would be solved by shipping his boat, *Elf Aquitaine,* back across the Atlantic but, instead of the ship dropping her off on the way, she carried on to Hamburg and there was then no time to get her to Plymouth. Robin did a rapid turn around in America, grabbing a totally unknown Frenchman, who spoke no English, to

crew for him on the return passage to Plymouth. It appears that the Frenchman was an excellent crew, and presumably they both became a little bit more bilingual, but they managed to arrive in Plymouth only 24 hours before the start of the race. In accordance with the rules, Robin was given an enormous, 19^1/$_2$ hour, penalty for arriving late in Plymouth. Lesser men would have chucked their hands in but Robin, encouraged by his fresh crew, Billy King-Harman, started on time. Behind him lay a double Atlantic crossing with one hectic day in harbour and, ahead, almost 2000 miles of very testing racing around Britain. I'm sure it was this extraordinary determination which prompted his fellow competitors to vote him the winner of the Henri-Lloyd Trophy which is awarded in the Round Britain Race, to the yacht, not being a major prizewinner, adjudged by the competitors to have achieved the most outstanding performance in completing the race within the time limit.

Philip Weld withdrew because he felt his newly rigged boat was not "raceworthy". Mike Birch had not sorted out boats and sponsors and Philippe Faque also withdrew. However, as far as the British entry was concerned the line-up was still formidable and included all our top contenders. In addition there was a good international spread with entries from 12 countries. The greatest feature of the Round Britain Race is the wonderful

Opposite page:
Rob and Naomi James sailed Colt Cars GB *to victory in the 1982 Round Britain and Ireland.*

collection of characters who are attracted by this form of sailing, the husbands and wives, the all-girl crews, the brothers and even the chaps who sail with other people's wives.

Husbands and wives were a particularly strong section led, literally, by Rob and Naomi James in *Colt Cars GB*, Walter Greene and his wife Joan, from America, sailed *A Cappella*, and Philip and Frances Walwyn were back again from St Kitts with *Skyjack*. David and Jane Ashe sailed their Rival 34, *Stormy Rival*, and, way down towards the bottom, in size though by no means performance, came Katie and Alex Allan in *Uncle John's Band*, Bob Menzies and Christine Bruet, later to become Mrs Menzies, were there in *Dancing Dolphin*.

Among the brothers sailing together were the identical twins Richard and John Oswald, destined to effect a very successful mid-ocean rescue on the third leg of the race. Three pairs of very experienced girls teamed up. Eve Bonham and Diana Thomas-Ellam, who had sailed together in the two-handed trans-Atlantic race the year before, sailed *Blue Nun*, a Contessa 32 belonging to Eve's mother. Mary Falk and Fiona Wylie sailed *Wild Rival*, a Rival 34, and June Clarke and Vicki de Trafford sailed a quarter tonner *Moondog*. *Moondog* was little more than an overgrown dinghy, very wet, almost totally devoid of any interior fittings relating to comfort, designed to be day-sailed and, in the modern fashion with lots of people with their legs over the side to keep her something approaching upright. They did find that without the weight normally supplied by a full crew they were forced to reduce sail to the detriment of the boat's performance.

A newcomer to the event was Walter Ehn, from Switzerland, who sailed *Scheat* with Kurt Meierhofer. During the pre-race round of social activities Walter had shown a tendency to fall asleep during the course of the evening and his fellow competitors soon developed a routine for seeing him home. When in Castle Bay, Barra, he attended a party given by Leslie Williams and Bob Fisher onboard their 80 foot (24.4 m) *Challenger*, which went on until it was time Leslie and Bob left on the next leg of the race. At the last minute the party goers were taken off by another yacht and very much at the last minute Walter was found curled up asleep in *Challenger's* sail bin, within an ace of becoming a stowaway. Walter enjoyed the race, and all that went with it, enormously and I think his fellow competitors enjoyed having him. I helped him pick up a mooring in Plymouth after he had finished the race and he described himself as being "the happiest man in the whole wide world". The successful completion of the Round Britain meant a great deal to him.

From South Africa, Bertie Reed and John Martin brought, the new *Voortrekker II*. They always enjoy themselves ashore but are totally dedicated afloat and brought *Voortrekker II* home first of the monohulls in 18 days 16 hours. Warren Luhrs, from America, was back with *Tuesday's Child*, her third appearance in these races. She retired in the 1980 OSTAR with structural problems, was back in 1981 for the two-handed transatlantic race and now in 1982 she came second of the monohulls in the Round Britain Race. Another interesting monohull was Chris Shaw's light, narrow *Micro Metalsmiths*, at 56 feet (17.1 m) two feet (0.6 m) longer than the also narrow *Tuesday's Child*, who managed to beat her home by a margin of just under 15 hours.

Some competitors in these races simply enter and then show up on the day. Others enter into a correspondence with the club at an early stage and then keep up a dialogue until they finally arrive in Plymouth for the start. In the latter category were Ian Johnston and Cathy Hawkins who, far away in Australia, were building a 31 foot (9.4 m) trimaran which they were to sail to Plymouth for the race. All this was done without any real sponsorship and with great determination and resourcefulness. By the time they arrived in Plymouth I really felt I almost knew them. I had certainly followed their progress from Australia with great interest. Their boat *Twiggy*, was designed by Lock Crowther and, before leaving Australia, they did very well in races there, so they left their native shores with confidence in the boat.

After crossing the Indian Ocean they stopped in Durban for four months, earning some well needed money and doing some modifications to the boat in the light of experience so far. They also needed to wait for the northern winter to abate. They arrived in Plymouth in very good time for the race having sailed 13,000 miles. Once racing, her placings for such a small boat, of 15th at Crosshaven and 13th at Castle Bay must have made them feel their long trek from Australia was worthwhile.

Ian Johnston and Cathy Hawkins enjoy a little peace in Millbay Docks after their sail from Australia.

After that, however, things went badly wrong. After being 2nd in Class 5 at Castle Bay they were hell bent on overtaking Walter and Joan Greene in *A Cappella* and, on Monday 19 July, when they were going up to the west of Orkney, they felt they might indeed be creeping up on them. Cathy was on the helm as they creamed along averaging 14 knots under full main, cruising spinnaker and No 2 headsail, with a westerly wind of about force 6. They had what they later described as a cross-swell sea. Without warning a sea came along which picked up the stern and, instead of sailing up the face of the swell ahead, the three bows dug into the sea and the yacht pitchpoled. Cathy was propelled out of the cockpit into the spinnaker which was by then in the water. Ian was below. They had given a great deal of thought to the problem of a capsize and what to do if and when it happened. They had already secured various important items in nets so that, if the boat was inverted, they would remain dry. The battery was gimballed so that it would

remain upright – it did. They had also agreed procedures to be followed after a capsize and now, with Cathy outside and Ian inside, they calmly followed the drill. Cathy found the axe and, reminded by Ian where to make the hole, cut a hole in the hull so that they could go in and out without having to dive down.

Inverted, *Twiggy* was a reasonable survival platform although they were, from time to time, thrown into the sea and forced to struggle back onto the hull. They had supplies for several days but their great danger was from the cold; only one of them had a survival suit. At daybreak they had lost faith in their EPIRB and had concluded that their best hope of rescue lay in another competitor coming upon them. In this they were quite right and at 1015, on the day following their capsize, they spotted a sail approaching. It was a yacht under spinnaker. Cathy started waving their orange sleeping bag and Ian reached for the flares from their dry stowage. The yacht came closer but

Twiggy *in Orkney. Note the hole in the main hull through which Ian emerged and the radar reflector still lashed to the bottom.*

did not seem to have seen them, so Ian loosed off a parachute flare and followed this with a red hand held flare. When the approaching yacht dropped her spinnaker they knew they had been seen.

The rescuers turned out to be the Oswald twins in their *Pepsi*. They left *Twiggy* drifting, and also her dinghy which had been used to transfer some items of equipment to *Pepsi*. Later *Boomerang* spotted the dinghy and spent some hours searching for Ian and Cathy. *Boomerang* reported finding the dinghy and this was the first news we had of *Twiggy's* accident. *Pepsi* was unable to report, being out of range of her VHF radio but later *Challenger* came upon the upturned *Twiggy* and, being within range of *Pepsi's* radio, heard of the rescue and was able to report it to shore with her more powerful transmitter.

The only other serious casualty in the race was another multihull, the catamaran *Jan II*, sailed by Robert Denny and Tony Smith, who capsized on the second leg, 20 miles south west of Mizzen

Head. Their EPIRB signal was heard by a civil airliner early on the morning of 14 July, which apparently did nothing about it. It was 1345 that day before the signal was picked up by an RAF Nimrod who homed a helicopter, and the Irish Naval vessel *Aisling,* to the scene. The crew of the yacht were rescued about two hours later and the *Aisling* tried to take the catamaran in tow. This was not practicable and the yacht was abandoned, and later reported sunk.

Although there were two capsizes the weather was in fact kind during the race. A number of notable multihull capsizes have been caused more by the sea than the wind. There comes an odd, rogue, wave which, by being larger, steeper or from a different direction to all the others, breaks the rhythm of what was a perfectly acceptable motion, and transforms the situation to one of acute danger, without any warning. Cruising yachtsmen are more able to ease up and allow for these rogue waves but racing skippers find the temptation to

press on conflicts with prudence.

In this particular race the feelings of some of the Class 6 crews were summarized in what became known as the Class 6 Round Britain Song: its theme was that this smallest class had been forgotten by everyone else. Words, and generally music as well, were provided by Katie Allan, skipper of *Uncle John's Band*. Katie's impromptu concerts at stopover ports were a popular feature of the race.

In the past we had always had a newspaper, or newspapers, sponsoring the races and it is not surprising that sponsors in the business of selling news know better how to feed their fellow media folk than sponsors geared to selling electronic equipment. Furthermore *The Observer* had a real live yachting correspondent in the shape of Frank Page who knew all about reporting yacht races. Binatone were new to the sailing scene and, with the sponsors of *Colt Cars* airlifting the media about and generally jollying them along, it was not surprising that *Colt Cars* got the lion's share of the coverage.

There was, of course, plenty to be interested in at the front end of the fleet. The first three yachts rang the changes on being first into each port. Rob and Naomi James were first into Crosshaven. On the next leg Mark Gatehouse and Peter Rowsell came up from 5th to be 1st into Castle Bay, then Chay Blyth and Peter Bateman took up the running and were 1st into Lerwick and then Lowestoft.

Among the leading yachts on the final leg, Rob and Naomi James brought *Colt Cars* across the finishing line first but Chay Blyth and Peter Bateman, in *Brittany Ferries GB,* were close behind them; so close in fact that they were actually in Plymouth Sound when *Colt Cars* finished, but there was so little wind that they took another 43 minutes to complete the course. The winning time of 16 days 15 hours and 3 minutes was a record for the course until 1989. Of that time 8 days had to be spent in harbour and their average speed, after the deduction of that time, was 9.1 knots. Third to finish was *Exmouth Challenge,* sailed by Mark Gatehouse and Peter Rowsell, just an hour after *Brittany Ferries GB.* Then there was a gap of 18$\frac{1}{2}$ hours until the next bunch of five boats

arrived, led by Peter Philips and Andrew Herbert in *Livery Dole III,* followed by Tony Bullimore and Nigel Irens in I.T. 82, who won Class 4, Brian Law and Dick Gomes in *Downtown Flyer,* Mike Whipp and Wil Hardcastle in *Gordano Goose* and then Walter and Joan Greene in *A Cappella,* who won Class 5.

As the first yachts were finishing in Plymouth the last one had not yet arrived at Lerwick. Worries over the four latecomers at Castle Bay had prompted a note in the watchkeepers' log at Plymouth, for the benefit of worried relations who rang up, which reminded them that, in 1978, the longest time for the second leg was 6 days and in 1974 five yachts took over 7 days. The latter times were due to strong contrary winds but in this, 1982 race, the delays were caused by light conditions and the last boat into Castle Bay took over 7 days. In the monohull fleet, *Voortrekker II* went out in front and steadily increased her lead over *Tuesday's Child* finally beating her by nearly 35 hours. Only 10 minutes behind *Tuesday's Child* came Robert Nickerson and Jeffrey Taylor in *RJN Marine.* This boat was really *Panic* and was sailed by Fred Dovaston and Jeffrey Taylor in the 1981 TWOSTAR under the name of *Inkel Hi-Fi. RJN Marine* had been well up throughout the race and had an interesting tussle with *Pepsi* and *Jeantex.* The former was a fellow Class 4 boat but *Jeantex* was in Class 2. Another monohull to outperform some of the much bigger boats was *Alice's Mirror,* designed, built and sailed by Adrian Thompson, with Max Noble as his crew. At 30 feet (9.1 m) she was at the top limit of Class 6. She was 36th overall and 2nd in her class. She had a terrific race with *Applejack* who, though the same length, was a trimaran, sailed by Julian Musto and Andrew Williams. *Applejack* led at Crosshaven and Castle Bay but *Alice's Mirror* slipped through to have a lead of 3 hours at Lerwick. By Lowestoft this lead had been narrowed to just 7 minutes and on the final leg *Applejack* went through to cross the line 18 minutes ahead. Amongst the little boats *Uncle John's Band,* Katie and Alex Allen, and *Mr Speedy,* Richard Moncad and David Craddock did very well to bring their 25 footers (7.6 m) home above so many larger boats. Luke Fitzherbert, who last time round enjoyed a more luxurious ride in Peter Jay's *Norvantes,* 47 feet (14.3 m), brought his gaff cutter *Falmouth Bay* home well off the bottom of the list with Jeremy Fordham as his crew. Not everyone thought that a gaff cutter would be their number one choice for this particular race.

Opposite page:
The rescue of the crew of Jan II *as seen from the* Nimrod *which co-ordinated the operation.*

15

Two French Winners

The Observer/Europe 1 Single-handed Transatlantic Race 1984

After the 1980 OSTAR, Jack Odling-Smee retired as Chairman of the Committee after more than 20 years. He could not possibly have imagined, as he saw the first five off in 1960, how the race would develop in those 20 years. He saw the race through the crisis years, 1975/76, and when he retired it was going along very much on an even keel. The race benefitted enormously from the continuity of his chairmanship and I believe the lack of that continuity, resulting from the current policy of having a new chairman for each race, is to be regretted.

Air Commodore Tom Pierce, who succeeded Jack, formed his committee in August 1980 and set straight to work on the rules for the 1984 race. Whilst it used to be fairly simple to get the rules out three and a half years in advance, the progress of sailing technology makes it more difficult to produce rules far in advance which will not need to be revised nearer the start. Quite apart from technology, there was, in this case, the basic question of what the race was to be called. Since the introduction of the very expensive ARGOS system, *The Observer* had needed a co-sponsor and they alone were involved in securing this assistance. It was not until November 1981 that they had assurances from Europe 1 that they would again sponsor the event.

The upper size limit for the race was raised by

four feet (1.2 m) and we had five classes instead of the three in 1980.

A new rule did away with the previous restrictions on overhangs by adopting overall length as the only measurement. Some feared this would lead to boats with vertical ends, though what was wrong with this was never clear. Despite pressure to raise the lower size the committee kept this at 25 feet (7.6 m) overall length. For the first time, the rules specifically excluded proas. This brought protests from Dick Newick, whose *Cheers* was the only proa ever to finish an OSTAR. He proposed a design for a boat which he described as an "asymmetrical trimaran", but it looked like a proa to the committee!

Entries were limited to 80, plus another 20 at the discretion of the committee. The aim was to get about 100 on the line on the day and this figure was derived from the number of ARGOS transmitters which Europe 1 would finance, and the fact that there was very restricted space available for the pre-race assembly. When entries closed on 14 April 1984 the list contained 105 names. By the end of the month that figure had dropped to 98 and both *The*

Opposite page:
Umupro Jardin V *to windward of* Travacrest Seaway *at the start.*

108

Paul Ricard *(note the foil below the starboard float) in apparently close company with* Shamrock *(69) and* Thursday's Child *before the start.*

The undaunted Florence Arthaud sailed Biotherm *but problems forced her into the Azores.*

Elf Aquitaine, L'Aiglon *and* Destination St Croix *at the start.*

Gespac *well reefed at the start. Note the Argos beacon on the after hatch just abaft the mainsheet track.*

Observer and Europe 1 were anxious that we should go on taking entries to bring the total to 100 on the day. However, at a meeting of the committee on 30 April it was agreed that we should not now start taking 'post entries'. This decision did not satisfy the sponsors and *The Observer* continued to press for more entries to be allowed. They were under pressure from France to get some heavily sponsored well known skippers in.

I had spent the last ten years corresponding with competitors and dealing with the entries and waiting lists. I tried to be scrupulously fair and to build up confidence in the system. I felt that any last minute acceptance of entries would undermine the confidence which I hoped existed. At the request of *The Observer* another meeting was called for 18 May, at which they put their case for allowing more entries. Before this meeting I explained to the Commodore and the committee Chairman that I felt so strongly about this that, if the committee agreed to *The Observer's* request they would have to find a new Secretary.

The meeting was, as one member of the committee recorded in his diary, "a bad meeting". The case for *The Observer* was put by Brian Nicholson its Joint Managing Director, and soon after he had spoken a vote was taken and by a

narrow majority his request was granted. The debate then continued and, had another vote been allowed, the decision would certainly have gone the other way! It was the end of the road as far as I was concerned. I duly resigned.

Quite apart from objecting to the agreed entry procedure being abandoned, I also felt that sponsors are sponsors and clubs should be left to run the race the way their experience tells them is right. Certainly race organizers must try to accommodate their sponsors as far as possible, but they must always be looking to the future, expecting that the event they are organizing will be repeated and mindful that any monkeying with the rules, for temporary expediency, will reverberate to their embarrassment in the future. So, the remains of the waiting list had to be scoured for skippers who, at this late stage, could get themselves organized in time to start. In the end the only takers were the three professionals, who Europe 1 had been plugging, and Timothy Hubbard who had been in Plymouth for nearly a year waiting for his name to come to the top of the list.

On the day of the race, 91 yachts started. The evening shipping forecast for that day was for the southeasterly winds to veer southwesterly and increase to force 7 or 8, in sea area Plymouth, and to become cyclonic then westerly 6 to 7 further west. This was not good news to competitors, who would not only have had little time in which to settle down but would still be in the approaches to the Channel and therefore concerned with dodging shipping as well as each other. Rising winds had their first victim when June Clarke, in her trimaran *Batchelors Sweet Pea (ex Downtown Flyer)* came to grief off the Cornish coast between Penzance and Land's End. The first the race office knew of this was a message from Falmouth Coastguard which was recorded as "Capsized trimaran off Tater Du light crew wearing lifejacket on bottom". Presumably the apparent confusion between the crew's and the trimaran's bottoms was due to the watchkeeper not being fluent in shorthand. That message was followed four minutes later by another which simply said "crew of yacht is a woman". This was soon followed by the yacht's number and we then had confirmation that it was June Clarke. June had actually capsized at 1700 but the first report came from the Coastguard at 2304. She had activated her EPIRB but it was never established whether it had operated correctly. It was obviously a great disappointment to June and, as the coxswain of the Penlee lifeboat who rescued her said, ironic considering that she was sponsored by a number of people, to the tune of about £10,000, in aid of a new lifeboat for the Channel Islands. One hopes the sponsors stood by their pledges notwithstanding the shortness of her voyage.

The first of six dismastings also took place on day one, when *Lada Poch,* was forced to retire, and American hopes of another win were reduced when Hugh McCoy, in his powerful 60 foot (18.3 m) catamaran *Fury* had to retire with rudder damage. He returned to Plymouth but was unable to re-start. There were dramas out in the front of the fleet. On 7 June *Credit Agricole* capsized in only 15 knots of wind. The skipper, Philippe Jeantot, was out on one of the floats, pumping it out, when the self steering gear failed and the yacht altered course bringing the wind abeam and over she went. Yvon Fauconnier, in *Umupro Jardin V,* went to the scene and took Philippe on board. He was loath to leave his yacht which he knew could be salvaged so they hung around until they were sure help was on the way. Philippe was then put back on his upturned boat and Fauconnier continued in the race. Patrick Morvan was out in front of the fleet when he hit a tree trunk and had to abandon his yacht. The lead was taken over by Gilles Gahinet, in *33 Export,* but

June Clarke was rescued from her capsized trimaran off the Cornish coast.

Philippe Jeantot found temporary refuge on board Umupro Jardin *after his capsize in* Crédit Agricole.

he had already reported that a crack had developed in his mast and was causing concern. At this point Peter Phillips in *Travacrest Seaway,* was lying second so, when Giles Gahinet turned for home, *Travacrest Seaway* took over the lead. Also well up was another British hopeful, Geoff Houlgrave, in *Colt Cars* but on 11 June his race ended when his mast came down damaging his starboard float. He was soon forced to abandon his yacht. Hopes of a British win ran high for a day or two with Peter Philips out in front, but Daniel Gilard, in *Nantes,* Olivier Moussy, in *Region Centre* and Marc Pajot, in *Elf Aquitaine II* were all challenging. Eric Tabarly too was not far away and gradually improving his position.

Crédit Agricole, *here moving fast under reduced sail, was later to capsize and cause a problem with the results table.*

As the front runners got to about 500 miles from Newport, the weather became lighter and Peter Philips, having suffered sail and gear damage earlier on, could not carry the sail he so desperately needed to hold on to his lead. Philippe Poupon in *Fleury Michon,* came through to take the lead with Marc Pajot hard on his heels. Philippe was first to reach the line and, he thought, to be the winner. Marc Pajot was only 23 minutes behind him and he was followed by Eric Tabarly and Peter Philips, in that order. Ten and a half hours after Philippe Poupon finished, Yvon Fauconnier arrived in *Umupro Jardin V.* In accordance with normal racing custom, Fauconnier had been awarded a time allowance for having stood by *Credit Agricole.* This amounted to 16 hours and was announced in a press release on 18 June, before any yacht had finished. This press release ended "The race officials remind the media that the first competitor to cross the line may not necessarily be the winner of the 1984 OSTAR".

The allowance was to be subject to examination of Fauconnier's log on arrival, and in due course, much to the agony of Philippe Poupon, Fauconnier was declared the winner.

Because of the unusual situation which had arisen, *The Observer,* made two special awards. These were, an award for first to finish for Philippe Poupon in *Fleury Michon* and a fourth prize for Eric Tabarly in *Paul Ricard,* who would have been third if Fauconnier had not been compensated for standing by another yacht. It is very important that this practice of allowing time is kept up because, in this increasingly commercial world, one could envisage a sponsor leaning on his skipper to abandon the humane customs of the sea, if he thought he was winning.

In the 1982 Route du Rhum race, Olivier Moussy rescued Ian Johnston, who had capsized, and was then told by radio that he had been disqualified for having two people on board. This was an unbelievable decision on someone's part and contrasted very strikingly with what had happened earlier that year when he and Cathy

Jeff Houlgrave

Olivier Moussy

Marc Pajot on board Elf Aquitaine II

Philippe Poupon exultant as he brings Fleury Michon *over the line first in a new record time.*

Yvon Fauconnier and Philippe Poupon shared the honours. Fauconnier was declared the winner and Poupon the record holder.

Hawkins had capsized, in the same boat, in the Round Britain Race. There they had been picked up by another competitor who finished that leg four up in a two-handed race and was given a time allowance for time lost during the rescue. Fortunately the decision to disqualify Moussy was rescinded later, but he was not given a poper time allowance to allow him to be appropriately placed in the results. In the 1982/3 BOC Around Alone Race, Richard Broadhead sailed back nearly 300 miles to rescue Jacques de Roux from his sinking yacht and was given an allowance of 145 hours to compensate for the delay it caused him. Another rescue by a fellow competitor occurred in the 1984 OSTAR when John Mansell's 35 foot (10.7 m) catamaran *Double Brown,* started to break up 400 miles east of St John's, Newfoundland. Alan Thomas in his 40 foot (12.2 m) monohull, *Jemima Nicholas,* diverted to his position and scooped him up just in time. He reckoned he lost 3½ hours doing this and was therefore allowed that amount of time off his total elapsed time. John was of

Alan Thomas who rescued fellow competitor John Mansell in the nick of time.

John Mansell

course not allowed to help in any way as regards sailing or navigating *Jemima Nicholas*. Whether or not having a survivor on board helps or hinders a single-hander when racing can be argued ad nauseam, but one thing is certain, no one must ever be disqualified for rescuing someone else.

It was no surprise that the first home were multihulls, but is was a surprise that no less than 12 boats beat Phil Weld's record of 17 days 23 hours, and two of these were monohulls. *Elf Aquitaine II* was alone, amongst the first boats home, in being

new and this could account for her not winning. Marc Pajot still had much to learn about his boat. Of the others, *Umupro Jardin* was originally *Exmouth Challenge, Fleury Michon* was well tried, *Nantes* was previously named *Royale,* and *Travacrest Seaway* (ex *Livery Dole III*) had done a Round Britain Race, Route du Rhum, Transat en Double and the Plymouth to Vilamoura, so she was certainly well tried.

There were three 60 foot (18.3 m) monohulls, producing a race within the race. Warren Luhrs'

Edoardo Austoni sailed his third OSTAR in Chico Boba III.

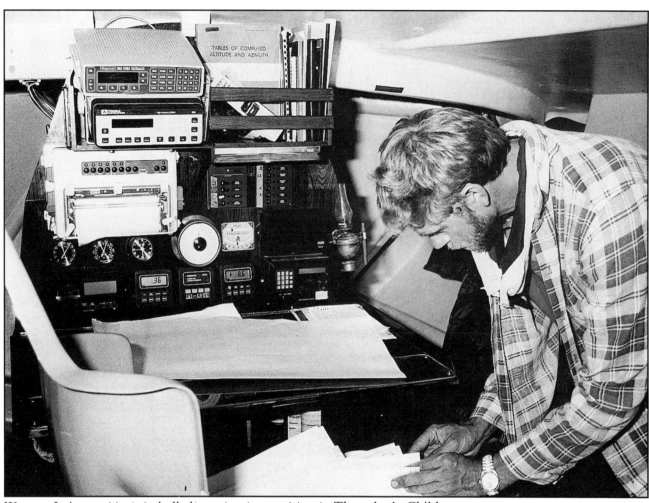

Warren Luhrs at his (gimballed) navigation position in Thursday's Child

Yves le Cornec triumphed over adversity.

Chris Butler won Class V despite various setbacks.

Tony Bullimore was luckier than Rachel Hayward; he found Brenton Reef Tower in daylight and good visibility.

Bob Menzies' Dancing Dolphin *sank under him.*

Jack Petith was first in Class III with his 38 foot (11.6m) trimaran Destination St Croix.

Rachel Hayward's race ended tragically on the rocks of Point Judith, after just missing the finishing line.

Luis Tonnizzo won class IV in City of Slidel

Bill Homeward was only 5¹/₂ hours behind Tonnizzo to make British Airways II *2nd in Class IV.*

Vasil Kurtev, the quiet man from Bulgaria, in probably the most basically equipped yacht in the race, Nord *(25 foot/7.6m), finished in 40¹/₂ days.*

Thursday's Child was the first monohull to finish as well as being the first American finisher. John Martin, in *Mainstay Voortrekker,* though nearly a day behind Luhrs, was still just inside Philip Weld's record. Edoardo Austoni, in *Chico Boba III,* was two and a half days behind *Thursday's Child.* Warren Luhrs was one of those who had taken advantage of the fact that the rules allow water ballast. He also had a pendulous rudder which could be adjusted to be vertical although the yacht was heeled. He did not have an entirely trouble-free trip. On the second day out he broke a steering cable and debated whether to return to Plymouth for repairs, but spent some three hours effecting makeshift repairs and then resumed the race. With about 1200 miles to go he lost the use of his principal working headsail so that when going to windward he was undercanvassed.

Of the many who triumphed over adversity, one who deserves special mention is Yves le Cornec who, in his 42 foot (12.8 m) trimaran *Idenek,* was well up with the leaders when he dropped his centreboard so hard that he demolished the centreboard casing. For two days he almost stopped while working in his flooded hull to put a patch over the hole. This he finally did and went on to finish a very creditable 16th overall and 3rd in class. Chris Butler, in *Swansea Bay,* was towed into

a buoy on the way out to the start. After repairs, he set off in pursuit of the fleet, but later noticed a crack which worried him into taking it easy when on the starboard tack. However he outgrew this cautionary habit and pressed on to win Class V despite losing all forms of self steering ten days before finishing.

Losses of yachts are always sad but more so when they are the skippers' pride and joy, paid for by him rather than out of some big company's advertising budget. This was the case with Bob Menzies' *Dancing Dolphin,* which sank under him on 26 June. She started making water and he was forced to press his ARGOS emergency push when he could not control the inflow of water. He was rescued but the yacht was lost. Bob and *Dancing Dolphin* had been in a number of our races and this was a sad ending to their partnership. Worse still was the disaster which befell Rachel Hayward in *Loiwing.* For the week before her final approach to Newport she had been without electric power, and now, in fog, with no satnav or sounder, she was groping for Brenton Reef Tower and the finishing line. She mistook the signal on Point Judith for that on the Brenton Reef Tower, and, having just missed the line, she drove up onto Point Judith doing about 6 knots. All that was left for her to do was to get out and walk.

16

Around in Gales

The City of Plymouth Round Britain and Ireland Race 1985.

For a time it looked as though the 1985 Round Britain Race might have no sponsor, but, in February 1985, the City of Plymouth came forward. This was their first full sponsorship of a yachting event, though for some years the city had shown an enlightened attitude towards sailing events in Plymouth, providing assistance in kind and entertaining visiting crews.

This was the last race for which the pre-race assembly was in the old Millbay Dock. In future, events would be in the modern yacht harbour of Queen Anne's Battery Marina. As this had been backed by the City of Plymouth, it was appropriate that the 1985 race should be started by the Lord Mayor. There were no naval vessels available and the Lord Mayor and the RWYC committee were embarked in the motor yacht *Trago Voyager*, kindly made available by Mike Robertson. With their necks on swivels, they anchored in the middle of the starting line with the motor yacht *Cordelia* marking the eastern end and the Queen's harbour master's launch *Swift* on the western end. The monohulls started on the western section and the multis the eastern end. Light westerly winds and a few calm patches later on made the first leg, to Crosshaven a slow one.

Among the fleet in 1985 Tony Bullimore had his designer, Nigel Irens, with him in *Apricot*, and *BCA Paragon* sailed by Mike Whipp was also

crewed by his designer, Adrian Thompson. These two started favourites, but there were a number of other yachts with a good track record. *Morr Energy* (ex *Travacrest Seaway* ex *Livery Dole III)* was sailed by Paul Hargreaves and Jeff Houlgrave, *Marlow Ropes* (ex *Umupro Jardin,* winner of the 1984 OSTAR and previously *Exmouth Challenge* was sailed by Mark Gatehouse and Peter Rowsell, and Don Wood had acquired the salvaged *Colt Cars* which Jeff Houlgrave had abandoned in the 1984 OSTAR and, with sponsorship from British Rail's parcel department, named her *Red Star/Night Star*. His crew was Butch Dalrymple-Smith. Robin Knox-Johnston and Billy King-Harman completed the top British line up and from the U.S.A., the formidable combination of Walter Greene and Philip Steggall sailed *Sebago*. The French end was kept up by Pierre le Maout and Antoine Pouliquen in the 40 foot catamaran *Macallan – Festival de Lorient*.

Only a minute separated *Apricot* and *Paragon* at Crosshaven. *Apricot* had halyard troubles during the second and third legs and had to have her mast lifted out in Lerwick. *Paragon,* despite having sail problems, beat the course record for the leg from Crosshaven to Castle Bay but was forced to retire into Peterhead, after leaving Lerwick, having suffered structural damage and a torn mainsail in 40 knot winds. *Red Star/Night Star* hit

Apricot with four crew members to windward in exhilarating conditions.

Tony Bullimore took Apricot's *designer, Nigel Irens, along as crew. A combination which proved very successful.*

an unlit buoy after leaving Crosshaven damaging the bow of her port float. This was the crew repaired under way with fibreglass cloth and epoxy resin. From all accounts Don Wood had as much of both on him as the boat by the time he had finished this balancing act. It was a considerable achievement. They had problems on the leg from Lerwick to Lowestoft which dropped them down to 6th place from which they only managed to climb one place by the finish. Peter Philips and Bob Fisher parted their main halyard on day one and went into Fowey to fix it, arriving in Crosshaven in 32nd place. Beset by rigging problems they retired and returned to Plymouth.

Nick Skinnard and Robert Moncur in Newcastle Brown Ale *showed once again what a Folkboat can do.*

Opposite page:
Don Wood sailed the previously abandoned Colt Cars, *now named* Red Star/Night Star, *with Butch Dalrymple-Smith.*

Among monohulls the contenders for best time were Warren Luhrs's *Thursday's Child* (60 ft/18.3 m), John Martin's *Voortrekker II* (60 feet/18.3 m) and Donald Parr's *Quailo of Wight* (63 feet/19.2 m). They finished in that order and *Thursday's Child* led them all the way. Following his resue by Alan Thomas in the previous year's OSTAR, John Mansell was crewing for Alan in *Jemima Nicholas*. This time he was allowed to help. In the middle of the fleet were many previous competitors on this course, back to settle old scores. A gale that savaged the leaders on the east coast of Scotland caused the smaller boats, still on the west side, considerable discomfort and delay. On 17 July 10 yachts were reported held up in Castle Bay due to weather. These were *Zeehaas, Sarie Marais, Silk, Max Factor, Shoki, Spring*

Gold, Taal, Quixote, Beefeater and *Robiijn.* They decided to leave together at 0730 the next morning but in fact never did so. *Sarie Marais* retired on medical advice directed towards the skipper, and *Max Factor* also retired. At this time there was concern for *Newcastle Brown Ale,* Nick Skinnard's little Folkboat crewed by Robert Moncur, but they battled their way into Castle Bay at 2040 on 17 at a time when winds there were reported between force 7 and force 9.

On 18 July the number holed up in the Castle Bay had risen to 23; however at 1830 that evening the weather had moderated sufficiently to allow about 15 of them to set off for Lerwick. The wind was then SW 6-7, moderating, and backing southerly. One not to be delayed by this storm was the little *Humberts,* sailed by the Trafford brothers, Richard and James. This J 24 class inshore racer had to be "stretched" by the addition of 12 inches, at the stern, for her to be admissible to the race. *Humberts* arrived in Castle Bay on the morning of 14 July, so was away again on 16 and in Lerwick three days later. On that leg they reported surfing at 15 knots under bare poles. They finally finished

33rd overall, the first monohull in their class and ahead of several class 4,5 and 6 boats.

There were a number of retirements at Castle Bay and Tobermory. Just how many of these were due to gear or boat failures, or simply an urge to change from racing to cruising the Western Isles, is not recorded but among those who went on were the Folkboat *Newcastle Brown Ale* and Christine Bryan and Sally Harrison in their 26 foot (7.9 m) *Sadler Girl*. In the end they were able to finish the race within the time limit. Another boat at the very bottom end of the size scale, was the 25 foot (7.6 m) Danish trimaran *Majic Hemple,* sailed by Eric Quorning and Eric Fruergaard, who managed not only to get around the gruelling course but finish in 18th place overall.

The Henri Lloyd Trophy for special endeavour, awarded by the votes of competitors, went to *Newcastle Brown Ale* with the following all not very far behind (not in sequence of votes scored) *Ghoster, Quixote, Sadler Girl, Intermediate Technology, Majic Hemple* and *Quickstep.*

Excluded from this prize under its rules were all those who had won a major award. The Boxall Trophy for the yacht with the highest speed to waterline ratio went to *Majic Hemple.* The tail enders were treated to another gale before they finally made Plymouth and with threats of storm force winds, a number of yachts sought refuge along the south coast between 2 and 4 of August. These delays were, in some cases just enough to force some retirements as time ran out for skippers and crews. Of the casualties during this race there were three dismastings, a number of rigging problems and some structural damage but the worst was the destruction of *Glucometer II* by a Dutch coaster of Beachy Head, on the last leg of the race. Fortunately her crew Simon Frost and Lock Crowther were rescued. Merchant ships, many of whom maintain a deplorably low standard of look-out remain the most dangerous thing yachts have to contend with in the English Channel.

17

A Low Key Transatlantic

The Carlsberg Transatlantic Race 1986.

After the success of the first two-handed transatlantic race in 1981, it was assumed that the second race in the series would attract even more entries than its predecessor. But the 1986 race suffered from a lack of a sponsor and alternative events elsewhere.

However Carlsberg Lager came in at the last minute with moderate funds (for instance, Argos could not be fitted to the fleet) and when the Danish star helmsman Paul Elvstrom fired the starting gun on 8 June there were only 49 yachts as opposed to the 103 who had started five years before.

One of the disappointing withdrawals was that of *Paragon,* a British multihull. After sweeping the board in the La Trinité series she must have had a very good chance, although only a Class II boat, of winning the TWOSTAR. Surprisingly, Mike Whipp the owner was unable to get sponsorship for the race and so put the boat on the market. There was a certain amount of quiet satisfaction in some quarters that the grand prix element was much diminished. Competitors in some of the smaller, less richly sponsored yachts, felt that there would be less thunder-stealing by the big boys and more interest in their section of the race.

When the committee first met, it was agreed that, as this was a two-handed race, proas would be allowed. But in the event they were specifically precluded as in the single-handed race. There seems to be no record of this change of heart being debated, so there is just the suspicion that the 1984 rules formed the basis for the 1986 ones and the unfortunate proas suffered from an oversight. Clearly they had no lively champion amongst the committee members. *Apricot* seemed to be the British favourite. Her owner Tony Bullimore had obviously got her going well and, after winning the Round Britain Race the previous year she looked set to do well in this event. Bullimore had acquired Walter Greene as his crew to complete the package. Recent performances had suggested that two people could handle a 60 footer (18.3 m) comparatively more efficiently than their counterparts in the big 80 footers (24.4 m) to the extent that the big yachts could lose the advantage their extra length gave them. This would of course depend upon the weather conditions and the amount of reefing and sail changing required. A long settled spell with the right sails set would allow the bigger yacht to build up a good lead over her smaller adversary. In this race *Royale,* 85 feet (25.9 m), was able to finish almost exactly 2 days ahead of *Apricot,* the first 60 footer (18.3 m). Robin Knox-Johnston's *British Airways I* was thought to be well suited to a windward flog, but the Plymouth to Newport course, while nearly always giving a measure of this sort of sailing,

By 1984 radio aids to navigation were allowed, but here Henk Jukkema does it the traditional way. (Courtesy of Henk Jukkema)

Round Britain competitors at anchor in Castle Bay, Barra. (1985) (Courtesy of Highlands and Islands Development Board)

In the 1985 Round Britain Race Jens Quorning and Bo Rasmussen in Quick Step *were only just beaten into second place in Class 6 by Terry Cooke. (Courtesy of Roger Lean-Varcoe)*

Eric Quorning and Eric Fruergaard had a wonderful race round Britain in their little 25 foot (7.6 m) trimaran Majic Hemple *in 1985. (Courtesy of Roger Lean-Varcoe)*

British Airways *was sailed by Robin Knox-Johnston and Bernard Gallay in the 1986 Transatlantic Race. (Courtesy of Roger Lean-Varcoe)*

In 1986 Kitty Hampton and Mary Falk sailed the 40 foot (12.2m) Sony Handycam. (Courtesy of Roger Lean-Varcoe)

Bepe Panada at the wheel of the ill-fated Berlucci *at the start of the 1986 Two-Handed Transatlantic Race.*
(Courtesy of Roger Lean-Varcoe)

The anatomy of a single-handed yacht, New Majic Breeze. *(1988) (Courtesy of Witze Van Der Zee)*

New Majic Breeze *was one of those in the 1988 OSTAR to retire after hitting flotsam. (Courtesy of Witze Van Der Zee)*

Dream Weaver *was back, after 8 years, for the 1988 race. This time sailed by Anthony Rowe. (Courtesy of Anthony Rowe/Billy Black)*

Peter Goss, Philippe Poupon and Tony Bullimore compare notes in Newport after the 1988 Single-handed Race. (Courtesy of James Boyd)

Mike Richey takes Jester *out of Plymouth for her 8th OSTAR, and last voyage, in company with* Invertex Voortrekker, *off on her 3rd OSTAR in 20 years, skippered by Bertie Reed.*

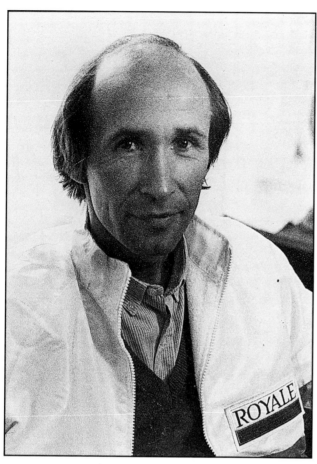

Loic Caradec sailed Royale *with Olivier Despaigne to victory.*

Opposite page:
Royale *retired from an earlier race to return to win the Carlsberg Race.*

seldom fails to produce some light weather conditions as the yachts approach the North American continent.

Philip and Frances Walwyn were back from St Kitts with their very well appointed 75 foot (22.9 m) schooner rigged catamaran *Spirit of St Kitts,* but, sadly, they developed leaks and decided to go straight home to the West Indies. *Novanet,* at 80 feet (24.4 m), the biggest British entry, was said by the *Western Morning News* to be equipped with "space age" sails. These were to arrive only two days before the start. The resultant lack of preparation meant that the skipper Peter Phillips, four days into the race, blew out the mainsail and was unable to complete the course. In the big monohull section, John Martin's *Tuna Marine Voortrekker, (Voortrekker II),* Guy Bernadin's

Biscuits Lu, Markku Wiikeri's *Colt International,* Robert Nickerson's *Cherry Valley Duck* and Beppe Panada's *Berlucchi* were all 60 feet (18.3 m).

In the 1986 race there were 23 monohulls out of a total of 36, which were between 35 (10.7 m) and 45 feet (13.7 m) inclusive. Amongst these was *Sony Handicam,* sailed by Kitty Hampton and Mary Falk. This boat was really *Ntombifuti,* designed by Ed Dubois and owned by Ian Radford who had sailed her very impressively in the Round Britain Race the previous year.

It was Ian who was the first person to sound out the committee on water ballast, which he installed in *Ntombifuti.* This, I seem to remember, led to Archimedes being drawn into the argument. I asked what would happen if he inadvertently went about and found he had all his water ballast down to leeward. "Oh," he says, "haven't you heard of Archimedes? Once down to leeward the water would have no weight." "Right," I replied, "but where you should have buoyancy you now have water and that cannot be good." This was finally agreed and, after the committee had agreed to water ballast, in principle, there seemed to be a need to specify how much such ballast a yacht could have. After consulting various designers, it was decided that when fully ballasted the resulting angle of heel must not exceed 10 degrees in still conditions. The rule also specifies that the water ballast must be contained in fixed tanks. The next question, inevitably, though not necessarily from Ian, was, may we transfer ballast by means of power driven pumps? Here there was some dilemma because the committee have always denied crews the use of power for sail handling but not for pumping bilges. It seemed as important to get the water on the right side of the boat as to get it out of the bilges, so the answer was, yes, you can use power to transfer water ballast. Water ballast remains strictly forbidden in conventional yacht racing.

Gerry Hannaford entered his 45 foot (13.7 m) *Hetaera,* designed by Michael Pocock with sailing to windward in fresh conditions very much in mind. Gerry and Michael Moody finished in just over 22 days to win Class IV, and beat all Class III, except the 50 foot (15.2 m) *Belmont. Belmont,* sailed by Harry Harkimo and Michaela Koskull, from Finland, finished in 22 days 1 hour to win Class III. The Bulgarians, Tenev Svetlozar and Vasil Poov brought their 38 foot (11.5 m) *Bulcan Star* in 22 days 9 hours to win Class V and achieve 13th place overall. This was a great achievement

Opposite page:
Tony Bullimore and Walter Greene teamed up to win Class II in Apricot.

and it was nice to see people, for whom entering an event of this sort is not easy, doing do well. In fact having 7 different nationalities in the first 13 places was very pleasing.

Kai Granholm, from Finland, by now a veteran in these races, having done the TWOSTAR 1981, OSTAR 1984 and the RBR 1985, sailed *Mobira*, a 40 footer (12.2 m) with Tapio Lehtinen and was narrowly beaten by Michael and Patricia Pocock in their 38 foot (11.5 m) *Blackjack*. Two Royal Marines, Chris Johnson and Peter Goss, sailed the Royal Marines' Sail Training Yacht, the OOD 34 *Sarie Marais*. This yacht started her career as the *Hindostan,* stationed at the Britannia Royal Navy College Dartmouth. On transfer to the Royal Marines she was renamed *Sarie Marais,* the march tune of the Commando Forces, Royal Marines. Chris and Peter showed that all their training in tenacity and persistence, and not a little courage, paid off as they baled their way to the finish with the keel emulating the clapper of a bell. They were, nevertheless, the second monohull in their class and made it in 25 days. The yacht was put up for sale after the race!

Whilst the 40 and 35 footers (12.2 m and 10.7 m) were finishing, anxiety was growing over the non-arrival of *Berlucchi*, the Italian 60 footer (18.3 m) sailed by Beppe Panada and Roberto Kramar. Quite early in the race she had reported that her radio was defective and her position reporting had ceased as a result. Now there was no question that she should have arrived. She had, in accordance with the rules, an EPIRB which had to be self activating should the yacht sink, but this had evidently not been heard. She could perhaps be dismasted and making slow progress under jury rig. However when the Coastguard had been persuaded that she was in fact overdue, an "all ships" was put out. We were back with the *Three Cheers* situation, except that there was absolutely no way in which any sort of datum could be established upon which to base a search. Once again we were faced with the problem of the North Atlantic being a very big expanse of sea over which it is quite impossible to search without some indication of where to look.

In fact *Berlucchi* had capsized after losing her keel; at least that is what must be deducted since she was found some months later floating upside down with no keel. Her crew were never found. This tragedy marred a race otherwise notable for the absence of dramas. All the other yachts having difficulties had managed to get themselves to port without assistance. The loss of *Berlucchi* is still, as I write, several years after the event, not a closed book. Regrettably the father of Roberto Kramar, Beppe Panada's crew, thought it necessary to bring an action against the Royal Western Yacht Club in the Italian courts. It appears that he cannot accept, as the crew members did when they signed the entry form, that competitors enter these events at their own risk. I feel sure that Beppe and Roberto would, as many of their fellow yachtsmen do, deplore the action which was taken. It is certainly a far cry from the original rule, written by Blondie Hasler, himself a competitor, which said ". . . Crews have no right to expect or demand rescue operations to be launched on their behalf."

18

Poupon in Ten Days!

The Carlsberg Single-handed Transatlantic Race 1988.

In 1988, the entry having been oversubscribed at 127 in January, 95 boats actually crossed the starting line. The French fielded a formidable team in the big class, in which British entries were not promising. Tony Bullimore's new *Spirit of Apricot* was insufficiently prepared and tried. Chay Blyth's late entry in *NCR* (ex *Red Star*/*Night Star* ex *Colt Cars*) never looked like a serious challenge since, amongst other things, he had recently broken a leg in a riding accident, and was hobbling about on crutches only days before the start. It became even more bizarre when, after retiring three days after the start, he announced to the press that the whole thing was dangerous and should be stopped, something which he had said four years earlier. Perhaps he had been reading *Yachting World* which in a recent article, was still crusading against single-handed racing, after so many years.

Richard Tolkien and his *Williams Lea* were also late off the mark in their preparations and he was granted an extension to his qualifying date. The yacht was originally *Exmouth Challenge* and later *Umupro Jardin,* lengthened to 55 feet (16.8 m). Apart from some very exciting new multihulls, there was the finest collection of monohulls I ever remember seeing in any of these races. The BOC Single-handed Round the World Race, spawned of the OSTAR, now contributes its own breed of yacht to the original event. Jean Yves

Philippe Poupon, current and previous record holder for the Plymouth to Newport course.

Terlain's UAP 1992 and Tituan Lamazou's *Ecureuil d'Aquitaine* were two such yachts. The space age appearance of UAP was, to some extent matched by the revolutionary *New Majic Breeze,* entered by Wijtze Van der Zee. Exactly 39 ft 11 in (12.2 m), she fitted neatly into Class III. Purpose built for single-handing she was designed to take full advantage of water ballast. This resulted in a very broad beamed yacht with the beam achieved by sponson-like construction.

Some years ago the committee appreciated that at some time someone would produce a monohull incorporating some features of a multihull, and they defined the difference. *New Majic Breeze,* on first sighting, seemed to be approaching such a boundary line. It was a great disappointment to her skipper that on 7 June, she hit something which removed the rudder and he was forced to retire to Cork.

John Martin was back from South Africa with *Voortrekker II,* now named *Invertex Voortrekker,* and another old friend, *Cherry Valley Duck* which Robert Nickerson had chartered to that popular Spanish veteran Jose Ugarte who sailed her under the name of *Castrol Solo.* Making a comeback, after 8 years, was *Dream Weaver* sailed in 1980 by James Kyle and in this race by Anthony Rowe, whose father was sailing *Piper Rising,* a 39 foot (11.9 m) monohull. Looking like a diminutive surfaced submarine, *Dream Weaver* was entered as being 26 feet (7.9 m) in length apparently having shrunk a foot over the 8 years. She fits the Blondie Hasler image of a specially built small single-hander. In 1980 she took just under 32 days to get to Newport, but Anthony Rowe did very well to finish in just under 29 days, only a day and nine hours after his father. Michael Richey, aged 72, started *Jester* in her eighth, and what was sadly to be her last transatlantic race.

Though much of the weather in the week before the start could only be described as morale sapping, when the morning of the start arrived it was almost ideal for getting the yachts out of the marina. When King Constantine of the Hellenes fired the starting gun at noon, there was enough wind to keep everyone moving nicely. The Navy had been unable to provide a starting ship and 29 Commando, Royal Artillery, based at the Citadel on Plymouth Hoe, airlifted in two 105 mm field guns to the starting point on Penlee Point where transit marks had been set up. For the first time, in a transatlantic race, Eddystone Lighthouse directly south of the starting area was a mark of the course,

Witze van der Zee

Jose Ugarte skippered Castrol Solo

a concession to the media before turning west. In fact this made little impact because a number of yachts held on to the south east before tacking to the westward. As the fleet emerged from the, initially, rather quiet conditions, there were no surprises, as far as positions were concerned, among the leaders who were fanned out, on 9 June, with a north/south spread of about 250 miles.

It very soon became apparent that new records were going to be set, as Nigel Irens, the designer of the yachts who would be first and second, predicted before the start. In an interview he had said, "The record is bound to be broken. The evolution in multihull design is taking place at a phenomenal rate. Today's 60 foot tri's have a 25% speed advantage over boats raced four years ago." He went on to say, "This race is, above all, a race of seamanship. To win you must first finish the race."

By the time I was to fly to Newport to open up the RWYC office, they were laying bets in Europe that Poupon would beat me to it. In fact I just made it and was on station at the Brenton Reef Tower to time in Philippe in the new, astonishing, record time of 10 days 9 hours 15 minutes. The chairman of the committee, John Lawson, arrived soon after. Our American friends were of course all there ready and waiting. Dr Fred Alofsin who, over the years, as Chairman of the Rhode Island State Yachting Committee, has seen to it that we are made welcome in Newport, was there as usual. Other familiar faces were there too but in a different place. Goat Island Marina was no longer available to us but its erstwhile manager, Pete Dunning, was our man in the race office together with his radios and infinite patience. Lois Muessel once again handled information and her husband, Bill, was still harbourmastering. That well known figure, George Monk, the Customs Officer was still there to smooth out customs and immigration problems and to reminisce about past races and those who sailed in them. On the subject of the new $25 arrival tax he said wryly, "Who's ever heard of a Frenchman with $25?" (In fact of course they have now gone to the top of the affluence table in these events.) Some day George will have to retire; when he does he will be sadly missed.

Apart from the fact that weather conditions were exceptionally favourable for the faster boats, Philippe's win was a highly professionally planned, prepared and executed achievement. He himself said that the hardest and most important work was done before the race. During the race, he was supplied with routeing advice enabling him to make the best use of the favourable winds which the unfolding weather pattern provided, a strategy pioneered by Geoffrey Williams in 1968, later outlawed and since allowed again. The almost unlimited funds available, Philippe's professional status, which allows him to dedicate himself totally to the project and to be fully practised in sailing the boat, coupled with the good design and construction of the yacht, all added up to success and were in marked contrast to some other professionally entered boats. There are still some who think they can throw the whole thing together in a few months, or even weeks, and get the odd gullible reporter to aver, for the benefit of the sponsor, that they have a good chance of success.

Mike Birch was one of several to have problems with whales. One damaged *Fujicolor* so badly that he was forced to send out a distress call. However he later decided to stay with the yacht and try to get her into port, although the main hull was flooded. Eleven days later he arrived, exhausted and without food for the last three days, in Belle Isle, from where the yacht was towed to La Trinité. This was a great feat of seamanship and endurance. At the time he hit the whale he was very well placed and stood a very good chance of being first.

The most extraordinary whale encounter was that of David Sellings, in *Hyccup*. Talking to Barry Pickthall by radio from the ship which rescued him, he described how he had been surrounded by whales for three days before he was attacked. He said "On the first night, I saw several whales in the distance. The next night I heard them grunting and squealing like pigs in a trough. They were clearly talking to each other and bringing other whales in. They went away and came back next morning. This time there were more of them, probably 50 to 60, they kept coming closer and closer, making an awful lot of noise and pushing up tight against the boat. There were two distinct bumps and that was it. The rudder was smashed and they had disabled the ship."

Sellings immediately put out a Mayday call and started collecting his belongings together. The

Opposite page:
Roel Engels was another victim of flotsam. He took this picture from his life raft of Doortje *sinking.*

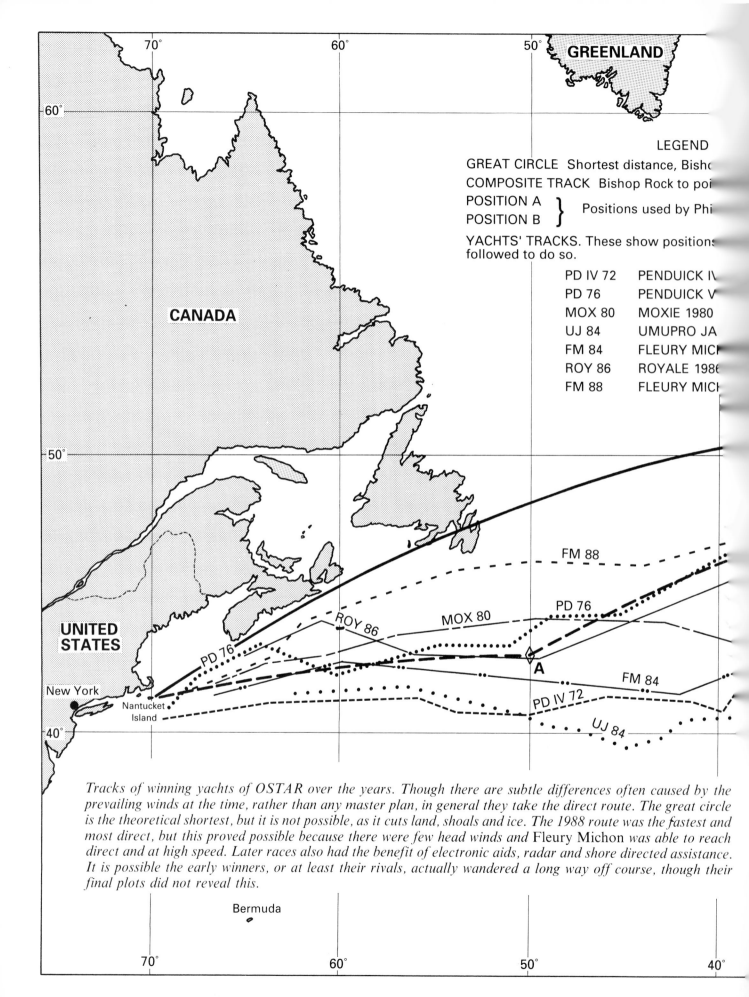

LEGEND

GREAT CIRCLE Shortest distance, Bisho...

COMPOSITE TRACK Bishop Rock to po...

POSITION A }
POSITION B } Positions used by Phi...

YACHTS' TRACKS. These show positions
followed to do so.

PD IV 72	PENDUICK I...
PD 76	PENDUICK V...
MOX 80	MOXIE 1980
UJ 84	UMUPRO JA...
FM 84	FLEURY MIC...
ROY 86	ROYALE 198...
FM 88	FLEURY MIC...

Tracks of winning yachts of OSTAR over the years. Though there are subtle differences often caused by the prevailing winds at the time, rather than any master plan, in general they take the direct route. The great circle is the theoretical shortest, but it is not possible, as it cuts land, shoals and ice. The 1988 route was the fastest and most direct, but this proved possible because there were few head winds and Fleury Michon was able to reach direct and at high speed. Later races also had the benefit of electronic aids, radar and shore directed assistance. It is possible the early winners, or at least their rivals, actually wandered a long way off course, though their final plots did not reveal this.

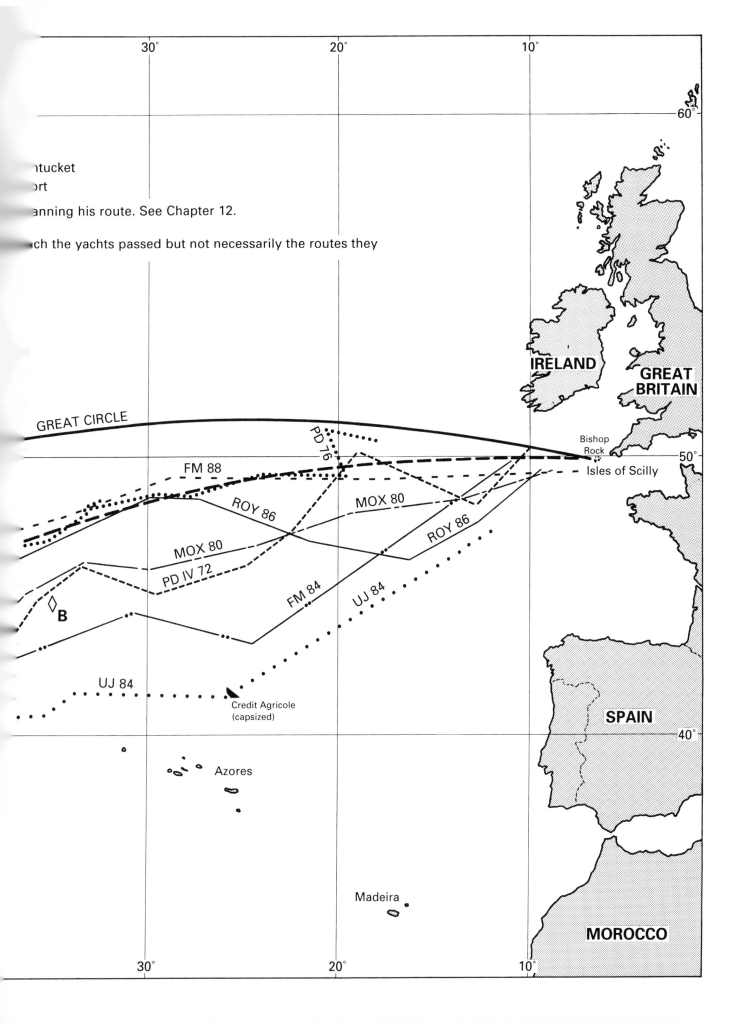

anning his route. See Chapter 12.

ntucket
rt

ch the yachts passed but not necessarily the routes they

GREAT CIRCLE

PD 76

Bishop
Rock

FM 88

Isles of Scilly

ROY 86

MOX 80

MOX 80

ROY 86

PD IV 72

FM 84

UJ 84

B

UJ 84

Credit Agricole
(capsized)

IRELAND

GREAT
BRITAIN

SPAIN

Azores

Madeira

MOROCCO

Mike Richie who took Jester *over from Blondie Hasler.*

next thing he heard was a crash. The whales had put a hole in the yacht and he only just managed to get his life raft inflated and board it before the yacht sank. He said, "The whales, which had been absolutely frenetic, churning up the water until then, suddenly went very quiet. Two or three circled the liferaft and then they all disappeared."

A look at the results table will show how many other yachts were to come to grief by hitting things, not necessarily whales. It must surely be possible to devise a small transmitter which would transmit a signal which would deter whales from coming too close. There is little one can do about flotsam except campaign for ships to be more careful in securing deck cargo and refrain from throwing buoyant objects overboard. The number of collisions with whales and other objects seems to be on the increase in recent years and, as the speed at

which the yachts are travelling increases, so does the seriousness of these collisions.

After a succession of 60 foot multihulls, mostly French, though Phil Steggall brought his *Sebago* in in fourth place to break the succession, there was an instant boost for British spirits when, out of the blue, came Nick Bailey in his 40 foot Trimaran *MTC* to finish 12th overall and the first yacht outside Class I, a remarkable achievement for a Class IV boat. When I told him over the VHF, as we towed him in from the finish, that he was the first finisher outside Class I there was a short pause, then, "Oh. That's quite made my day!" Of the arch rivals he must have been thinking about, *Triton Sifo* was having problems and was to be towed in to Nantucket the following day, and *Holsten Ocean Surfer* finished a day and a half after him.

For the leaders, the race was, comparatively, plain sailing, but the middle of the fleet and later finishers had some nasty weather to contend with when approaching the North American coast. Several skippers who had been nursing leaking or damaged boats were forced to put in to various ports either for repairs or to retire. Alan Thomas had been sailing *Triton Sifo* with a replacement mainsail for some time when he had trouble with a leak in his starboard float. He pressed on as best he could but an unlucky turn in the weather finally forced him to take a tow from a US Coastguard vessel. After a very difficult night, towing on the end of a long warp in nasty conditions at 8 knots, during which the visibility sometimes obscured the towing vessel, he arrived in Nantucket. Jacqueo Dewez had also had a leak in *Sperone* and for some days he was on the verge of becoming a casualty. He finally called it a day and ended up in Nantucket.

Another to end up in that part of the world was Noelle Corbett in *Outrageous,* who had had a number of problems and had been delayed to the extent that she became assessed as overdue. Ships were asked to keep a look-out for her and she was located by a fishing vessel, who reported that she was "in fine shape, becalmed, with most of her navigation equipment out of action". She reported, after having been towed in to Woods Hole, on the southwest tip of the Cape Cod peninsula, that it was a desperate situation, she had lost her boom, had only one headsail she could use, had lost her running backstay, her autopilot was broken and she had neither power nor aerials. "The fisherman shouted at me that I was causing quite a stir ashore and that I should get my act together and call the Coastguard. What else could I do?"

On 15 July, with some 600 miles still to go to Newport, *Jester* suffered a knockdown in the course of which her starboard hatch was lost, admitting huge amounts of water. Mike Richey, his charts, almanacs and other gear all saturated was unable to stem the inflow of water, and operated his EPIRB. He was found by a Canadian aircraft which dropped supplies and a radio to him. The M/V *Nilam* stood by and finally took Mike onboard and the yacht in tow. I'm sure none of them really thought that they would be able to tow the disabled *Jester* all the way to port, but it was a gesture. They were later forced to abandon the tow and *Jester,* a tragic moment for Mike after all the crossings of the Atlantic he had made in her and a tragic way for *Jester* to end her 8th OSTAR.

As each race goes by there always seems an ever widening gap between the highly professional yachts in the front and the family owned and maintained yachts further down the results table. Pondering on this with an American competitor, from the second category, who had finished and was out with us in the committee boat *Sally Forth,* I suggested that perhaps the time would come when there would have to be two races. His reaction was immediate, no, never do that, he said, it is a great privilege for us to be in this great race and we enjoy being part of it. Conversely I have heard several of the professional "stars" say how much they enjoy all the others being in it. It looks therefore as though it would be a retrograde step to do anything to divide the race. However what clearly needs to be done is to examine the finances of the race and see if the amateurs in their own boats can be assisted financially so that they can still afford to take part. Their costs have risen markedly in recent years and we need to get back to the situation where they were subsidized by the race sponsors through their entry fees being kept low. It would not be right for me to quote figures in relation to race sponsorship but I will say that the amount of actual money that race sponsors have paid to the organizers has not kept pace with the enormously increased cost of running these races.

I said earlier that I found the finish of these races exciting, and I'm sure many others do too, but after three visits to Newport to officiate at finishes, I have to say that I am amazed at the lack of interest shown by the American public, and even yachtsmen. I have been saddened, when towing in a yacht which has just raced across the Atlantic, be it with either one or two people on board, to pass countless yachts, few of whose crews get around to a wave by way of a greeting. It is always obvious what the yacht in tow has been up to, because the towing craft proclaims it in banners and flags. I always feel that if it was me arriving I would appreciate acknowledgement of my achievement by a friendly wave.

When *Fleury Michon* was towed in after her record breaking 10½ day passage from Plymouth, the Bermuda Race fleet, big fully crewed American ocean racers, was assembled in the marina we were sharing. The crews of some yachts on the water front waved and clapped but others nearby in the marina just went on with their chores on board, not even raising an eye to observe a man and his boat who had made a little bit of history.

Comparison of times is revealing in the cases

of the 1984 and 1988 races where the top class had the same upper, but not lower, limit and four of the other classes had the same limits but not the same class numbers. The winning times in the comparable classes are shown in the table below.

CLASS WINNERS
1984 and 1988

	1984				1988			
Up to 60 ft	Philippe Poupon	16d	12h	25m	Philippe Poupon	10d	09h	15m
40 to 45 ft	Olivier Moussy	16	12	48	Michael Reppy	19	08	28
35 to 40 ft	Jack Petith	18	12	31	Nick Bailey	16	17	03
30 to 35 ft	Luis Tonizzo	20	23	40	Richard Wilson	21	17	17
25 to 30 ft	Chris Butler	30	14	48	Roderick Stuart	21	06	16

CHANNEL HANDICAP RESULTS 1988

As there were some yachts in the race who had Channel Handicaps a prize was offered to the one with the best corrected time and the results were:

		Elapsed time			H'cap	Corrected time			Place
Temaraire	D. Rice	32d	09h	42m	0.864	28d	01h	40h	1
Amnesty International	M. Petrovsky	32	04	48	0.874	28	03	25	2
Spirit of Ipswich	J. Hall	29	23	35	0.952	28	13	03	3
Largo	J. Passmore	32	21	40	0.876	28	19	45	4

19

Short Handed Elsewhere

Following two successful OSTARS the Royal Western Yacht Club launched the two-handed Round Britain Race. After this had been a success as well, thoughts of yachtsmen around the world turned to this short-handed form of ocean racing. Apart from the concept of sailing single or two-handed, the other aspect which appealed was the freedom to experiment without the binding restrictions imposed by any rating rules. The races also provided an opportunity for multihulls to race offshore with monohulls.

After the Round Britain Race the first offspring was a single-handed round the world race with no stops. This was for prizes put up by the Sunday Times. There was no formal start and competitors could select their own start date, within certain limits. Nine competitors started out at various times in 1968. The two things that most people remember about this race were that Robin Knox-Johnson, in the elderly *Suhaili,* who was the only finisher, became famous as the first man to sail round the world non-stop, and Donald Crowhurst cruised around the South Atlantic pretending, through his radio messages, that he was going around the world. Robin left Falmouth on 14 June 1968 and returned there on 22 April 1969. In fact Bernard Moitessier, who started in the race, but decided to go on eastwards after rounding Cape Horn, became the first solo round the world

single-hander because he crossed his outward track six weeks before Robin Knox-Johnston. However Robin had the record for going from one home port and back. One can "sail around the world" covering far less miles than from Falmouth back to Falmouth. Also in this race, Nigel Tetley, in his trimaran *Victress,* which he had sailed in the 1966 Round Britain Race, became the first single-hander to round the "five Capes" in a multihull during a circumnavigation. He did not finish the race because *Victress* sank when he was pressing her hard in an effort to beat Crowhurst who, to judge by his radio messages, was apparently beating him.

In 1977 there were four new races. The Bermuda One-Two was originated by Jerry Cartwright. In this event yachts sail from Newport, Rhode Island, to Bermuda single-handed and return two-handed. Some people had complained that it took too long to compete in the OSTAR and for them the Royal Cornwall Yacht Club started the Azores and Back Race, AZAB. This started as a single-handed event but in its second race the option of doing one or both legs two-handed was introduced. It had proved a popular race having a low upper size limit and no big commercial starters.

The third race to start that year was the Round North Island (New Zealand) Race run by the Devonport Yacht Club. Martin Foster, a past Commodore of that Club, was the first chairman of the race committee, aided and abetted by Peter Blake who had sailed in *Burton Cutter* in the 1974 Round Britain Race. The marked similarity between the rules for the Round North Island Race and the Round Britain Race was due to considerable liaison between the Devonport Club and the Royal Western. The New Zealand race follows the pattern of the Round Britain with three compulsory stops, going counter clockwise. Multihulls were precluded in the first Round North Island race but have since been admitted.

The fourth race to start in 1977 was the Mini-Transat. In the wake of an OSTAR in which one yacht was 236 feet long it was felt by some that there was a need for a race in which small yachts, not costing a fortune, could race without being overshadowed by the monsters. Bob Salmon organised the Mini-Transat, which was for boats not exceeding 21.3 feet ($6^1/2$ metres) LOA. The race was from Penzance to Tenerife and then on to Antigua. There were some, including some OSTAR-philes, who thought this race was overdoing it and altogether too hairy, but in fact, because it was well run, it was successful and certainly as far as the French were concerned, a good proving ground for skippers seeking to make sufficient of a name for themselves to attract sponsorship for bigger yachts in other events. What is more Bob Salmon took part himself. He managed to run this, with no club or other backing for four events at two yearly intervals before it became too much for him. Then when no club or organization in this country would take it on it passed into French hands, where it has continued but over different courses. It was interesting that even in this unashamedly "poor man's OSTAR", hi-tech crept in and exotic materials appeared in the construction of boats thus failing to keep costs down.

In the aftermath of the 1976 OSTAR, with the Royal Western announcing that there was to be a drastic cut in the size of yachts in the next single-headed race, the French, with lots of large, heavily sponsored yachts, and, apparently, no "authorities" breathing down their necks, decided they must organize a race in which these yachts could compete. Obviously this must be from one French port to another and so the Route du Rhum was born. This started at St Malo and finished in Guadeloupe. The main problem with this race seems to be that, if you want to arrive in the West Indies at a good time of year, clear of hurricanes, and in nice weather, you have to leave Europe at a bad time of year for sailing. November starts from St Malo can have problems.

The first Route du Rhum in 1978 was very nearly won by a monohull. Michel Malinovsky sailed a light displacement 70 footer (21.3 m) called *Kriter V*. As he came towards Guadeloupe and the finish he saw Mike Birch in this trimaran *Olympus Photo* (Walter Greene's *A Cappella*). As they approached to finish, *Kriter* was in the lead but, with a mile to go, Mike Birch overtook him to win by 98 seconds. This was an exciting end to this new and exciting race. Sadly it was marred by the tragic loss of Alain Colas who with his trimaran *Manureva*, in which he had done his record breaking one-stop circumnavigation and also won the 1972 OSTAR (under the name of *Penduick IV*) disappeared without trace.

In the following year the French came up with another new race. This time it was a two-handed event, which started from Lorient, went to a mark off Bermuda and then returned to Lorient. As if to emphasise that this was a race for dedicated racing yachtsmen, there was no stopover for a run ashore in Bermuda. The race was called the Transat en Double. Like the Route du Rhum, the first race produced a nail biting finish. Eric Tabarly had led around the Bermuda mark and a little later *VSD* put in to Bermuda for repairs. By the time she left, her skipper Eugene Riguidel and his crew Gilles Gahinet faced the seemingly impossible task of catching Eric Tabarly and Marc Pajot who were 62 hours ahead. There were others between them and the leader, but gradually *VSD* caught them all up and, as they approached the finish, came in sight of *Paul Ricard* and Eric and Marc. With spinnakers set they duelled for a short time and then *VSD* went ahead to win by $4^1/2$ minutes. The Transat en Double was repeated in 1983 when Jean François Fountaine and Pierre Follenfant sailing *Charante Maritime* reduced the winning time from 35 to 23 days. Four years later the race was replaced by an event for fully crewed big monohulls over a different course, so was unusual in being a reversal of the short-handed trend.

The first of the Royal Western's two-handed transatlantic races was sailed in 1981 and the following year came the BOC Around Alone Race. This single-handed round the world event was the brainchild of David White and it is said to have been born in the Pub on Goat Island, a place where singlehanders used to congregate and exchange ideas. *BOC* came to sponsor the race because Richard Broadhead asked them to sponsor him and they said they would rather sponsor the whole race. They appointed Robin Knox-Johnston as the chairman of the organizing committee.

The race started and finished at Newport, Rhode Island and the stopover ports were Cape Town, Sydney and Rio de Janeiro. Multihulls were not allowed. There were 17 starters with a good leavening of OSTAR veterans. Philippe Jeantot, who at that time had not sailed an OSTAR, won handsomely in *Credit Agricole*. When about 2000 miles west of Cape Horn, Jacques de Roux's *Skoiern III* started to sink after having been pitchpoled in a storm, and Richard Broadhead sailed back 300 miles to rescue him just before the yacht sank. For this Richard received several awards in Britain and France. The BOC race was repeated in 1986 and was due to be sailed again in 1990.

And then, it had to happen, the French have organized another round the world race, this time without any stops. It has been described as the Course du Monde en Solitaire, and the 89-90 Globe Challenge, the latter title presumably recalls the fact that the first single-handed round the world race, in 1968/69 was for the Sunday Times Golden Globe Trophy. The race is to start and finish off Les Sables d'Olonne, on the Atlantic coast of France.

There are, or have been, a number of other single and two-handed races in various parts of the world, notably in the Pacific and the seas surrounding Australia and New Zealand, and I think it is fair to say they are all children of the OSTAR and the Round Britain Races. In 1988, the Australians ran a race around Australia as part of their bicentennial celebrations. This had two-handed and fully crewed divisions. It was an extremely tough race with 7600 miles of testing sailing starting with a blow which resulted in one crew member being lost on the first leg. In the two-handed division, Peter Blake and Mike Quilter of New Zealand won in their 60 foot (18.3 m) trimaran *Steinlager I*. They were followed by Cathy Hawkins and Ian Johnston, from New South Wales, in their 40 foot (12.2 m) trimaran *Verbatim*, successor to *Twiggy*, which they capsized in the 1982 Round Britain Race and in which Ian repeated the act in the Route du Rhum the same year. Verbatim, ex-*Bullfrog*, ex-*Balena*, has been very successful and is the culmination of a great deal of perseverance and patient endeavour.

20

Psychology of a Strange Sport

Early in the history of single-handed racing, scientists realised that these races provided an ideal field in which to study the physiological and psychological problems of persons subjected to a prolonged period of stress. The period involved would, in many cases, be longer than that provided by the other situations available for study. In the case of the competitors in these events there was an almost unique combination of factors; the most important, though not necessarily in this order, were (a) danger: the need to preserve the skipper and his yacht from stress of weather, shipwreck and collision, (b) physical exertion: trimming and changing sails and steering the yacht, (c) mental exertion: navigating, assessing the weather and planning the route, and (d) competitiveness: the need to keep the boat sailing as fast as possible over a long period.

The study of these problems is by no means purely academic, and those who do the studying and those who provide the data, by taking part in the studies, all combine to build up a store of knowledge which can be utilized by a wide variety of people for whom physical and mental endurance is important. I can think of numerous instances, in my naval service, when a better understanding of efficient sleep patterns would have been of great value, particularly in wartime, when one never knew how long one would have to keep going. In

the OSTAR, competitors had always to bear in mind that the last lap may be the slowest and the last day may be spent groping for the finishing line in fog. One important aspect of the study of competitors in a race is that, to some extent, their individual patterns of behaviour can be related to their performance in the race, and this enables certain, though necessarily broad, conclusions to be arrived at. It has to be remembered that the competitiveness in these races varies from the 100% dedicated professional to the amateur to whom just finishing is the predominant ambition. In between these there are all sorts.

In 1972, Dr Glin Bennet, of the Department of Mental Health at the University of Bristol, undertook a study by getting a number of competitors in the OSTAR to complete a questionnaire and to keep records for him. From these and from interviews with competitors after the race, he produced a paper which appeared in the Lancet in October 1973. In Glin Bennet's study his subjects varied enormously, not only as I have suggested in the degree of dedication to winning, but in age, background and sailing experience. There were 19 British, 2 Australian, 5 American, 3 French, 2 West German, 2 Polish and 1 Italian.

The mean age was 40 (range 26 to 57), 25 were married, or had been married, and 9 were single. Two were grandfathers. There were 7 serving or retired officers, 7 in various branches of engineering, 3 journalists, 4 who were professionally concerned with yachting, a newspaper publisher, a dentist, a bank manager, a shop proprietor, a pharmacist, an architect, a farmer, a croupier, a lawyer, an editor, a band leader, an actor and director and a freelance photographer. In 1972 there were some competitors who could be described as regulars, some of whom were to go on to full professionalism, but the professional as we see him today was yet to come.

Of his study of sleep patterns he says, "5 managed to sleep for not more than 1 hour at a time for practically the whole crossing (24 to 52 days), and the most rigorous of these (a lawyer) woke himself every half hour, day and night, for 38 days. The others were the bank manager, the dentist, a journalist and the actor." Since then, catnapping has become more refined among experienced competitors. Bennet recorded that "all competitors were apprehensive of the time when the need to give continual attention to the boat would outrun their ability to stay awake." This worry must diminish with experience and regular competitors in these events must have worked out a routine which approaches perpetual motion. Indeed one of Bennet's subjects said, "my mind was completely separated from my body, I just used my body to get me around the boat."

To a large extent the effects of profound tiredness are predictable, and most of us have experienced them at some time or another. Other quotes from his study were:- "Eventually there was no difference between sleeping and waking. You went about in a kind of 'sleep-wake'." Another recognized stages in his own reactions: "Kept dozing off. Mentally numb. Took hours to do everything, then you find you have hoisted the sail upside down", "Almost like being drunk or high on pot". Bennet continues, "All had had previous experience of sleep loss which helped them to some extent." One of the skippers said, "Tiredness varies with experience. I get less tired than formerly because I do things more efficiently and with less effort. The boat is better prepared, too, so you're less anxious." Another commented, "I worked in a very low key, did everything slowly, even thought slowly." A Polish competitor used a dialogue method to help impose control on his powers of reasoning. "I was very tired and the RDF showed me heading for Sable Island. I tacked away for half an hour, then talked out loud about what to do,

and carried on a conversation in several languages. I spoke, and another person answered in a different language." When Bennet considered "Performance Errors", he mentioned navigation as being the greatest single subject for error. In those days competitors relied upon sextants and a lot of delving into tables from which the right figures had to be extracted. Mercifully, the sextant has, for many competitors become the secondary means of establishing their position, with the advent of Satnav and Loran. However, even with these aids there is scope for performance errors both in navigation and other activities. These errors are induced by tiredness or physical exhaustion due to some particularly strenuous task.

For instance one competitor, aged 51, found one of his lower shrouds lying on deck one night. It was dark and there was a heavy swell following a gale. Aware of the dangers of ill-judged action, he considered the problem for two hours and "discussed everything out loud". Eventually he was ready, and, having put the boat on a point of sailing which would minimise the motion, he climbed the 30 feet (9.2 m) to the point where the shroud had come adrift. He took 2 hours, with 5 trips up and down the mast to resecure the shroud. By that time it was 0500 on day 8 of the race. The next day he recorded "found it extremely difficult to think clearly due to tiredness and apprehension regarding shroud breaking – it was difficult exercise for anyone fresh." He found it hard to remember things. He would go below to fetch something and then forget what he had gone for. He also recorded: "I thought I heard voices." He had not slept all that night, but he rewarded himself with three tins of lobster soup. The record showed an uncharacteristic tension, and lack of confidence in the boat.

On day 10 he "tried to put a saucepan away in cutlery drawer". He had a total of 4 hours sleep and was still apprehensive about the integrity of the boat. Day 11: "Made a pot of tea this morning which I had been looking forward to – left it for 15 minutes to draw, having promptly forgotten about it (not distracted by any other important duty)." Apart from this, function was returning to normal and sailing conditions were good.

Bennet went on to record perceptual experiences; he records that "hearing, vision, smell, and sense of space gave seriously inaccurate information on many occasions, and nearly always there was a correlation with external events of the competitor's level of function." On day 2 a

145

competitor in a 25 foot (7.6 m) boat recorded: "Someone knocked on the side deck as if asking to come in – I was petrified. Found stanchion (guard rail support) loose." Another, also on day 2: "Usual voices in the rigging – calling 'Bill, Bill', rather high pitched. Dreams of people and boats. Neglected cleaning up the cabin, and cooking supper last night because of motion of yacht and queasiness." Another skipper reported visual experiences. On day 10 "Spots before my eyes when looking in the sky. I feel my tactics in staying south and east so long have backfired with this weather and more or less put me out of the competitive race." He was sleeping adequately but feeling tense and physically uncomfortable. On day 26 "spots before my eyes again. Not serious and only occasional . . . I think I have been spoiled by all that calm weather. Conditions have not been all that rough but I'm really exhausted." Then, on day 35 he goes on to record "Usual spots before my eyes when tired. Three days of gales and storms. Very miserable. Poor progress". He had little sleep during this period, made errors in navigation and sail handling: a tape recording made at the time records his distress and despair in most poignant fashion.

Another competitor described, on day 26, a rather more organized perception: "While at the helm last night I saw what looked like the reflection of a window moving down the port side, say 20 feet (6.1 m) below the surface. It was very faint and passed three or four times. There were a few stars but no moon. It did not worry me." He had just left the iceberg area with calms and some fog, and was now approaching the coast and in shipping lanes. He made one navigation error that day.

Another skipper was setting his twin foresails for the first time in the race at about noon on day 33, in good visibility, when he saw an object in the water. "A baby elephant." He thought: "A funny place to put a baby elephant." A little later, looking at the same object: "A funny place to put a Ford Popular." He accepted these observations without question until, on closer inspection, he realised that the object was a whale. This occurred 3 days before arrival, and he was feeling alert, only trying out a manoeuvre for the first time that might have presented problems if the wind had got up suddenly.

Much more complex visual experiences were reported in the qualifying cruise, not in the race. One man had been continuously at the helm for 56 hours because of bad conditions, and was making do with only occasional snacks. He saw his father-in-law at the top of the mast. They were aware of one another's presence, and the experience was in no way alarming. At the top of the mast there is a metal radar reflector. A short time later the same evening he looked down into the cabin and saw his wife, then his mother, and then his daughter lying on the bunk where a sleeping bag was stretched out. Later again, he was up in the bows changing a sail and saw in the water, by the bows, a large flat fish like a ray – very unlikely off the coast of England – which was probably a misinterpretation of the boat's bow wave, as indeed were the other experiences misinterpretations of the radar reflector and the sleeping bag.

The skipper of a trimaran was sailing up from the Bay of Biscay around Ushant. Because of shipping and navigational hazards, he was very short of sleep. Furthermore he had only enough food for one more day, and this as it turned out had to last for six days. He was lying on his bunk when he heard a man putting his boat about on the other tack. He had "seen" nothing at that point, but when he went on deck to investigate the man passed him, coming down as he went up. The boat had indeed been put about and was on the correct course. This process was repeated several times. The man was not recognizable. Glin Bennet only records one case of a skipper experiencing an inexplicable smell. In this case the man smelled coffee. "A strong smell of coffee coming from the west. Clear visibility and no ship in sight." He said it was like the smell outside a shop where coffee is being roasted. He had had some calms and fog and was approaching the iceberg area. The next day the smell returned and lasted about half an hour. He did not drink coffee during the race.

One skipper had spatial experiences. Several times he had "this strong feeling of locality – in this case for where I have been becalmed for close on 24 hours. I keep thinking of it as a place I have been to before and can almost picture it". Sometimes he felt "as though I had just left somewhere familiar". A few days later he wrote, "I still have this preoccupation with place, to the extent that if I did not have a compass it would be very easy to become unbalanced about it. It is as though the time and weather conditions constituted a locality. 'I did not like that place last night' etc." These feelings tended to be associated with calms and the consequent frustration.

On premonitions and dreams, Bennet says,

"Amongst single-handers the difference between sleeping and waking was often blurred even when apparently well rested, so what was a premonition, while awake, and what was a dream, dreamed in sleep, was hard to distinguish. Three people reported premonitory experiences either while awake or which woke them from a dream." The first of these subjects recorded, on day 1, "Strange dream during the half hour of sleep. Can't remember it." Day 2: "Still vivid dreams saying that I haven't started the race. Major preoccupation is sickness." Day 5, after a good day's run of 121 miles, "Slept through the midnight alarm. Woke at 0100 from a dream, with someone shaking my shoulder telling me to go on deck as there was shipping about, and not to forget to drop my wife off at Lugo. I don't know who the figure represented, but I knew he was a friend." He woke to find there were many ships about. Lugo was the site of a radio beacon situated well inland in Spain. The second subject wrote, on day 16, "I looked out yesterday morning convinced there were people about. Shortly afterwards a Portuguese survey vessel came over the horizon." There was no asdic or other noise from the ship familiar to him. He had made one navigational error that day but was well rested and conditions were good. The third skipper had three experiences of waking a very short time before a ship came over the horizon, and none of these were associated with excessive tiredness or any unusual occurrence.

In summing up his paper Glin Bennet said: "The physical findings speak for themselves – what is striking is the frequency and range of the psychological phenomena reported. Taken out of context they might be said to provide evidence of severe mental disorder, but what is their significance in context? Is there something special about the business of single-handed sailing that makes such phenomena common, or are they due to some peculiarity in the sailors themselves? Experimental work on sensory deprivation and sleep deprivation shows that gross disorders of perception and thinking processes can be produced quite reliably. Further, these reactions are more likely if the subject is fatigued or anxious. The sustained exposure to the elements, the seasickness, and lack of nourishment certainly contribute to the development of fatigue. Sensory deprivation also occurred, but mainly in the form of reduced patterning. The whine of wind in the rigging, the steady noise of the waves, the lack of anything on the surface of the sea or in the sea or in the sky, especially in foggy conditions, all reduce the sensory input and increase the likelihood of the development of visual and auditory experience from within. It is the exposure to combinations of these factors that renders the yachtsman so liable to these perceptual disturbances, but they are not peculiar to the sea. They have been described in the Polar regions and on mountains at high altitude.

"In these situations there seems to be a progression up to what one would call a frank hallucination as the apparatus that receives and interprets the visual input becomes more and more fatigued. A continuum begins with the unorganized "spots before my eyes", then the sighting of "the reflection of a window . . . 20 feet below the surface". Later there is frank misinterpretation, mistaking a whale for, first a "baby elephant", and then "a Ford Popular", and more elaborate again with the man who saw his father-in-law at the top of the mast where the radar reflector was secured. Finally there was the instance when there was another man on board helping with sailing the boat.

"There is also perhaps a parallel progressive loss of insight. The experiences were completely "real" but, for example, the man did not think his father-in-law was actually at the top of the mast, but it is all somewhat relative, like the reality of the experience of a dream of a horror film. The man who experienced someone else on board who was helping him to handle the boat certainly never questioned his reality at the time, only later.

". . . all errors, episodes of forgetfulness, hearing voices, visual misinterpretations, and the like can usefully be seen as manifestations of impaired function, and these in turn can be related to problems with the boat and the external environment. A sensitivity to the early evidence of impaired performance, such as forgetfulness, thinking the radio is on when it is not, spots before the eyes, can warn the sailor to rest if he can and to take extra care if he cannot. It applies equally to the motorist and the pilot."

Glin Bennet was not the only one to spot that single-handers are good subjects for research. Dr Claudio Stampi, now at the University of Ottawa, is also the President of La Barca Laboratorio (Bologna, Italy), a research society which undertakes biomedical and marine biology research projects on board *La Barca Laboratorio,* which he skippered in the 1981/82 Whitbread Round The World Race. Claudio is at present writing a book about ultrashort sleep strategies during extreme or continuous work situations. He studied sleep patterns of competitors in the 1980 OSTAR, the 1982 Round Britain Race and in the 1983 Mini Transat, and he is, as I write, analyzing recordings made during the 1988 Carlsberg Single-handed Race when a number of competitors were carrying automatic sleep recorders.

In 1980 he set out to study "how a group of selected individuals, who are extremely motivated to find an efficient sleep strategy under prolonged sustained operations would solve the problem." He wanted to analyze the main characteristics of spontaneous sleep patterns adopted by the competitors, their adaptability to such patterns and possible correlations between the sleep pattern adopted and any particular individual characteristic. Finally he wanted to assess the effects of adopted sleep patterns on race performance. His hypotheses were that at least some of the skippers would adopt ultra-short sleep/wake routines to which they would adapt easily and that ultra-short sleep/wake routines would produce better race results than other sleep patterns.

It has to be remembered that Glin Bennet's subjects in 1972 were basically amateurs whereas by the time Claudio Stampi started his investigations professionalism was growing fast, and his subjects have been progressively more competitively minded. Although even in 1972 it was apparent, perhaps not surprisingly, that too much or too casually arranged sleep was not good for competitiveness. As in many things, there is a world of difference between what is theoretically desirable and what is practically possible. For instance, a single-handed race competitor should, ideally, start his or her intended sleep pattern some days before the race, because any change from the normal routine takes time to achieve. However most competitors have a very busy preparation and social programme in the days before the race and can't therefore do this. The basic human is designed, or has become accustomed to, taking his or her sleep in one whack, that is at night, though

some, particularly in the hotter places of the world, have a siesta some time after noon. This after-lunch zizz is anathema to some but essential for others and, interestingly, some studies have shown that at this time of the day it is possible to re-charge one's batteries quicker than at any other period of the 24 hours. There is also much to be learned about storing up sleep in advance of a period of prolonged activity as well as recuperating afterwards. One thing seems certain however, that any drug taken to prolong one's wakefulness only defers the need for sleep. In other words it will catch up with you in the end.

Stampi's study of the 1980 OSTAR showed that, as he suspected, the shorter the competitor's individual periods of sleep the better was his performance. However, when plotted on a graph, performance showed a marked decrease between durations of two to three hours. The graph went up again at four hours, ran straight to six hours and then plunged to its lowest point at seven hours. In other words those who, when they could, took all their sleep ration at one time did badly. The best performance was achieved by those having mean sleep episode durations between 20 minutes and one hour. When considering the toal amount of sleep taken in each 24 hours, the best performancee was by those who took a total of between $4^1/2$ and $5^1/2$ hours, and over $5^1/2$ hours the performance fell away quite sharply.

Of the three races Stampi looked at, the skippers in the mini-transat, on average, had less total sleep, and took it in shorter periods, than those in the OSTAR or RB & IR and, not surprisingly the RB & IR competitors fared better than those in the other two races. Somewhere the relative physical fitness of the competitors must come in to influence their performance but this would be difficult to evaluate. Somewhere also there must come the factor contributed by their diet. Without mentioning names, whisky and sardines can't really be a winning diet!

Results

(M = Monohull, C = Catamaran, T = Trimaran)

1960 PLYMOUTH – NEWPORT (for actual race name see relevant Chapter)

STARTERS 5
FINISHERS 5
STARTED 11 June

	Yacht	Type	LOA	Class	Elapsed Time	Place o/a	Nation
Francis Chichester	GIPSY MOTH III	M	40	–	40 12 30	1	British
Blondie Hasler	JESTER	M	26	–	48 12 02	2	British
David Lewis	CARDINAL VERTUE	M	25	–	55 00 50	3	British
Val Howells	EIRA	M	25	–	62 05 50	4	British
Jean Lacombe	CAP HORN	M	21.5	–	74	5	French

1964 PLYMOUTH – NEWPORT

STARTERS 15
FINISHERS 14
STARTED 23 May

	Yacht	Type	LOA	Class	Elapsed Time	Place o/a	Nation
Eric Tabarly	PEN DUICK II	M	44	–	27 03 56	1	French
Francis Chichester	GIPSY MOTH III	M	40	–	29 23 57	2	British
Val Howells	AKKA	M	35	–	32 18 08	3	British
Alec Rose	LIVELY LADY	M	36	–	36 17 30	4	British
Blondie Hasler	JESTER	M	26	–	37 22 05	5	British
Bill Howell	STARDRIFT	M	30	–	38 03 23	6	Australian
David Lewis	REHU MOANA	C	40	–	38 12 04	7	British
Mike Ellison	ILALA	M	36	–	46 06 26	8	British
Jean Lacombe	GOLIF	M	22	–	46 07 05	9	French
Bob Bunker	VANDA CAELEA	M	25	–	49 18 45	10	British
Mike Butterfield	MISTY MILLER	C	30	–	53 00 05	11	British
Geoffrey Chaffey	ERICHT 2	M	31	–	60 11 15	12	British
Derek Kelsall	FOLATRE	T	35	–	61 14 04	13	British
Axel Penderson	MARCO POLO	M	28	–	63 13 30	14	Danish
Robin McCurdy	TAMMIE NORIE	M	40	–	Retired		British

1966 ROUND THE BRITISH ISLES

STARTERS 16   STARTED 2 July
FINISHERS 10

Skipper	Co-skipper	Boat	Type		Elapsed Time	Pos'n o/a	
Derek Kelsall	Martin Minter-Kemp	TORIA	T	42	19 17 23	1	British
Don Robertson	David Cooksey	SNOW GOOSE	C	36½	20 09 16	2	British
Mike Ellison	Peter Ellison	IROQUOIS XIII	C	30	21 00 50	3	British
J.L.E. Willis	Rod Macalpine-Downie	STARTLED FAUN	T	33	22 11 46	4	British
S. Fearon-Wilson		MIRRORCAT	C	40	23 10 27	5	British
Nigel Tetley	J.M.M. Field	VICTRESS	T	40	24 21 56	6	British
A. Wheeler	A.M. Buchan	SEVERN	M	47½	25 04 16	7	British
Leslie Williams	D.D. Mathews	BLUE SALUKI	M	36½	27 00 04	8	British
A. Smith	W.H. Berry	DINAH	M	33	28 17 36	9	British
B.C. McManus	J.A. Macadam	MABEL AMELIA	M	41½	30 01 05	10	British
K.P. Pearce	J. Fenwick	WHIPLASH	M	31	Retired. Masthead fitting problem.		
R. Gibbon	W.H.F. Gibbon	MANITO	C	30	Retired at Barra – business reasons.		
H.G. Hasler	Bridget Hasler	SUMNER	M	45½	Retired during 3rd leg – rudder damaged.		
L.G. Turner	G.L. Plum	MATAMONA	T	41	Retired in Lerwick – crew had to go home.		
H.R.A. Edwards	R.J. Burrough	TAO	T	30	Disqualified – finished with only 1 crew member on board.		
James Wharram	M. Hempel	TIKI ROA	Double outrigger	38	Retired.		

The Elapsed Time includes time spent in the stop-over ports

1968 PLYMOUTH – NEWPORT

STARTERS 35   FINISHERS 18   STARTED 1 June

	Yacht	Type	LOA	Class	Elapsed Time	Place o/a	Nation
Geoffrey Williams	SIR THOMAS LIPTON	M	57	—	25 20 33	1	British
Bruce Dalling	VOORTREKKER	M	50	—	26 13 42	2	S.Africa
Tom Follett	CHEERS	P	40	—	27 00 13	3	U.S.A.
Leslie Williams	SPIRIT OF CUTTY SARK	M	53	—	29 10 17	4	British
Bill Howell	GOLDEN COCKEREL	C	42.5	—	31 16 24	5	Australia
Brian Cooke	OPUS	M	32	—	34 08 23	6	British
Martin Minter-Kemp	GANCIA GIRL	T	42	—	34 13 15	7	British
N.T.J. Bevan	MYTH OF MALHAM	M	40	—	36 01 41	8	British
B. de Castelbajac	MAXINE	M	34.5	—	37 13 47	9	French
Jean Yves Terlain	MAGUELONNE	M	35	—	38 09 10	10	French
N.S.A. Burgess	DOGWATCH	M	27	—	38 12 13	11	British
Andre Foezon	SYLVIA II	M	36	—	40 00 16	12	French
B. Enbom	FIONE	M	20	—	40 14 13	13	Swedish
Claus Hehner	MEX	M	37	—	41 10 46	14	German
Revd. Stephen Packenham	ROB ROY	M	32.5	—	42 03 49	15	British
Colin Forbes	STARTLED FAUN	T	33	—	45 10 08	16	British
B. Rodriguez	AMISTAD	T	25	—	47 18 05	17	U.S.A.
Michael Richey	JESTER	M	26	—	57 10 40	18	British
Ake Matteson	GOODWIN II	M	19.5	(50 19 48 – disqualified)			Swedish
Eric Tabarly	PEN DUICK IV	T	67	Collision damage & gear failures Retired			French
Eric Willis	COILA	T	50	III, bad water, taken off			British
Alex Carozzo	SAN GIORGIO	C	53	Rudder trouble – retired			Italian
David Pyle	ATLANTIS III	M	26.5	Torn sails, self steering, toothache, ret'd to Azores			British
W. Wallin	WILECA	M	27	Retired after 5 days, no damage			Swedish
Comdt. B. Waquet	TAMOURE	T	26	Ret'd at once due to Air France strike. They were to help him navigate			French
Edith Bauman	KOALA III	T	39.5	Abandoned ship in difficulties and breaking up			German
Robert Wingate	ZEEVALK	M	39.5	Self steering and leak, ret'd			British
M.J. Pulsford	WHITE GHOST	T	34	Float attachment, rudder, ret'd			British
Egon Heinemann	AYE-AYE	M	33	Self steering, ret'd to Falmouth			German
Guy Piazzini	GUNTAR III OCEAN	M	41	Mast step fitting broken, ret'd			Swiss
A. Munro	HIGHLANDER	C	45	Dismasted, sailed back, ret'd			British
L. Paillard	LA DELIRANTE	M	36	Retired to France			French
Marc Cuiklinski	AMBRIMA	M	37	Dismasted, hull damaged, taken in tow but yacht sank			French
Joan de Kat	YAKSHA	T	50	Broke up in heavy seas, crew resc'd			French
Alain Gliksman	RALPH	M	58	Steering trouble, ret'd to St Johns			French

151

1970 ROUND BRITISH ISLES

STARTERS 25 FINISHERS 20 STARTED 4 July

		Yacht	Type	LOA	Place at stopovers				Final place o/a	Elapsed Time#
					CR	CB	LK	LO		
Leslie Williams	Robin Knox-Johnston	OCEAN SPIRIT	M	71	2	1	1	1	1	20 21 10*
Don Robertson	David Cooksey	SNOW GOOSE	C	36	4	5	4	2	2	22 08 43
Philip Weld	Bob Harris	TRUMPETER	T	44	1	4	3	4	3	22 22 29
Gerald Boxall	Stuart Nairn	MINNETAREE	C	30	7	6	5	5	4	23 01 58
Bill Howell	Murray Sale	GOLDEN COCKERELL	C	45	11	10	6	6	5	24 12 52
John Beswick	Roger Gull	LEEN VALLEY VENTURER	T	42	3	7	7	7	6	24 14 54
Mike Wigston	Bill Davies	ELECTRON OF PORTSEA	M	36	13	12	9	9	7	25 08 34
D. Butcher	M.A. Shuttleworth	GANCIA GIRL(ex-TORIA)	T	42	16	11	14	8	8	25 13 06
Mary Bevan	Noel Bevan	MYTH OF MALHAM	M	36 1/2	8	8	8	11	9	25 14 50**
Andrew Simpson	Mike Ellison	THREE FINGERED JACK	T	26 1/2	15	14	12	12	10	25 17 27
John Lawson	Jeremy Yonge	RINALDO	M	35	14	13	11	13	11	25 22 16
M. Simonds	J. Simonds	ISHKOODAH	M	28	17	9	10	14	12	26 04 05
B.E. Evans	Michael Eddings	CYMRO	M	43	19	15	15	16	13	26 16 57
Ewen Southby-Tailyour	Roger Dillon	SPEEDWELL OF CREMYLL	M	49	21	16	13	10	14	27 02 48
Mike McMullen	Martin Read	BINKIE	M	25 1/2	20	19	16	17	15	27 15 08
Mike Perry	Guy Hornett	BLUE SMOKE	M	26	22	17	17	18	16	28 05 27
J.F. Fenwick	L. Wakefield	HURRYING ANGEL	M	27	24	18	18	19	17	29 05 17
G. O'Brien Kennedy	Ean McCarron-Miller	KERRY BLUE	M	27	18	21	20	20	18	29 07 06
Michael Pipe	Arthur Holt	SLITHY TOVE	M	48	5	2	19	15	19	29 18 35
J.E.C. Perry	Bill Logie	RENEW	T	30	25	20	21	21	20	30 18 40
Mike Butterfield	Peter Ellison	APACHE							Capsized	
James Wharram	Margaret Oliver	SUNDANCER	C	40	6	3	2	3	Retired	
Bill Cherry	John Westell	TEHINI	C	52	23				Backstay parted, mast damaged, retired	
		TRIXIA	T	28 1/2	12					
John White	Rod Macalpine Downie	WARLORD	C	40	9				Steering problems, retired	
Derek Kelsall	W. Goodman	SIDEWINDER	Proa	51 1/2	10				Teething troubles, retired	

* Includes 12 hr penalty
** Includes 1 hr 10 m penalty
# Elapsed Time includes time spent in stop-over ports

Stop-over ports CR Crosshaven
CB Castlebay, Barra
LK Lerwick
LO Lowestoft

1972 PLYMOUTH – NEWPORT

STARTERS 55
FINISHERS 40 (+ 3 late arrivals)   STARTED   17 June

Name	Boat	Type	LOA	Time	Pos'n o/a	Nationality
Alain Colas	PEN DUICK IV	T	70	20 13 15	1	French
Jean-Yves Terlain	VENDREDI TREIZE	M	128	21 05 14	2	French
Jean-Marie Vidal	CAP 33	T	53	24 05 40	3	French
Brian Cooke	BRITISH STEEL	M	59	24 19 28	4	British
Tom Follett	THREE CHEERS	T	46	27 11 04	5	U.S.A.
Gerard Pesty	ARCHITEUTHIS	T	55	28 11 55 *	6	French
Martin Minter-Kemp	STRONGBOW	M	65	28 12 46	7	British
Alain Gliksman	TOUCAN	M	34.5	28 12 54	8	French
Franco Faggioni	SAGITTARIO	M	50.5	28 23 05	9	Italian
James Ferris	WHISPER	M	53.5	29 11 15	10	U.S.A.
Marc Linski	ISLES DU FRIOUL	M	48	30 02 45 *	11	French
Krzysztof Baranowski	POLONEZ	M	45	30 16 55	12	Polish
Mike McMullen	BINKIE II	M	32	31 18 10	13	British
Marie-Claude Fauroux	ALOA VII	M	35	32 22 51 *	14	French
Lt Col Jock Brazier	FLYING ANGEL	M	46	33 09 21	15	British
Joel Charpentier	WILD ROCKET	M	63	34 13 38	16	French
Yves Olivaux	ALOA I	M	35	34 17 30	17	French
Guy Piazzini	CAMBRONNE	M	45.5	35 10 24	18	French
Pierre Chassin	CONCORDE	M	43	36 01 19	19	French
Bruce Webb	GAZELLE	M	47.5	36 02 07	20	British
John Holtom	LA BAMBA OF MERSEA	M	34	36 04 30	21	British
Lt. Guy Hornet	BLUE SMOKE	M	26	36 21 26	22	British
Wolf-Dietrich Kirchner	WHITE DOLPHIN	M	32	38 07 17	23	German
Jock McLeod	RON GLAS	M	47	38 09 50	24	British
Richard Clifford	SHAMAAL	M	25.5	38 10 30	25	British
R. Lancy Burn	BLUE GIPSY	M	28	39 08 30	26	U.S.A.
Philip Weld	TRUMPETER	T	44	39 13 25	27	U.S.A.
Claus Hehner	MEX	M	35	40 08 23	28	German
Ambrogio Fogar	SURPRISE	M	38	41 04 45 *	29	Italian
Capt. P. Chilton R.N.	MARY KATE OF ARUN	M	38	41 17 17	30	British
Lt Cdr (SCC) Eric Sumner RNR	FRANCETTE	M	25	43 09 38	31	British
Zbigniew Puchalski	MIRANDA	M	39	45 10 05	32	Polish
Heiko Krieger	TINIE	M	26.5	46 15 30	33	German
Jerry Cartwright	SCUFFLER III	M	32.5	49 02 00 [4]	34	U.S.A.
Christopher Elliott	LAURIC	M	34	51 14 33 [2]	35	British
Andrew Spedding	SUMMERSONG	M	28	51 23 05 [3]	36	British
David Blagden	WILLING GRIFFIN	M	19	52 11 06	37	British
Teresa Remiszewska	KOMODOR	M	42	57 03 18	38	Polish
Michael Richey	JESTER	M	26	58 08 18	39	British
Anne Michailof	PS	M	30.5	59 06 12 *	40	French
Richard Konkolski	NIKE	M	22.5	60 13 12 [1]	Outside time limit	Czech.
Martin Wills	CASPER	M	31	63 22 00	Outside time limit	British
Peter Crowther	GOLDEN VANITY	M	38	88		British

* Times marked thus include a time penalty.

PENALTIES

Boat	Penalty	Reason	Nationality
SAGITTARIO	18 Hrs	Late qualifying	Italian
KOMODOR	Started 18/6	Late arriving	British
ARCHITEUTHIS	24 Hrs	Late arriving	Australian
MEX	24 Hrs	Late arriving	British
PS	24 Hrs	Late arriving	
WHITE DOLPHIN	Started 18/6	Late arriving	
ISLES DE FRIOUL	75 mins	Over the line	
ALOA VII	50 mins	Over the line	

1 Dismasted, returned Plymouth, restarted 29/6
2 Started 1000 4/7 = actual passage time 34d 16h 33m
3 In collision, restarted 24/6
4 Leak, left Falmouth 27/6
5 Split sails, left Plymouth 20/6

Skipper	Boat		Rating	Notes	Nationality
Carlo Mascheroni	CHICA BOBA	M	41	Retired to Gibraltar	Italian
H.G. Mitchell	TULOA	M	33	Put back to Plymouth leaking	British
Bill Howell	TAHITI BILL	C	43	In collision, towed to Newport	Australian
Bob Miller	MERSEA PEARL	M	43	Dismasted, abandoned, crew resc'd	British
Gerard Dikstra	SECOND LIFE	M	71	Dismasted, retired to St Johns	Netherlands
Osca Debra	OLVA II	M	46.5	Fuel leak, retired	Belgian
Francis Chichester	GIPSY MOTH V	M	57	Skipper sick, assisted to Plymouth	British
Murray Sayle	LADY OF FLEET	C	41	Dismasted, towed to Newport	Australian
Bob Salmon	JUSTA LISTANG	M	25	Dismasted, picked up by ship	British
Eugene Riguidel	ONYZ	M	43	Rigging trouble, retired	British
Sqd. Ldr A. Barton	BRISTOL FASHION	M	24.5	Dismasted twice, retired	French
Eduardo Guzzetti	NAMAR IV	M	32.5	Retired to Azores	British / Italian

1974 ROUND BRITISH ISLES

STARTERS 61   STARTED 6 July

FINISHERS 39 plus one over time limit

Skipper	Co-skipper	Yacht	Type	LOA	CR	CB	LK	LO	O/A	H'Cap	Elapsed time	Nat.
Robin Knox-Johnston	Gerald Boxall	BRITISH OXYGEN	C	70	1	2	3	1	1	26	18 04 26	
Mike McMullen	Martin Read	THREE CHEERS	T	46	2	4	1	2	2	18	18 05 37	
Philip Weld	David Cooksey	GULF STREAMER	T	60	4	4	2	3	3	23	18 07 48	U.S.A.
Alain Colas	Jean-François Colas	MANUREVA	T	70	10	5	4	4	4	31	19 03 15	French
Nick Keig	Peter Keig	THREE LEGS OF MANN	M	35	5	6	5	5	5	17	19 12 13	
Leslie Williams	Peter Blake	BURTON CUTTER	M	80	11	7	6	6	6	24	19 18 29	
Donald Parr	Stephen Allinson	QUAILO III	T	55	8	9	8	7	7	11	20 01 37	
Brian Cooke	Eric Jensen	TRIPLE ARROW	T	49	3	3	11	8	8	30	21 01 30	
David Palmer	Luke Fitzherbert	F.T.	T	35	7	10	10	9	9	22	22 06 14	
A.J.Smith	Robin Burrows	SUPERSTAR	M	35	26	17	12	10	10	29	23 08 40	
Gustaff Versluys	Fred Schulpen	TYFOON V	M	34½	23	20	15	14	11	9	23 16 51	Belgian
Mike Birch	Josephine Birch	JOSEPHINE M	M	35	17	22	14	13	12	6	23 21 30	
Leslie Dyball	Larry Pardey	CHOUGH OF PARKSTONE	M	30	27	23	18	15	13	1	23 22 27	
John Holmes	John Tanner	FRIGATE	C	39	12	13	22	16	14	19	23 23 52	
John Hart	John Bennett	SNOW GOOSE OF WIGHT	C	37	19	24	19	12	15	27	24 01 14	
Jack Fenwick	Phoebe Mason	MORNING SONG	M	33½	21=	18	16	17	16	12	24 04 11	
John Beswick	Jacques Redon	OUTLAW	M	48½	28	25	20	19	17	28	24 06 15	
Harold Hudson	Martin Challis	ALBIN BALLAD	M	30	31	27	21	18	18	7	24 07 02	
David Cannell	Chris Gill	LOIWING	M	34½	24	26	23	23	19	13	24 18 12	
Beat Guttinger	Albert Schiess	PETIT SUISSE	M	25	38	29	25	22	20	2	24 19 18	Swiss
Richard Wood	Andrew Scott	EROICA II	M	31	36	30	24	20	21	5	24 23 41	
Clare Francis	Eve Bonham	CHERRY BLOSSOM	M	33	37	33	26	21	22	3	25 00 13	
Brian Cook	Harry Harrison	ZEE VALK	M	39½	32	28	27	26	23	16	25 11 38	
Richard Clifford	David Barrie	SHAMAAL II	M	25½	35	32	29	25	24	4	25 20 30	
Stuart Nairn	Michael Mahoney	MINNETAREE	C	30	14	16	30	24	25	33	25 23 39	
Richard Burrows	John Burrows	SHESH	M	29	34	31	28	27	26	8	26 00 39	
Jock McCleod	Julian van Hasselt	RON GLAS	M	47	46	36	32	29	27	15	27 14 30	
Claus Hehner	Cay Hehner	MEX	M	35	33	34	31	28	28	25	27 15 06	German
Gerd Bucking	Wolfgang Quix	HELENE II	M	26	42	37	33	30	29	10	27 16 05	German
Stuart Rogers	Mike Best	CRODA WAY	T	35	6	14	43	37	30	36	28 23 35	
Peter Crowther	Tony Addiss	GALWAY BLAZER OF DART	M	42	52	38	36	35	31	21	29 01 43	
Tony Bullimore	Arthur Ellis	GANCIA GIRL	T	42	39	47	37	32	32	37	29 03 38	
David Dillistone	Martin Baldwin	CATCH 34	C	34	29	35	34	31	33	35	29 07 28	
Michael Teal	Norman Holland	BOULE D'ECUME	M	26	50	39	35	33	34	14	29 13 33	
David Cowper	Colin Lindsay-MacDougall	AIREDALE	M	29½	48	46	38	36	35	20	30 17 20	
Stanley Merer	David Furse-Roberts	PULA TIGA	T	44	21=	42	41	34	36	38	30 19 25	
Pat Patterson	Tom Rees	HEAVENLY TWINS	C	26	56	45	39	38	37	34	31 02 46	
Alan Perkes	Charles Gautier	SHERPA	M	26	54	43	42	39	38	32	31 14 20	
Andrew Spedding	Mervyn Wheatley	ECLIPSE OF MYLOR	M	28	61	49	45	40	39	-	37 22 30	

The following yacht finished but outside the (extended) time limit

Gerry Norman / John Reynolds	WINDSOR LIFE	M	24	60	50	44	41	-			38 13 30

*Elapsed time includes time in stop-over ports

Crew	Boat	Class						Remarks
Richard Gatehouse / Edmund Gatehouse	SKOL	M	25	44	41	-	-	Retired to Clyde
Roger Justice / Chris Haskell	CONTESSA CAROLINE	M	25½	47	44	-	-	Retired at Barra
Stephen Pakenham / Elizabeth Pakenham	BATTLE ROYAL	M	37½	55	-	-	-	Retired after 1st leg
John Perry / Paul Goodall	PETER PETER	C	48	16	11	7	11	Retired at Lowestoft
Ewen Southby-Tailyour / Brian Cox	BLACK VELVET	M	24	57	-	-	-	Almost reached Barra but retired to land exhausted crew.
Jeremy Hurlbatt / Malcom Bird	FIDGET	M	30	51	-	-	-	Retired to Oban
Dick Crowe / Tony Barber	MUD SLIDE SLIM	T	36	15	19	-	-	Retired to Islay
David Harris / Richard Hargreaves	COUP DE SABRE	M	27	43	-	-	-	Retired to Tiree
Barton Evans / Guy Hornett	CYMRO	M	43½	18	21	17	-	Retired to Granton
Martin Wills / Colin Hoare	TOWER CASPER	M	31	53	40	40	-	Disqualified, landed crew to continue single-handed.
Colin Pote / John Harris	BACARDI SPIRIT	M	29½	41	48	-	-	Retired at Barra
William Serjeant / Frederick Serjeant	SHYAUK	M	24	59	-	-	-	Retired to Scillies
Robert Evans / Margaret Oliver	TEHINI OF DAGANWY	C	54	30	-	-	-	Retired after 1st leg
Graham Rates / Alastair Mitchell	TANE NUI	C	28	45	-	-	-	Retired after 1st leg
Michael Pipe / Ian Porter	SLITHY TOVE	M	48	9	8	-	-	Retired to Lerwick with rigging problems
John Westell / Bill Cherry	JOHNWILLIE	T	46	13	12	9	-	Broke up, abandoned, crew rescued.
David Bishop / Brian Walton	BLUE SQUIRREL	M	30	49	-	-	-	Retired to Galway
Mike Ellison / Jim Lloyd	MANTIS IV	T	35	40	-	-	-	Retired at Crosshaven with structural problems
Alan Goodfellow / Trevor Harvey	HIPPOKAMPUS	M	45	25	15	13	-	Retired
John Dicks / Ric Carpenter	KASANTI	C	40	20	-	-	-	Retired to Galway
Rod White / Dan Hogarth	BLUFF	M	24	58	-	-	-	Retired Blacksod

1976 PLYMOUTH – NEWPORT

STARTERS 125 (plus 1 disq. before start)
FINISHERS 73 (plus 5 late arrivals)

STARTED Saturday 5 June

CLASSES	Length overall	Waterline length
JESTER	up to 38 ft	up to 28 ft
GIPSY MOTH	up to 65 ft	up to 46 ft
PENDUICK	No upper size limits	

+ = Multihull

Skipper	Yacht	Type	LOA	Class	Time	Position o/a	Class	H'cap	Nation
Eric Tabarly	PEN DUICK VI	M	73	P	23 20 12	1	1	32	French
Mike Birch	THE THIRD TURTLE	T	32	J	24 20 39	2	1	1 +	Canadian
Kazimierz Jaworski	SPANIEL	M	38	P	24 23 40	3	2	6 +	Polish
Tom Grossman	CAP 33	T	53	P	26 08 15	4	2	5 +	U.S.A.
Alain Colas	CLUB MEDITERRANEE	M	236	P	* 26 13 36	5	3	60	French
Jean Claude Parisis	PETROUCHKA	M	47	GM	27 00 55	6	1	16	French
David Palmer	F T	T	35	J	27 07 45	7	3	4 +	British
Walter Greene	FRIENDS	T	30	J	27 10 37	8	4	3 +	U.S.A.
Jaques Timsit	ARAUNA IV	M	38	GM	27 15 32	9	2	7	French
Alain Gabbay	OBJECTIF SUD 3	M	38	GM	28 09 58	10	5	19	French
Francis Stokes	MOONSHINE	M	40	GM	28 12 46	11	3	15	U.S.A.
Carlo Bianchi	VENILIA	M	54	GM	29 00 15	12	4	31	Italian
Clare Francis	ROBERTSON'S GOLLY	M	37.5	J	* 29 04 22	13	6	8	British
Gustav Versluys	TYFOON V	M	34.5	J	29 21 12	14	7	9	Belgian
John de Trafford	QUEST	T	54	GM	30 07 30	15	5	9 +	British
Yves Anrys	PAWN OF NIEUPORT	M	30	J	30 15 34	16 =	8 =	4	Belgian
Eugene Riguidel	NOVA	T	33	J	30 15 34	16 =	8 =	2 +	French
Gilles Vaton	ACKEL FRANCE	M	38	J	31 03 12	18	10	26	French
Daniel Pierre	LORCA	M	29.5	J	31 14 45	19	11	17	French
Patrice Dumas	SIRTEC	M	39	GM	31 23 09	20	6	25	French
Guy Hornett	OLD MOORE'S ALMANAC	T	42	GM	32 02 06	21	7	7 +	British
Bill Howell	TAHITI BILL	C	43	GM	* 32 05 19	22	8	6 +	Australian
Geoff Hales	WILD RIVAL	M	34	J	32 13 48	23	12	1	British
Bernard Pallard	PETIT BRETON	M	33.5	J	32 19 57	24	13	24	French
Folkmar Graf	DADZTOY II	M	38	J	32 20 55	25	14	22	German
Ernesto Raab	CARINA	M	41	GM	33 01 22	26	9	39	Italian
Rome Ryott	ADHARA	M	33.5	J	33 02 54	27	15	13	British
Pierre Riboulet	PIERRE	M	38	J	33 03 39	28	16	34	French
Gerd Bucking	HELENE III	M	35	J	33 08 41	29	17	5	German
Richard Clifford	SHAMAAL II	M	25.5	J	33 12 51	30	18	3	British
E. Everett-Smith	WIND QUEST	M	40	GM	34 08 44	31	10	42	U.S.A.
Burg Vennemans	PYTHEAS	M	38	J	34 10 10	32	19	43	Holland
Nicholas Clifton	AZULOA	T	32	J	35 03 35	33	20	8 +	British
John Mansell	INNOVATOR OF MANA	M	28	J	35 12 25	34	21	12	New Zealand
Philip Howells	FROMSTOCK FILIUS	M	28	J	35 16 07	35	22	40	British
D.H. Clark	FREEMERLE	M	32	J	35 22 50	36	23	11	British
Georgi Georgiev	KOR KAROLI	M	30	J	36 01 50	37	24	21	Bulgarian
Yves Olivaux	PATRIARCHE	M	33.5	J	36 05 14	38	25	37	French
Ian Radford	JABULISIWE	M	28	J	38 08 44	39	26	10	British
Lars Wallgren	SWEDLADY	M	27.5	J	36 11 10	40	27	14	Swedish

157

Pos.	Skipper	Yacht	Cl.	Rating	Div.	Elapsed Time			Nationality
41	Edoardo Austoni	CHICO BOBA	M	41	GM	37 06 00	45	11	Italian
42	Ida Castiglioni	EVA	M	34.5	J	*37 10 20	30	28	Italian
43	Elie Labourgade	EVALOA	M	34	J	37 10 24	27	29	French
44	Klaus Schrodt	LILLIAM	M	29.5	J	37 21 25	23	30	German
45	Jock McCleod	RÓN GLAS	T	47	GM	38 17 40	38	12	British
46	Rory Nugent	EDITH	M	31	J	39 04 30	10 +	46	U.S.A.
47	Chris Butler	ACHILLES NEUF	M	30	J	39 06 02	41	32	British
48	Juan Guiu	CRISAN	M	38	GM	39 08 15	55	13	Spanish
49	Richard Konkolski	NIKE	M	22.5	J	39 10 49	2	33	Czech.
50	James Young	ENGLISH ROSE	M	30	J	39 11 29	20	34	British
51	Peter Crowther	GALWAY BLAZER	M	42	GM	39 12 57	46	14	British
52	David White	CATAPHA	M	32	J	39 17 15	36	35	U.S.A.
53	H.G. Mitchell	TULOA	M	33	J	41 11 59	18	36	British
54	Enrique Vidal Paz	CASTENUELA	M	34	J	42 10 10	54	37	Spanish
55	David Pyle	WESTWARD	M	30	J	42 10 11	44	38	British
56	Zbigniew Puchalski	MIRANDA	M	38	GM	42 13 14	49	15	Polish
57	Wolfgang Wanders	AMITIE	M	35	J	42 17 30	58	39	German
58	Henk Jukkema	HESPERIA	M	29.5	J	42 21 18	53	40	Netherlands
59	Max Bourgeois	ACHILLE	M	33	J	43 08 41	52	41	French
60	Corrado di Majo	TIKKA III	M	37	J	44 00 37	61	42	Italian
61	David Sutcliffe	LADY ANNE OF ST DONATS	M	25.5	J	44 03 47	33	43	British
62	Angelo Preden	CAIPIRINHA	M	30	J	44 04 45	56	44	Italian
63	Stuart Woods	GOLDEN HARP	M	30	J	44 19 14	59	45	Irish
64	Martin Wills	CASPER	M	31	J	44 21 05	29	46	British
65	Richard Elliott	LAURIC	M	34	J	45 02 29	47	47	British
66	Henry Pottle	JANINA	M	25	J	45 03 12	28	48	British
67	Michel Bourgeois	DRAGON	M	37.5	GM	45 12 45	62	16	French
68	Nigel Lang	AIREDALE	M	29.5	J	46 11 17	35	49	British
69		GALADRIEL OF LOTHLORIEN	M	25.5	J	48 03 10	50	50	British
70	Rodney Kendall	SONGEUR	M	24	J	49 05 40	48	51	New Zealand
71	Gerard Dijkstra	BESTEVAER	M	54	GM	#49 07 22	63	17	Netherlands
72	Eilco Kasemier	BYLGIA	M	40	GM	49 10 34	57	18	Netherlands
73	Bob Lengyel	PRODIGAL	M	25	J	49 19 30	51	52	U.S.A.

* Times marked thus include a time penalty

PENALTIES:-

CLUB MEDITERRANEE	58 Hrs, infringement of Rule 22	
ROBERTSON'S GOLLY	2½ Hrs – Late arrival	
TAHITI BILL	24 Hrs – Late arrival	
EVA	2 Hrs – Late arrival	

\# Restarted from Plymouth after repairs 1200z 30/6

Skipper	Yacht	Cl.	Rating	Div.	Nationality	
Rod White	BLUFF	M	26	J)	British	Finished but outside the time limit
Peter Evans	MEINWEN	M	32	J)	British	
Jean Ropert	BIGOUDEN BRISE	M	27.5	J)	French	
Dr F. Sloan,	BALLYCLAIRE	M	33.5	J)	British	
Anthony Lush	ONE HAND					
	CLAPPING	M	28	J)	U.S.A.	Skipper lost overboard.
Mike Flanagan	GALLOPING GAEL	M	38	J	U.S.A.	
Tony Bullimore	TORIA	T	42	GM	British	Fire, yacht abandoned, crew safe

Skipper	Yacht		No.		Notes	Nationality
Jean Yves Terlain	KRITER III	C	70	P	Broke up and sank, crew safe	French
Pierre Fehlman	GAULOISE	M	57	GM	Sank in storm 49°2'N, 14°W crew saved	French
Dominique Berthier	5100	M	37	J	Sank after collision with M/V 11/6 rescued following day	French
P. Szekely	NYARLATHOTEP	M	42	GM	Abandoned after structural failure. Rescued	French
Mike McMullen	THREE CHEERS	T	46	GM	Skipper and yacht lost	British
Kees Roemers	BOLLEMAAT	M	45	GM	Unable charge batteries, ret'd	Netherlands
Heiko Krieger	TINIE II	M	36	J	Retired to Azores	German
R.J. Ogle	JADE	M	51	GM	Electrical problems, ret'd to Corunna	British
Jock Brazier	FLYING ANGEL	M	63	GM	Self steering & electrical problems, returned to Plymouth	British
Hans Schulte	SILKE	M	25	J	Steering gear, mast & hull damage, ret'd to Amsterdam	German
Mike Richey	JESTER	M	26	J	Retired in favour of Irish cruise, no damage	British
Val Howells	UNIBRAS BRYTHON	M	38	J	Crew injured in fall, ret'd to SW Ireland.	British
Ambrogio Fogar	SPIRIT OF SURPRISE	C	25	J	Structural failure, ret'd to the Azores	Italian
Yvon Fauconnier	ITT OCEANIC	M	128	P	Crew injured, sails damaged, towed into St John's	French
Andre de Jong	AQUARIUS	M	28	J	Self steering failure, ret'd to Guernsey.	Netherlands
John Christian	ET SOEKI	M	27	J	Paraffin stove fire, returned to Plymouth	British
Christian le Merrer	ACTEIA II	M	36	J	Ret'd after collision with Spanish fishing vessel	French

Skipper	Boat				Remarks	Nationality
Edoardo Guzzetti	NAMAR V	M	45	GM	Steering gear failure, ret'd to Brest.	Italian
Paolo Sciarretta	VALITALIA	M	42	GM	Retired to Horta	Italian
Pierre Yves Charbonnier	KARATE	M	33	J	Injured arm, ret'd Fowey 8/6	French
Michael Kane	SPIRIT OF AMERICA	T	62	P	Hull damage ret'd Plymouth	U.S.A.
Chris Smith	TUMULT	M	23	J	Retired to Azores due sickness	British
Hywell Price	MC ARTHUR	M	35	J	Retired 9/6 rudder failure	British
Gerard Frigout	PEN AR BED	M	40	GM	Hit log, damaged self steering, ret'd 15/6	French
Doi Malingri di Bagnolo	CS & RB II	M	60	GM	In collision with unknown ship rigging damage, small hole	Italian
Marc Linksy	OBJECTIF SUD I	M	38	J	Self steering damage, hull leaking ret'd to Azores.	French
Angus Primrose	DEMON DEMO	M	33	J	Dismasted in capsize 14/6, ret'd Plymouth under jury rig	British
C.S.W. Ward	ALTERGO	T	39	GM	Retired with broken rudder quadrant.	British
Patrick O'Donovan	SILMARIL	T	31	J	Dismasted 43°N, 65°W, towed to U.S. port.	British
Mike Best	CRODA WAY	T	35	GM	Damaged float returned to Plymouth unaided.	Irish
Guy Cornou	KERVILOR	M	34	J	Skipper slipped disc, rescued by French Navy	British
Jean Claud Montesinos	KEEP CAP D'AGDE	M	53	GM	Hit drifting buoy, damaged self steering gear.	French
Paolo Mascheroni	PANDA 31	M	32	J	Retired – cause unknown	French
Mike Richardson	ARCTIC SKUA	M	31	J	Damaged self steering gear	Italian
Andrew Bray	GILLYGALOO	M	32	J	Self steering damaged by whale. Rigging problems	British
						British

Skipper	Yacht		No.	Class	Remarks	Nationality
Colin Drummond	SLEUTH HOUND	M	32	J	Knocked down in force 11 winds, thrown overboard, saved by harness but injured. Sails etc damaged. Ret'd Falmouth	British
Joel Charpentier	WILD ROCKET	M	63	P	Storm damage to sails & rigging	French
Aline Marchand	LOGO	M	38	J	Dismasted, made Azores under jury rig	French
Guy Brunet	IRONIGUY	M	32	J	Steering gear failure	French
Jonathan Virden	SHARAVOGE	M	25	J	Retired to Bermuda. No wind	French
C.H. Le Moing	PRONUPTIA	M	43	GM	Went to Azores for sail repairs then ran out of wind	British
Alain Marcel	DRAKKAR III	M	39	GM	Entered Falmouth 12/6, self steering failure, after repairs in France re-started but no wind.	French
Oscar Debra	VANESSA	M	43	GM	Sails, self steering damaged in storm 49°N, 30°W	French
Simon Hunter	KYLIE	M	26	J	Retired in Azores, calms and head winds.	Belgian
Yann Nedellec	** OBJECTIF SUD 2	M	38	J	Capsized 3 times, dismasted, skipper rescued by RFA OLNA, yacht later recovered.	British
Brian Start	TRUE NORTH	M	36	J	Retired to Halifax N.S.	French
						Canadian

** Not qualified under Rule 8 but started with the race unofficially.

1978 ROUND BRITISH ISLES

STARTERS	74	STARTED 8 July
FINISHERS	57	plus 5 outside time limit

CLASSES
1 Monohulls over 35'
2 Monohulls 35' and under
3 Multihulls over 35'
4 Multihulls 35' and under

Skipper	Yacht	Type	LOA	Class	Place at stopovers CR	CB	LK	LO	Final placing O/A	Cl	H'cap	Time	Nation
Chay Blyth	GREAT BRITAIN IV	T	54	3	6	3	3	3	1	1	31	21 01 24	British
Nick Keig	THREE LEGS OF MANN	T	53	3	2	2	2	1	2	2	38	21 13 59	British
Philip Weld	ROGUE WAVE	T	60	3	1	4	4	4	3	3	47	21 15 05	U.S.A.
Walter Greene	A CAPPELLA	T	35	4	4	5	6	4	4	1	18	22 13 14	U.S.A.
Nigel Irens	JAN OF SANTA CRUZ	T	31½	4	7	7	5	7	5	2	12	22 23 47	British
Dirk Nauta	TIELSA II	M	54	1	5	4	10	5	6	1	28	* 23 01 04	Netherlands
Martin Read	RFD	T	32	4	15	9	11	9	7	3	14	23 04 14	British
Michael Pipe	SLITHY TOVE	M	48	1	11	12	9	8	8	2	21	23 07 56	British/U.S.A.
R.M. Norris	DAY TRIPPER	T	33½	4	8	6	9	10	9	4	23	23 09 21	British
Philip Walwyn	WHISKY JACK	T	34	4	13	10	14	11	10	5	17	23 11 11	Kittitian
Beat Guttinger	PETIT SUISSE	M	35	2	14	13	7	13	11	1	7	23 11 37	Swiss
Robin Knox-Johnson	GREAT BRITAIN II	M	77	1	3	8	12	6	12	3	54	23 12 15	British
Robert Nickerson	CHERRY VALLEY DUCK	M	35	2	12	11	15	12	13	2	8	23 12 52	British
Bill Cherry	JOHNWILLIE	T	46	3	9	14	16	15	14	4	30	23 14 03	British
Peter Jay	NORVANTES	M	47	1	25	16	13	16	15	4	9	23 16 05	British
T.Romke de Vries	N.S. 44	T	28	4	10	15	23	14	16	6	20	* 23 22 38	Netherlands
Charles Dennis	GAZELLE	M	35	2	33	26	18	21	17	3	15	24 05 32	British
Fred Dovaston	KURREWA	C	32	4	16	18	21	19	18	7	5	24 07 17	British
Mike Ellison	COMANCHE	M	33	4	19	20	19	20	19	8	16	* 24 10 45	British
Yves Anrys	YAMAHA D'IETEREN	T	35	4	17	17	20	22	20	9	2	24 11 45	Belgian
Tony Bullimore	RUN AROUND	M	32	2	23	22	17	17	21	4	49	* 24 13 57	British
Stephanie Merry	MEZZANINE	M	32	2	21	19	26	18	22	5	4	* 24 14 12	British
Jeremy Hurlbatt	ATTILA	M	34	2	20	21	24	23	23	6	13	* 25 00 34	British
Niels Svendsen	JAWS	T	35	4	28	27	22	24	24	10	11	25 01 07	British
Frank Wood	LYDIA CARDELL	M	45	1	24	24	25	25	25	5	37	25 18 00	British
Kees Roemers	BOLLEMAAT IV	M	36	1	18	23	28	26	26	6	44	26 02 18	Netherlands
Alan Perkes	SHERPA BILL	M	32	2	26	30	32	27	27	7	3	26 19 08	British
William Ker	ASSENT	M	40	1	29	29	33	30	28	7	6	26 21 57	British
Richard Wood	ULTIMA THULE	M	37½	1	39	43	35	31	29	8	51	28 17 37	British
Geoff Hales	LONE RIVAL	M	37½	1	42	42	27	32	30	9	46	28 17 54	British
Richard Clifford	ROBERTSON'S GOLLY	M	37½	1	36	33	29	35	31	10	48	28 20 45	British
Mike Richey	GIPSY MOTH V	M	57	1	22	44	30	29	32	11	61	28 21 13	British
Tony Smith	TELSTAR	T	26	4	43	53	34	34	33	11	57	29 01 23	British
Rodney Barton	CHECKMATE	M	32	2	30	36	39	33	34	8	35	29 03 05	British
Hywell Price	LYDNEY MAID	M	50	1	47	37	41	38	35	12	60	29 03 59	British
John Bradley	TSUNAMI	M	30	2	32	34	37	36	36	9	19	29 08 59	British
Andrew Spedding	SLIGHTLY	M	28	2	37	42	38	35	37	10	32	29 11 37	British
Tony de Sousa	KASS-A-NOVA	M	28	2	44	44	44	39	38	11	45	29 16 14	British
Daniel Russell	HAIGRI	M	37½	1	57	53	43	42	39	13	52	29 17 39	British
John Dungey	OCEAN BEETLE	M	29	2	34	36	40	40	40	12	1	29 21 00	British

Skipper	Crew	Yacht	Class										Elapsed Time	Nationality
David Pyle	Patrick Gateley	PYLEDRIVER	M	30	2	48	46	51	46	41	14	24	29 21 18	British
Richard Gatehouse	David Robinson	SKOL II	M	25	2	40	48	54	52	42	15	22	29 23 03	British
Donald Whistance	Peter Smith	ELLA	M	25½	2	50	47	58	53	43	16	36	30 05 08	British
John McKillop	Charles Steinly	ELENA	M	50½	1	58	38	34	43	44	14	55	30 06 00	British
C.P. Lee	Paul Jeffes	LARA OF BOSHAM	T	36	3	55	40	36	37	45	5	59	30 06 32	British
Desmond Hampton	Kitty Hampton	WILD RIVAL	M	34	2	51	57	56	45	46	17	41	30 06 48	British
John Cunnington	Bob Lush	TARNIMARA	M	32	2	61	59	55	44	47	18	39	30 07 30	Canadian
Graham Rates	John Thewlis	AREOI	C	35	4	67	58	42	41	48	11	58	30 07 33	British
Herman Struijk	Dick Struijk	SAGITTA	M	30	2	60	55	53	48	49	19	34	30 07 36	Netherlands
Tassilo Metternich	Mark Kemmis-Betty	HAJJI BABA	M	34	2	63	63	57	50	50	20	42	30 07 55	British
Roger Corrall	Stewart Alexander	CONTAGIOUS	M	32	2	41	61	48	51	51	21	50	30 14 38*	British
Trevor Harvey	Brian Sismey	B.P.CATCATCHER	C	30	4	46	41	46	48	52	12	62	30 18 32	British
Ulf Olhagen	Tudor Barnard	MELODICUM III	M	27½	2	62	54	49	49	53	22	27	30 18 33	Swedish
Jock McCleod	David Cowper	RON GLAS	M	47	1	64	51	52	54	54	15	33	30 19 35	British
Gavin Howe	Mike Owen	YACHT & BOATBUILDER	M	24	2	53	56	59	56	55	23	10	31 01 10	British
Robin Lloyd-Williams	R.A.Adamson	WESTWIND	M	32	2	45	50	50	55	56	24	40	31 04 29	British
Paul Rodgers	Bruce Henly	CHRISTIAN SAUL	M	30	2	54	62	61	58	57	25	29	31 08 39	British

The following yachts finished but outside the time limit

Skipper	Crew	Yacht	Class										Elapsed Time	Nationality
Frank Esson	James Oliver	MELMORE	M	46	1	72	68	67	59	58	16	25	31 21 20	British
Chris West	Michael Moulin	SUPER ACHILLES	M	24½	2	59	60	63	62	59	26	56	31 22 30	British
Peter Crowther	Anthony Addis	GALWAY BLAZER	M	42	1	71	66	65	57	60	17	43	31 23 12	British
Michael Hall	Ronald Baker	BIRD	M	32	2	69	67	66	64	61	27	53	32 02 25	British
Chris Shaw	John Bunting	M.M.MICROWAVE	M	25½	2	65	64	62	60	62	28	26	32 11 30	British

The following yachts did not finish

Skipper	Crew	Yacht	Class							Remarks
Eric Mayne	Colin Young	DYTISCUS III	M	30	2	74				Retired to Baltimore – no progress
Peter Phillips	Nick Gray	HERETIC	T	35	4	31				Ret'd on 2nd leg – leak
Hugh Tusting	Morris Arthur	ANGLIA PIPEDREAM	Proa	35	4	49	49	61	61	Ret'd – ran out of time
Donald Clark	Syd Rudge	FREEMERLE	M	32	2	56	56			Ret'd – skipper with bad back
Peter Blomeley	Stuart Johnston	HINDOSTAN	M	35	2	27	25			Rigging trouble – motored – disqualified
Eric Jaques	Chris Lee	WILY BIRD	M	32	2	44	52	47	63	Ret'd off Isle of Wight – no wind
Eric Cameron	Christopher Lane	CUTLER HAMMER								
Trevor Marriott	Jerry Freman	EUROPA	M	26½	2	66	65	64	47	Retired – ran out of time
Robert Evans	Peter Wyatt	BBC RADIO BIRMINGHAM	M	27	2	73				Retired to Shannon
Pippa Longley	Katie Clemson	FRYGGA OF CYMRU	C	40½	3	70				Retired, crew sick
Angus Primrose	Robert Hurst	NIKONOS III	M	36½	1	35	32			Rigging trouble – used motor – disqualified
John Turner	David Etheridge	DEMON	M	2	52	45	45			Ret'd off Lowestoft – ran out of time.
		NIMONIC	M	27	2	68				Retired after first leg.

Elapsed Time includes time in stopover ports.
*Times marked thus include a time penalty, as follows, for late arrival in Plymouth before the race:
TIELSA II 3 h 15 m, N.S.44 – 8 h, YAMAHA D'IETEREN 11 m, RUNAROUND 8 h, MEZZANINE 2 h 32 m
CONTAGIOUS 14 h 15 m

1980 PLYMOUTH – NEWPORT

STARTERS 90
FINISHERS 72 (plus 2 outside time limit)
STARTED 7 June

CLASSES: JESTER (J), GIPSY MOTH (GM), PENDUICK (P)
Waterline Length: Up to 26 ft / 26 to 36 ft / 36 to 46 ft
Overall Length: Up to 32 ft / 32 to 44 ft / 44 to 56 ft

Name	Yacht	Type	LOA	Class	Elapsed Time	Overall Posn	Class Posn	Nation
Philip Weld	MOXIE	T	51	P	17 23 12	1	1	U.S.A.
Nick Keig	THREE LEGS OF MANN III	T	53	P	18 06 04	2	2	British
Philip Steggall	JEANS FOSTER	T	38	GM	18 06 45	3	1	U.S.A.
Mike Birch	OLYMPUS PHOTO	T	46	P	18 07 15	4	3	Canadian
Walter Greene	CHAUSSETTES OLYMPIA	T	35	GM	18 17 29	5	2	U.S.A.
Kazimierz Jaworski	SPANIEL II	M	56	P	19 13 25	6	4	Polish
Edoardo Austoni	CHICA BOBA	M	56	P	20 02 30	7	5	Italian
Daniel Gilard	BRITTANY FERRIES I	M	44	GM	*21 00 09	8	3	French
Richard Konkolski	NIKE II	M	44	GM	21 06 21	9	4	Czech
Tom Grossman	KRITER VII	T	56	P	*21 08 01	10	6	U.S.A.
Wolfgang Wanders	STADT KREFELD	M	44	GM	21 14 22	11	5	German
Gustaf Versluys	TYPHOON VI	M	44	GM	21 15 01	12	6	Belgian
Alain Labbe	HYDOFOLIE	T	42	GM	21 15 51	13	7	French
Olivier de Kersauson	KRITER VI	M	54	P	*21 20 30	14	7	French
Pierre Sicouri	GUIA FILA	M	44	P	22 02 34	15	8	Italian
Robert James	BOATFILE	T	31	GM	22 22 55	16	8	British
Dennis Gliksman	FRANCE LOISIRS	M	44	GM	23 10 00	17	9	French
Bertie Reed	VOORTREKKER	M	49	P	23 12 42	18	9	S. African
Eugene Riguidel	V.S.D.	T	52	P	*24 01 27	19	10	French
Philippe Fournier	HAUTE-NENDAZ	M	36.5	GM	24 03 05	20	10	French
Jean Pierre Millet	OPEN SPACE	M	52	P	25 01 05	21	11	French
Victor Sagi	GARUDA	M	48	P	25 08 23	22	12	Spanish
Francis Stokes	MOONSHINE	M	40	GM	25 14 07	23	11	U.S.A.
Naomi James	KRITER LADY	M	53	P	25 19 12	24	13	British
Bill Homewood	THE THIRD TURTLE	T	32	GM	25 20 13	25	12	U.S.A.
Robert Bocinsky	AMBERGRIS	M	37	GM	26 00 39	26	13	U.S.A.
Jean-Jaques Jaouen	LES MENUIRES	M	44	GM	26 15 21	27	14	French
Jerzy Rakowicz	SPANIEL	M	38	GM	26 19 29	28	15	Polish
John Chaundy	FREE NEWSPAPERS	M	32	J	28 00 56	29	1	British
William Doelger	EDITH	T	31	GM	28 04 10	30	16	U.S.A
Uno Hylen	YOLDIA	M	37	GM	28 05 48	31	17	Swedish
Desmond Hampton	WILD RIVAL	M	34	GM	28 13 44	32	18	British
John Charnley	ATLANTIC HARP	M	43	GM	29 06 21	33	19	British
Ian Radford	JABULISIWE	M	28	J	30 14 38	34	2	British
John Oswald	MOONSHADOW	M	37.5	GM	30 15 30	35	20	British
Oscar Debra	BASILDON	M	43	GM	30 16 32	36	21	Belgian
Richard Clifford	WARRIOR SHAMAAL	M	35	GM	30 16 45	37	22	British
Henk Jukkema	VICTORIA	M	31	J	30 18 02	38	3	Netherlands

Skipper	Boat		Rating	Class	Time	Pos.	No.	Nationality
Chris Smith	SADLER BLUEJACKET	M	25	J	30 19 20	39	4	British
Chris Butler	ACHILLEA	M	28	J	30 20 49	40	5	British
Kees Roemers	BOLLEMAAT IV	M	44	GM	30 21 24	41	23	Netherlands
Angus Primrose	DEMON OF HAMBLE	M	33	GM	30 23 08	42	24	British
Roger Forkert	PARISIEN LIBERE	T	38	GM	31 10 45	43	25	French/U.S.A.
Guy Bernadin	RATSO II	M	38	GM	31 11 45	44	26	French
James Kyle	DREAM WEAVER	M	27	J	31 23 05	45	6	U.S.A.
Alain Veyron	CAT MARINE	T	28	J	32 02 50	46	7	French
Don Clark	ABACUS	M	41.5	GM	32 07 17	47	27	British
Thomas Gochberg	MISTRAL	M	41.5	GM	32 18 35	48	28	U.S.A.
Luis Tonizzo	EGRET	M	27	J	33 05 25	49	8	U.S.A.
Nikolay Djambazov	TANGRA	M	36	GM	34 10 53	50	29	Bulgarian
Wijtze van der Zee	BLACK PEARL	M	41	GM	35 11 20	51	30	Netherlands
Jose Ugarte	NORTH WIND	M	39	GM	36 06 43	52	31	Spanish
Henk van de Weg	TJISJE	M	29.5	J	36 22 22	53	9	Netherlands
Paul Rodgers	CHRISTIAN SAUL	T	34	GM	37 03 11	54	32	British
Wolfgang Quix	JEANTEX	M	31	J	38 03 02	55	10	German
Giampaola Venturin	CECCO	M	26	J	38 08 55	56	11	Italian
Juin Guiu	CRISAN	M	38	GM	38 14 33	57	33	Spanish
J.R. Verwoerd	SEAGULL II	M	33	GM	38 17 00	58	34	Netherlands
Bob Lush	OLYMPUS SAILING	M	25	J	39 01 46	59	12	Canadian
Tony Lush	ONE HAND CLAPPING	M	32	J	39 06 56	60	13	U.S.A.
Andre de Jong	LA PELIGROSA	M	30.5	J	39 16 55	61	14	Netherlands
Bon Lengyel	PRODIGAL	M	25	J	40 06 09	62	15	U.S.A.
Tom Ryan	PEGGY	T	31	GM	* 40 20 16	63	35	U.S.A.
Ernest Sonne	ELBE	M	36	GM	41 10 45	64	36	U.S.A.
John Hunt	CRYSTAL CATFISH	M	31	J	41 13 18	65	16	U.S.A.
John Beharrell	MISCIN	M	38	GM	42 10 00	66	37	British
Beppe Panada	MULAT	M	56	P	* 42 18 20	67	14	Italian
Per Mustelin	MARE	M	30	J	43 03 34	68	17	Finnish
William Wallace	NOVIA	M	30	J	44 10 42	69	18	U.S.A.
Martin Wills	CASPER	M	31	J	* 46 13 52	70	19	British
Burg Veenemans	PYTHEAS II	M	47	P	* 49 08 16	71	15	Netherlands
Jerry Cartwright	LE FIRST	M	32	J	26 22 55	Disqualified (Rule 21)		U.S.A.
Michael Richey	JESTER	M	26	J	Outside time limit			British
Anthony Vassiliadis	OLD NAVY LIGHTS	M	34.5	GM	Outside time limit			Greek

*Times marked thus include a penalty: PENALTIES KRITER VII   40 min

		h		min	(Late arrival Plymouth)
MU LAT		12			(Late arrival Plymouth)
PYTHEAS		3		40	,,
V.S.D.				20	,,
PEGGY		16		20	,,
CASPER		35		00	,,
OLD NAVY LIGHTS		76		50	,,
KRITER VI		10		00	(Wrong side of line at start)

Piet ter Laag	LADY DONA	M	34	GM	Retired to Falmouth – skipper sick.	Netherlands
Jacques Timsit	MOTOROLA	M	38	GM	Hit submerged object, sank, skipper rescued	French
Hans Schulte	SILKE	M	38	GM	Retired to Fowey, broken forestay fitting	German
Nicholas Clifton	FLEURY MICHON	Proa	42	GM	Capsized, yacht abandoned	British
Eric Loizeau	GAULOISE IV	M	53	P	Retired La Trinité, hull damage	French
J.C. Parisis	CHARLES HEIDSIECK II	M	48	P	Retired to France, broken rudder	French
Michel Horeau	MAURICE LIDCHI	T	51	P	Broke float spar, ret'd to Brest	French

Skipper	Yacht		Length	Class	Notes	Nationality
Warren Luhrs	TUESDAY'S CHILD	M	54	P	Structural problems, returned to Plymouth, re-started but had to retire.	U.S.A.
Simon Hunter	JOMADA	M	30	J	Fell and was badly concussed, returned to Plymouth	British
Theo Cockerell	ROUNDABOUT	M	36.5	GM	Yacht destroyed by fire off Azores	British
Bernard Pallard	BRITTANY FERRIES II	M	29.5	J	Damaged, returned to France	French
Peter Philips	LIVERY DOLE	T	35	GM	Capsized after damaging float, yacht abandoned.	British
Czeslaw Gogol-kiewicz	RACZYNSKI II	M	56	P	In collision in fog approaching finish, towed to Pt Judith	Polish
Mac Smith	SEA QUEST	M	39	GM	Rigging problems, towed to Halifax	U.S.A.
Antonio Chioatto	MATTIA III	T	36	GM	Capsized, rescued after 3 day air search	Italian
Judith Lawson	SERTA PERFECT SLEEPER	M	32	GM	Dismasted, skipper and yacht picked up by M/V and landed in Gibraltar	U.S.A.

1981 NEWPORT – PLYMOUTH

STARTED 6 June

STARTERS 103
FINISHERS 76

CLASSES

Over 60 ft to 85 ft	I
Over 45 ft to 60 ft	II
Over 40 ft to 45 ft	III
Over 35 ft to 40 ft	IV
Over 30 ft to 35 ft	V
Over 25 ft to 30 ft	VI

Skipper	Crew	Yacht	Type	LOA	Class	Elapsed Time	Pos'n o/a	Pos'n Class	Nation
Chay Blyth	Rob James	BRITTANY FERRIES GB	T	65.5	I	14 13 54	1	1	British
Marc Pajot	Paul Ayasse	ELF AQUITAINE	C	59	I	15 06 03	2	2	French
Eric Loiseau	Halvard Mabire	GAULOISE IV	T	44	III	15 06 52	3	1	French
Robin Knox-Johnston	Billy King-Harman	SEA FALCON	C	70	I	15 22 38	4	3	British
Bruno Bacilieri	Marc Vallin	FARAM SERENISSIMA	M	66	I	16 01 25	5	4	Italian
Florence Arthaud	Francois Boucher	MONSIEUR MEUBLE	M	69	I	16 03 57	6	5	French
Paolo Martinoni	Enrico Sala	STARPOINT	T	53	II	16 04 58	7	1	Italian
Eugene Riguidel	Jean-Francois Coste	LESIEUR-TOURNESOL	M	54	II	16 05 22	8	2	French
Alain Gabbay	Andre Beranger	CHARLES HEIDSIECK III	M	65	I	16 05 59	9	6	French
Daniel Gilard	Lionel Pean	BRITTANY FERRIES FR	T	45	III	16 07 21	10	2	French
Michel Malinovsky	Joel Charpentier	KRITER	M	75	I	16 08 48	11	7	French
Gerard Pesty	Jean-Paul Griziaux	GEPE PAPIERS PEINTS	T	43	III	16 23 54	12	3	French
Philippe Poupon	Charles Capelle	CHAUSSETTES KINDY	T	38	IV	17 21 30	13	1	French
Warren Luhrs	Jim Stanek	TUESDAY'S CHILD	M	54	II	18 07 24	14	3	USA
Philip Walwyn	Frances Walwyn	SKYJACK	C	45	III	18 23 35	15	4	Kittitian
Fred Dovaston	Jeffrey Taylor	INKEL HI-FI	M	38	IV	19 14 54	16	2	British
Bertie Reed	John Martin	VOORTREKKER	M	49	II	19 20 49	17	4	S.African
Olivier Moussy	Louise Chambaz	S. MARINE	M	44	III	20 00 28	18	5	French
Philippe Fournier	Yann Nedellec	TECHNICA	T	36	IV	20 06 40*	19	3	Swiss
Annick Martin	Annie Cordelle	SUPER MARCHES BRAVO	M	45	III	21 04 28	20	6	French
Patrice Carpentier	Jean Michel Carpentier	BMW MARINE	M	38.5	IV	21 05 28	21	4	French
Jean Pierre Derunes	Andre Wilmet	FLEURY MICHON	M	44	III	21 10 42	22	7	French
Patrick Elies	Dominique Hardy	PHILIPS RADIO OCEAN	M	34.5	VI	21 14 51	23	1	French
Mark Gatehouse	Patrick Holmes	MARK ONE TOOL HIRE	T	30	VI	22 08 26	24	1	British
Simon Frost	Eugene Wade-Brown	TRI-DEXTROSTIX	T	40.5	III	22 12 58	25	8	British
Alain Petit-Etienne	Michel Liot	LAUNET ENTREPRISE	M	56	II	22 18 00	26	5	French
Patrick Morvan	J.P. Vambacas	TRANSPORTS JET	M	39	IV	22 18 35	27	5	French
Rodney Barton	Mike Pocock	BLACKJACK	M	38	IV	23 05 38	28	6	British
John Dean	Richard Reddyhoff	POPPY II	M	35	V	23 05 46	29	2	British
Yvan Griboval	Francois Carpente	FIRST	T	34.5	V	23 10 22	30	3	French
Michel Horeau	Olivier Despaigne	DICTIONNAIRE ROBERT	M	56	II	23 10 52	31	6	French
Claire Marty	Catherine Hermann	F. MAGAZINE	M	37	IV	23 15 31	32	7	French
Marie Noelle Dedienne	Isabelle Bernadin	FESTIVAL DE LORIENT	M	41	III	23 15 33	33	9	French
Gustave Brun Lie	Thorleif Thorleifson	NOR-AM FRIENDSHIP	M	37	IV	23 19 00	34	8	Norw'gn
Joe Seeten	Sylvain Vergnot	LADY OF SAILOMAT	M	40	IV	23 20 56	35	9	French
John Sweeney	David White	MISANTHROPE	M	43	III	23 21 14	36	10	U.S.A.
Giles Chichester	Brian Gladstone	GIPSY MOTH V	T	57	II	24 03 09	37	7	British
Dominique Montesinos	Malou Montesinos	VILLE DE St NAZAIRE	M	39	IV	24 04 51	38	10	French
Enrique Curt	Bernard Oliva	PICANCEL	M	38	IV	24 09 12	39	11	Spanish
Paul Vinck	Gerrit D'Haeseleer	PATRICK III	M	45.5	II	24 09 53	40	8	Belgian
Tom Perkins	Phyllis Aschenbrenner	HEART	M	29	VI	24 17 23	41	2	U.S.A.
Valerio Monaco	Giorgio Masala	BELLA BLU	M	39	IV	24 17 45	42	12	Italian
Edoardo Guzzetti	Sergio Rigo	NAMAR V	M	41	III	25 07 21	43	11	Italian
Marc Guillemot	Bertrand de Broc	COATHALEM	M	30	VI	25 08 19	44	3	French
Alan Perkes	Tim Rees	SHERPA BILL	M	36	IV	25 08 24	45	13	British
Brian Wells	Barry Sanders	ASSASSIN	M	38.5	IV	25 08 27	46	14	British
Kai Granholm	Klaus Koskimies	OLYMPUS CAMERA	M	35	V	25 09 40	47	4	Finnish
Didier Greggory	Alain Caudrelier-Benac	PORT DU CROUESTY	M	34.5	V	25 09 57	48	5	French
Peter Philips	Keith Brimacombe	LIVERY DOLE II	T	35	V	25 10 25	49	6	British
Jan Pinkiewicz	Wojciech Krupski	KAPITAN II	M	43	III	25 13 12	50	12	Polish

167

Skipper	Yacht	Type	Rating	Class	Elapsed Time	Finish No.	Place in Class	Nationality
Gerard Hannaford	AIRSTRIP	M	29	VI	25 13 48	51	4	British
John Ross	THUNDERER RAOC	M	32.5	V	25 14 44	52	7	British
Olivier Dardel	ALCATEL	M	37.5	IV	25 15 22	53	15	French
Eve Bonham	HELLO WORLD	M	35	V	25 18 21	54	8	British
Guy Bernadin	RATSO II	M	38	IV	25 18 34*	55	16	French/British
Jaques Jean	MOODY BLUE	M	48.5	II	26 02 45	56	9	French
Jeremy Tetley	CARTE BLANCHE	M	36	IV	26 04 53	57	17	British
Graham Adams	ADFIN'S RIVAL	M	37.5	IV	26 07 24	58	18	British
S.C.J. van Hagen	BETELGEUZE	M	42	III	26 08 28	59	13	Neth'lds
Kitty Hampton	WILD RIVAL	M	34	V	26 17 15	60	9	British
Wojciech Jeziorski	RETMAN III	T	52.5	II	27 09 49**	61	10	Polish
Jerzy Colojew	CARMEN	M	30	VI	27 05 21***	62	5	Polish
Jose Luis Ferrer	PUETO PRINCIPE	T	39.5	IV	27 10 27	63	19	Spanish
Cyril Simpson	PHANTOM	M	35	IV	27 12 57	64	20	British
Martin Minter-Kemp	EXCHANGE TRAVEL	M	38	IV	27 17 32	65	21	British
William McClure	THISTLEDOWNE	M	28	VI	27 22 20	66	6	U.S.A.
Kees Roemers	BOLLEMAAT IV	M	44	III	28 05 22	67	14	Neth'lds
Bob Menzies	DANCING DOLPHIN	M	37	IV	28 10 54	68	22	British
Julian Benson	THERM-A-STOR MERMAID	M	32	V	29 12 17	69	10	British
Frank Esson	MELMORE	M	46	II	30 07 52	70	11	British
Slade Penoyre	TELSTAR SP	T	26	VI	31 01 24	71	7	British
Luc Lafortune	BOURLINGUEUR III	M	26.5	VI	32 00 49	72	8	Canadian
Lennart Koskinen	FISKARS FINNSAILER	M	34	V	32 07 02	73	11	Finnish
Anne Hammick	MISS ALFRED MARKS	M	33	V	32 22 23	74	12	British
David Kayll	WILD THYME OF DURHAM	M	41.5	III	33 18 04	75	15	British
Jean Lacombe	YANG	M	25	VI	41 16 12	76	9	U.S.A.

* Includes 36 hour penalty for last minute change of crew
** Includes 9 hour 26 minute penalty for late arrival Plymouth
*** Includes 3 hour 26 minute penalty for late arrival Plymouth

Skipper	Yacht	Type	Rating	Remarks	Nationality
Alain Labbe	D'AUCY	T	39.5	Dismasted in collision with SUDINOX at the start	French
Guy Delage	SUDINOX	PROA	56	Damaged in collision, ret'd Plymouth under own sail	French
Loic Caradec	ROYALE	T	60	Dismasted soon after start, towed to Plymouth	French
Michel Ralys	PETIT REQUIN	T	49	Retired to Cherbourg with jib furling gear problems	French
Joseph Leguen / Jean Yves le Hir	BREST JUSANT	T	38	Entered Brest for repairs, left 7/6 later dismasted, ret'd Brest	French
Philip Steggall	BONIFACIO	T	45	Capsized 7/6 S.A.R. initiated on EPIRB signal and later ARGOS, Crew picked up by M/V ANGEL HAPPINESS then transferred to H.M.S. CARDIFF	French
Mike Stuart	AMP U.K. OVERSEAS	M	40	Ret'd Falmouth 8/6, acute seasickness	U.S.A.
Roland Lucas	ANTARES	M	60	Retired 9/6 due to injury	French
Nigel Irens	GORDANO GOOSE	T	40	Retired to Scilly, rudder problem	British
Jacques Thouverez	OVUM	M	40	Ret'd Le Havre 10/6 yacht making water, crew seasick	French
Christian Adam	PRESSE DE LA MANCHE	M	36	Ret'd 10/6 crew injured	French
Eric Tabarly	PAUL RICARD	T	52.5	Ret'd to Cherbourg 10/6 with structural damage	French
Edoardo Austoni / Carlo Sciarrelli	CHICA BOBA	M	56	Ret'd with broken boom	Italian
Jean Marie Vidal / Elie Aigon	ETERNA ROYAL QUARTZ	PROA	55.5	Dismasted 11/6 tried to make Spain under jury rig, more damage, activated EPIRB French A/C directed M/V to rescue crew, yacht abandoned	French

Crew	Yacht	Type	Points	Remarks	Nationality
Lars Netler, Peter Johansson	FOR FUN	M	44	Lost rudder & self steering gear 13/6. Crew resc'd by H.M.C.S. HURON yacht abandoned	Swedish
Rene Coucy	UTOPIE	M	37	Ret'd to Calais, no reason rept'd	French
Jean Yves Terlain	GAUTIER II	T	45	Damaged rudder and sails 17/6 ret'd but arr Newport 3/7	French
Bruno Peyron	TAKARA	C	56	Ret'd 17/6, structural damage	French
Jean Jacques Vuylstekker	JEREMI V	M	35	Retired to Calais, rigging trouble	French
Jean Michel Bouillet, Clive Green, Tim Thornton	QUARTZLOCK	M	33.5	Retired to Plymouth 14/6 with multiple defects inc water tank ruptured, autohelm, mainsail track slides broken, floors adrift	
Mike Birch, Walter Greene	TELE-7-JOURS	T	53	Hull damaged due to weakness of hull structure. Tried to reach N.S. under own power but was finally towed into Liverpool N.S.	British
Frank Wood, Michael Hampson	TRIPLE JACK	T	45	Dismasted about 160' SE of Halifax crew & yacht picked up by M/V and deposited off Newport to be towed in	Canadian
John Oakley, Laurel Holland	KRITER LADY II	M	68.5	Problems with mast steps. Ret'd to motor sail in to Newport. Short of time	British
Jacques Palasset, Jean-Alain Rondeleux	CHAMPAGNE DELAFON	M	32	Retired to Calais, no reason given	French
Jerzy Siudy, Wojciech Kaliski	CETUS	M	44.5	Ret'd to Lisbon. Forestays carried away	Polish
Herman de Vries, Sipke Castelein	FRISIA'S VIKING	M	30.5	Steering problems. Ret'd Falmouth 13/6	Neth'lds
Olivier de Kersauson, Gerard Dijkstra	JACQUES RIBOUREL	T	78	Dismasted 12/6	French

Summary
Capsized 1, Dismastings 6 (1 in collision), Steering gear 4, Hull damage 4, Rigging 5 (apart from the dismastings), Sickness/injury 3, No reason given 2.
YACHTS LOST:- 3 BONIFACIO, ETERNA ROYAL QUARTZ, FOR FUN.
103 yachts started – 76 finished (73%) 27 retired or were lost – of these
TRIMARANS   11 out of 28 = 39%
CATAMARANS   1 out of 4 = 25%
PROAS   2 out of 2 = 100%
MONOHULLS   13 out of 69 = 19%

1982 ROUND BRITISH ISLES

STARTERS 85
FINISHERS 69
STARTED 6 July

CLASSES
1 Over 60 ft to 85 ft
2 Over 45 ft to 60 ft
3 Over 40 ft to 45 ft
4 Over 35 ft to 40 ft
5 Over 30 ft to 35 ft
6 Over 25 ft to 30 ft

Positions at stop-over ports: CR, CB, LK, LO

Skipper	Crew	Yacht	Type	LOA	Class	CR	CB	LK	LO	O/A	CL	Elapsed time	Nation
Rob James	Naomi James	COLT CARS GB	T	60	2	1	1	1	2	1	1	16 15 03	British
Chay Blyth	Peter Bateman	BRITTANY	T	65	1	2	2	2	1	2	1	16 15 46	British
Mark Gatehouse	Peter Rowsell	FERRIES GB EXMOUTH CHALLENGE	T	53	2	5	1	3	3	3	2	16 16 42	British
Peter Philips	Andrew Herbert	LIVERY DOLE III	T	60	2	3	4	4	4	4	3	17 11 15	British
Tony Bullimore	Nigel Irens	IT82	T	40	4	6	5	5	5	5	1	17 14 26	British
Brian Law	Dick Gomes	DOWNTOWN FLYER	T	38	4	8	7	7	7	6	2	17 15 17	British
Mike Whipp	Wil Hardcastle	GORDANO GOOSE	T	40	4	7	8	8	8	7	3	17 15 43	British
Walter Greene	Joan Greene	A CAPPELLA	T	35	5	12	11	10	10	8	1	17 22 15	U.S.A.
Terry Cooke	Andrew Hall	TRIPLE FANTASY	T	34	5	10	14	11	9	9	2	18 07 21	British
Philip Walwyn	Frances Walwyn	SKYJACK	C	45	3	9	9	9	11	10	1	18 07 27	St Kitts
Robin Knox-Johnston	Billy King-Harman	SEA FALCON	C	70	1	4	6	6	6	11	2	*18 09 08	British
Bertie Reed	John Martin	VOORTREKKER II	M	60	2	17	10	12	12	12	4	18 16 19	S. African
Donald Young	Shirley Weese	HUMDINGER	M	35	5	16	15	13	14	13	3	18 21 37	U.S.A.
Frank Wood	Michael Hampson	TRIPLE JACK	T	45	3	14	12	14	13	14	2	18 22 40	British
Bertrand Harin	Herve Harin	ARRAOK	T	36	4	13	26	20	18	15	4	20 02 40	French
John Perry	Charles Prendergast	CRUSADER SEA WOLF	C	50	2	19	35	26	25	16	5	20 03 01	British
Warren Luhrs	John Luhrs	TUESDAY'S CHILD	M	54	2	21	16	16	15	17	6	20 03 03	U.S.A.
Robert Nickerson	Jeffrey Taylor	RJN MARINE	M	39	4	23	25	22	16	18	5	20 03 13	British
Kitty Hampton	Geoff Hales	QUEST	T	54	2	18	17	15	19	19	7	20 03 23	British
Leslie Williams	Bob Fisher	CHALLENGER	M	80½	1	24	22	17	21	20	3	20 04 57	British
J.W. Simonis	A.W. Simonis	BOOMERANG	C	44½	3	28	21	23	17	21	3	20 05 23	Netherlands
Cees Visser	Chris Court	TRIPLE TRAPPEL	T	31½	5	27	23	24	20	22	4	#20 06 31	Netherlands
Paul Jeffes	Bryan Collins	S-L SIMPSON LAWRENCE	T	33½	5	25	20	21	23	23	5	20 08 54	British
Wolfgang Quix	Lothar Koehler	JEANTEX II	M	54	2	26	18	18	24	24	8	20 09 22	German
John Oswald	Richard Oswald	PEPSI	M	39½	4	31	19	19	22	25	6	20 09 22	British
Fred Dovaston	John Wetherup	KURREWA	M	35	5	32	24	25	26	26	6	20 17 00	British
Chris Shaw	Chris Cannon-Brookes	MICRO METALSMITHS	M	56	2	30	28	28	27	27	9	20 17 53	British
John Dean	Richard Reddyhoff	POPPY II	M	35	5	36	27	27	28	28	7	21 10 51	British
Michael Cozens	Ian Atkins	GEMERVESCENCE	M	39½	4	33	29	29	29	29	7	+22 04 20	British
Bent Lyman	Ulla-Britt Lyngkjaer	GHOSTER	M	57	2	34	46	32	30	30	10	22 11 06	Danish
John Oakley	Robert Oakley	FREEDOM FLIGHT	M	33	5	40	39	37	36	31	8	22 11 10	British
Frank Esson	Martin Walker	MOODY EAGLE	M	41	3	38	31	36	31	32	4	22 16 21	British
Greg Bertram	Johan Bruwer	KREEPY KRAULY	M	34	5	42	34	30	33	33	9	22 17 38	S.African
Rodney Barton	Peter Johnson	BLACK JACK	M	38	4	41	33	33	32	34	8	22 19 22	British
Julian Mustoe	Andrew Williams	APPLEJACK	T	30	6	29	38	39	35	35	1	23 01 24	British
Adrian Thompson	Max Noble	ALICE'S MIRROR	M	30	6	45	40	31	34	36	2	23 01 42	British
Mark Heseltine	Mick Underdown	PROVEN SHARPE II	M	33	5	39	36	34	38	37	10	23 13 46	British
Gerald Tatton-Brown	John Everton	WHISPERER	M	30	6	47	49	44	42	38	3	23 16 13	British
Robin Tatam	John Clayden	ANCASTA MARINE	M	30	6	54	43	41	39	39	4	23 19 37	British
W.R. Lawes	J.H.P. Reid	CAMELOT OF WESSEX	M	36	4	46	52	42	41	40	9	23 21 37	British
Martin Sadler	Peter Foot	SADDLER TWO NINER	M	28½	6	51	45	43	44	41	5	23 22 51	British
Edward Bourne	Alan Perkes	EILA ROSE	M	38	4	43	32	40	43	42	10	23 22 54	British
Donald Clark	Nick Starkey	ABACUS	M	41½	3	44	37	38	40	43	5	24 00 09	British

Skipper	Crew	Yacht	Type	LOA	No.					Place	Class	Elapsed time	Nationality
Hywel Price	Keith Fennell	TAAL	M	35	5	37	30	35	37	44	11	24 04 11	British
Robin Sargent	Terence Jenkins	SEA NYMPH OF SOUTHWICK	M	34	5	48	48	45	45	45	12	24 04 36	British
John Chaundy	Christian Delaisse	ROO	M	32	5	50	44	49	46	46	13	24 14 56	British
Eve Bonham	Diana Thomas-Ellam	BLUE NUN	M	32	5	55	47	51	48	47	14	24 18 07	British
Walter Ehn	Kurt Meierhofer	SCHEAT	M	31	5	71	59	53	52	48	15	24 23 11	Swiss
David Searle	Roger Downham	RUINED BRUIN II	M	30	6	53	51	48	50	49	6	24 23 26	British
Jerry Freeman	Roger Utting	TORTOISE	M	28	6	52	41	46	49	50	7	25 00 35	British
Katie Allan	Alexander Allan	UNCLE JOHN'S BAND	M	25½	6	60	50	47	47	51	8	25 01 06	British
Andrew Bray	Hugh Cartwright	FOOTLOOSE	M	28½	6	56	58	54	54	52	9	25 02 32	British
Richard Moncad	David Craddock	Mr SPEEDY	M	25½	6	57	57	56	54	53	10	25 11 15	British
Max Ekholm	Johan von Willebrand	GEFION	M	30	6	63	54	55	56	54	11	25 11 24	Finnish
Nigel Southward	R.H. Devitt	SKAT	M	32	5	58	53	52	53	55	16	25 13 14	British
Richard Linnel	Russell Calderwood	QUELLE SURPRISE	M	26	6	69	62	59	60	56	12	25 14 14	British
Luke Fitzherbert	Jeremy Fordham	FALMOUTH BAY II	M	29	6	64	55	57	58	57	13	25 15 04	British
Stuart Hatcher	Sarah Meyhew	RTZ COMPUTER SYSTEMS	M	37½	4	49	42	50	51	58	11	25 16 14	British
Jane Ashe	David Ashe	STORMY RIVAL	M	34	5	66	60	61	59	59	17	25 16 25	British
Michael Hall	Michael Moulin	P&O CRUISING WEST	M	35¼	4	62	56	58	57	60	12	26 07 00	British
Nigel Wollen	Mick Bettesworth	WISH HOUND	M	33	5	72	61	60	61	61	18	26 14 15	British
Mary Falk	Fiona Wylie	WILD RIVAL	M	34	5	74	63	62	62	62	19	26 18 27	British
June Clarke	Vicki de Trafford	MOONDOG	M	30	6	70	66	64	64	63	14	27 05 34	British
Jocelyn Waller	Brian Hall	PLUNDER	M	31½	5	67	65	65	63	64	20	27 17 15	British
John Boyd	Geofrey Dean	FOREIGN EXCHANGE	M	34	5	77	67	68	65	65	21	28 07 51	British
Bob Menzies	Christine Bruet	DANCING DOLPHIN	M	37	4	68	64	63	66	66	13	29 05 47	British
Andre de Jong	Dick Van Geldere	LA PELIGROSA	M	31	5	79	69	67	67	67	22	29 13 27	Netherlands
S. Whiting	R. Davies	GIBBS II	M	28	6	78	68	66	68	68	15	29 19 17	British
Ann Fraser	Jack Marr	GOLLY WOBBLER	M	32	5	75	70	69	69	69	23	31 02 25	British
John Clark	Jack Hooper	LAUREL	M	30	6	73	72	70	70			33 00 03	British
Roger Burt	Christopher Hughes	GREY WANDERER	M	29½	6	80	73					Did not finish	British
Ian Johnston	Cathy Hawkins	TWIGGY	T	31	5	15	13					Capsized	Australian
Mike Cox	John McKillop	DELTA SHRIKE	M	34½	5	76	71					Retired, slow progress	British
George Jepps	Harold Young	SEA MIST OF RHU	M	25	6	82	74					Retired, slow progress	New Zealand
Robert Denney	Tony Smith	JAN II	C	35	5	11						Capsized	
Patrick Tiercelin	Francis Tiercelin	TRIMAMA	T	40	4	20						Retired – various problems	French
Bernard Letellier	Jean-Pierre Strowski	HELIODE	T	42	3	22						Retired – mast problems	French
David Bains	Humphrey Trusswell	AQUA BLUE	T	40	4	35						Retired – centreboard problems	British
Barry Sullivan	David James	MARITIME ENGLAND	M	27	6	59						Retired – crew sick	British
John Dungey	John Mullins	OCEAN BEETLE	M	28	6	61						Retired – crew sick	British
Geoffrey Cook	Peter Porter	ANOUKI	C	35	5	65						Retired crew called home	British
Mike Butterfield	Bill Howell	ADVOCAT	C	35	5	81						Retired various problems	British
Mike Ellison	David Ellison	SABU	T	26½	6							Retired with structural problems	British
Simon Beeson	John Gill-Murray	PASSING WIND	C	40	4							Dismasted	British
Richard Tolkien	David Tolkien	DOUCHKA	M	34	5							Rudder carried away – towed in.	British

Elapsed times include time spent in stop-over ports.

TIME PENALTIES			
*	SEA FALCON	19 h 33 m	Late arrival in Plymouth
#	TRIPLE TRAPPEL	2 h	Finished through Eastern Entrance to Plymouth Sound
+	GEMERVESCENCE	5 h	Non compliance with rule regarding qualifying cruise
@	DANCING DOLPHIN	1 h	Late arrival in Plymouth

1984 PLYMOUTH – NEWPORT

STARTERS 91 FINISHERS 64 STARTED 2 June

CLASSES		
I	Over 45 ft	
II	40 to 45 ft	
III	35 to 40 ft	
IV	30 to 35 ft	
V	25 to 30 ft	

Skipper	Yacht	Type	LOA	Class	Elapsed Time	Penalty/Allwnce	Time	Place O/A	Place in Class	Nation
Yvon Fauconnier	UMUPRO JARDIN V	T	53	I	16 22 25	– 16h (a)	16 06 25	1	1	French
Philippe Poupon	FLEURY MICHON	T	56	I	16 11 55	+ 30m (b)	16 12 25	2	2	French
Marc Pajot	ELF AQUITAINE II	C	59	I	16 12 18	+ 30m (b)	16 12 48	3	3	French
Eric Tabarly	PAUL RICARD	T	60	I	16 14 21		16 14 21	4	4	French
Peter Philips	TRAVACREST SEAWAY	T	60	I	16 17 23		16 17 23	5	5	British
Daniel Gilard	NANTES	T	60	I	16 17 51		16 17 51	6	6	French
Olivier Moussy	REGION CENTRE	T	45	II	16 18 46	+ 30m (b)	16 19 16	7	1	French
Bruno Peyron	L'AIGLON	C	60	I	16 19 51	+ 30m (b)	16 20 21	8	7	French
François Boucher	KER CADELAC	T	50	I	16 21 18	+ 30m (b)	16 21 48	9	8	French
Warren Luhrs	THURSDAY'S CHILD	M	60	I	16 22 27		16 22 27	10	9	U.S.A.
Vincent Levy	KERMARINE	T	50	I	17 03 58	+ 30m (b)	17 04 28	11	10	French
John Martin	MAINSTAY VOORTREKKER	M	60	I	17 22 02		17 22 02	12	11	S.African
Denis Gliksman	LESSIVE ST MARC	T	50	I	17 21 47	+ 30m (b)	17 22 17	13	12	French
Jack Petith	DESTINATION St CROIX	T	38	III	18 09 09	+ 2h 52m (c)	18 12 31	14	1	U.S.A.
Didier Munduteguy	COTE BASQUE	T	45	II	18 11 31	+ 1h 33m (c)	18 13 34	15	2	U.S.A.
Yves le Cornec	IDENEK	T	42	II	18 13 49		18 13 49	16	3	French
Philippe Fournier	GESPAC	T	40	III	19 07 50		19 07 50	17	2	Swiss
Walter Greene	SEBAGO	C	45	II	19 10 08	+ 30m (b)	19 10 38	18	4	U.S.A.
Edoardo Austoni	CHICA BOBA III	M	60	I	19 10 41		19 10 41	19	13	Italian
Tony Bullimore	CITY OF BIRMINGHAM	T	35	III	19 22 05	+ 30m (b)	19 22 35	20	3	British
Luis Tonizzo	CITY OF SLIDEL	M	54	I	20 23 40		20 23 40	21	14	U.S.A.
Jack Boye	CARTERET SAVINGS	T	31	IV	21 01 50		21 01 50	22	1	U.S.A.
Bill Homewood	BRITISH AIRWAYS II	M	45	II	21 05 04	+ 30m (b)	21 05 34	23	5	U.S.A.
Patrice Carpentier	CENET	C	60	I	21 06 02		21 06 02	24	15	French
Alain Petit-Etienne	REGION DE PICARDIE	M	40	III	21 04 43	+ 4h 4m (c)	21 08 47	25	4	French
Kai Granholm	PATRICIA OF FINLAND	M	44	II	21 13 04		21 13 04	26	6	Finnish
Guy Bernadin	BISCUITS LU	M	35	III	21 18 05	+ 30m (b)	21 18 35	27	5	French
Tony Lush	SURVIVAL TECH GROUP	M	45	II	22 02 39		22 02 39	28	7	U.S.A.
Jose Ugarte	ORION IRU	M	40	III	22 15 53		22 15 53	29	6	Spanish
Ian Radford	NTOMBIFUTI	M	35	III	22 16 13		22 16 13	30	7	British
Jim Bates	BIG SHOT	C	37.5	III	22 18 09		22 18 09	31	8	U.S.A.
Alain Veyron	VINGT SUR VANNES	M	40	III	23 09 15	+ 4h 29m (c)	23 13 44	32	9	French
Olivier Dardel	ALCATEL	M	40	III	24 13 10		24 13 10	33	10	French
John Shaw	MS PATTY	C	40	III	23 23 59	+ 14h 24m (c)	24 14 53	34	11	British
Wijtze van de Zee	ROYAL LEERDAM	M	40	III	24 18 08		24 18 05	35	12	Netherlands
Bruno Fehrenbach	DOUCHE CHAMPION	M	35	IV	25 03 53		25 03 53	36	13	French
Simon van Hagen	BETELGEUZE	M	42	IV	25 05 20	+ 30m (b)	25 05 50	37	8	Netherlands
Henk Jukkema	LDS SAILER	M	33	IV	25 09 12		25 09 12	38	2	Netherlands
Colin Laird	LA BALEINE	M	44	III	25 15 29		25 15 29	39	9	Trinidadian
Tom Donnelly	LONE EAGLE	M	36	III	26 06 46		26 06 46	40	9	U.S.A.
Alan Wynne Thomas	JEMIMA NICHOLAS	M	40	III	26 21 51		26 21 51	41	10	British
Jerry Freeman	ABACUS	M	42	III	27 11 11	– 3h 30m (e)	27 11 11	42	11	British
Alan Perkes	SHERPA BILL	M	36	III	27 11 50		27 11 50	43	16	British
David White	GLADIATOR	M	55	I	28 04 38		28 04 38	44	16	U.S.A.
Brian O'Donoghue	GAMBLE GOLD	M	33	IV	29 15 55		29 15 55	45	8	British
Mac Smith	QUAILO	M	44	III	29 23 10		29 23 10	46	11	U.S.A.
Hans van Hest	OLLE P2	M	38.5	III	30 04 10		30 04 10	47	12	Netherlands
Spencer Langford	SUMMER SALT	M	38	III	30 12 43		30 12 43	48	13	U.S.A.

Skipper	Yacht	Class	Rating	Div	Elapsed Time	Penalty/Allowance	Finish	Pos	Nationality
Chris Butler	SWANSEA BAY	M	27	V	30 14 48		49	1	British
Michael Petrovsky	TIMPANI	M	30	V	30 23 58		50	2	British
David Ryan	PHAGAWI	M	29	V	31 01 50		51	3	U.S.A.
Albert Fournier	EL TORERO	M	30	V	31 07 55	+ 5h 58m c	52	4	U.S.A.
Robert Scott	LANDS END	M	39.5	III	31 08 25	+ 30m b	53	14	U.S.A.
Bertus Buys	SEA-BERYL	M	35	IV	31 23 10		54	9	Netherlands
Jan van Donselaar	SHAMROCK	M	30	V	32 14 09		55	5	Netherlands
Alan Armstrong	MITSUBISHI ELECTRIC	M	35	V	32 13 20	– 4h f	56	6	British
John Howie	FREE BIRD	M	29.5	V	32 20 45		57	10	U.S.A.
Lloyd Hircock	MOUSTACHE	M	31.5	IV	35 04 33	+ 2h d	58	7	Canadian
Dick Hughes	GLADYS	M	29.5	V	35 15 57		59	11	Netherlands
Vassil Kurtev	NORD	M	34	IV	39 06 56		60	8	Bulgarian
Timothy Hubbard	JOHAN LLOYDE	M	25	V	40 16 38		61	12	U.S.A.
Jack Coffey	MEG OF MUGLINS	M	32	IV	41 04 30		62	13	Irish
Goos Terschegget	DE VOLHARDING	M	35	II	41 16 30		63	12	Netherlands
John Hunt	CRYSTAL CATFISH	M	31.5	IV	44 14 22		64	14	U.S.A.

PENALTIES AND ALLOWANCES

a Allowance for standing by CREDIT AGRICOLE
b Penalty for crossing wrong starting line
c Penalty for late arrival in Plymouth
d Used engine during the race
e Allowance for rescuing skipper of DOUBLE BROWN (John Mansell)
f Allowance for assisting DANCING DOLPHIN

Skipper	Yacht	Class	Rating	Notes
June Clarke	BATCHELORS SWEET PEA	T	40	Capsized off Cornish coast, rescued by lifeboat yacht recovered.
Loick Peyron	LADA POCH	C	54	Dismasted – made own way to Dartmouth.
Eric Loizeau	ROGER & GALLET	T	45	Returned to Plymouth, sail and centreboard problems.
Hugh McCoy	FURY	C	60	Retired to Plymouth with rudder damage.
Monique Brand	ALIANCE KAYPRO	M	44	Reported dismasted, towed to Scillies by H.M.S. JERSEY.
Thomas Veyron	RIZLA +	T	30	Dismasted, made own way to Port Navalo.
Chris Smith	RACE AGAINST POVERTY	M	30	Sprang a leak, pressed Argos emergency push but later reported he was able to make port under own power.
David Duncombe	GO KART	M	29	Hit by whale – returned to Plymouth un-aided on 9th June. Retired 12th June.
Gustav Versluys	TYPHOON VI	M	44	Retired to Falmouth with steering problems.
Jean-Jacques Vuylsteker	JEREMI V	M	35	Damaged sails, retired to Peros-Guirec 10th June.
Bob Lenguel	PRODIGAL	M	34	Returned to Plymouth, re-started but retired to Falmouth with steering problems.
Andre de Jong	LA PELIGROSA	M	31	Same as PRODIGAL.
Geoff Hales	QUEST FOR CHARITY	C	29	Hull leaking retired to Penzance.
Philippe Jeantot	CREDIT AGRICOLE	C	60	Capsized. UMUPRO JARDIN stood by till help on the way. Yacht salvaged.
Patrick Morvan	JET SERVICES	C	60	Holed by tree trunk. Ship directed to pick up skipper.
Florence Arthaud	BIOTHERM II	T	60	Put in to Azores with rigging problems, found she had hull problem as well so retired, continued later to Newport with crew.
Geoff Houlgrave	COLT CARS GB	T	60	Hull damaged during dismasting, yacht abandoned and skipper rescued by ship after location by R.C.A.F.
Frank Wood	MARSDEN	T	45	Dismasted 6th June, arrived Leixeos (near Oporto) and retired there.
Michel Horeau	MARCHES DE FRANCE	T	50	Developed mast trouble and returned to France arriving there 21st June.
Gilles Gahinet	33 EXPORT	C	60	Mast problems, retired to La Trinité.
John Mansell	DOUBLE DROWN	C	35	Yacht abandoned with structural problems, rescued by fellow competitor, Alan Wynne Thomas and taken to Newport.
Henk van de Weg	TJISJE	M	29 1/2	Hit by whale, pressed Argos emergency push, located by aircraft and rescued by helicopter all between 1100 and 1500 G.M.T.
Bob Menzies	DANCING DOLPHIN	M	37	Yacht abandoned in sinking condition, skipper rescued by merchant ship. (Argos alarm)
Karl Peterzen	KARPETZ	M	31 1/2	Hit drifting buoy, resulting leak became worse so he pressed Argos emergency push. Rescued by merchant ship.
Bill Wallace	NOVIA	M	30	Dismasted. Pressed Argos alarm button. Yacht located by aircraft who directed ship to scene. Ship recovered yacht and skipper.
Rachel Hayward	LOIWING	M	35	Ran aground on Point Judith having mistaken that fog signal for the one on Brenton Reef Tower.
Michael Richey	JESTER	M	26	Sail damage, unable to go to windward, finally reached Halifax N.S. and retired there.

1985 ROUND BRITISH ISLES

STARTERS	74
FINISHERS	51

STARTED 6 July

CLASSES

1	Over 60 ft	to	85 ft
2	" 50	"	60
3	" 45	"	50
4	" 40	"	45
5	" 35	"	40
6	" 30	"	35
7	" 25	"	30

(e.g. a yacht of exactly 40 ft was in Class 5)

Skipper	Crew	Yacht	Type	LOA	Class	Place at stopovers				Final placing		Elapsed Time #	Nation
						CR	CB	LK	LO	o/a	Class		
Tony Bullimore	Nigel Irens	APRICOT	T	60	2	1	2	8	1	1	1	17 07 33	British
Paul Hargreaves	Jeff Houlgrave	MORR ENERGY	T	60	2	7=	10	8	4	2	2	17 23 07	British
Mark Gatehouse	Peter Rowsell	MARLOW ROPES	T	53	2	4	5	6	3	3	3	17 23 26	British
Robin Knox-Johnston	Billy King-Harman	BRITISH AIRWAYS I	C	60	2	10	5	6	2	4	4	18 03 27P	British
Don Wood	Butch Dalrymple-Smith	RED STAR/NIGHT STAR	T	60	2	3	3	3	6	5	5	18 04 51	British
Pierre le Maout	Antoine Pouliquen	MACALLAN-FESTIVAL DE LORIENT	C	40	5	5	4	7	5	6	1	18 09 44P	French
Walter Greene	Philip Steggall	SEBAGO	C	45	4	7=	11	7	8	7	1	18 15 49	U.S.A.
Phillip Walwyn	Roger Spronk	SPIRIT OF ST KITTS	C	75	1	6	9	9	7	8	1	18 16 52	St Kitts
Terry Cooke	Robert Freemantle	YACHT PAINT CENTRE	T	34½	6	9	12	10	9	9	1	19 03 46	British
Jens Quorning	Bo Rasmussen	QUICK STEP	M	35	6	13	8	14	13	10	2	19 06 51	Danish
Warren Luhrs	Ola Wettergren	THURSDAY'S CHILD	M	60	2	12	13	12	12	11	6	19 07 19P	U.S.A.
Richard Tolkien	David Bartlett	THE SCANNER	M	40	5	8	15	11	10	12	2	19 07 36	British
John Martin	Murray Webber	VOORTREKKER II	M	60	2	22	16	16	15	13	7	19 20 23	S. African
Mark Pridie	Angus Pridie	GORDANO GOOSE	T	40	5	17	17	17	14	14	3	19 21 14	British
Peter Hopps	Vivien Cherry	SANSKARA	T	41	4	30	21	23	16	15	2	20 12 40	British
Rupert Kidd	Nic Bailey	LASMO EXPLORER	T	30	7	28	20	18	17	16	1	20 16 15	British
Donald Parr	Stephen Allinson	QUAILO OF WIGHT	M	63	1	33	23	22	19	17	2	20 17 18	British
Eric Quorning	Eric Fruergaard	MAGIC HEMPLE	T	25	7	11	16	15	18	18	2	20 18 16	Danish
John Chaundy	Mike Bradley	MEMEC & CHIPS	M	34	6	24	22	19	20	19	3	20 18 38	British
Ian Radford	Rod White	NTOMBIFUTI	M	40	5	26	24	21	21	20	4	20 19 39	British
John Dean	Richard Reddyhoff	HYTHE MARINA VILLAGE	M	50	3	14	18	20	22	21	1	20 23 09	British
Roger Bryan	Nigel Theadom	CONSTANCE	C	39	5	27	26	25	25	22	5	21 13 52	British
Herve Cleris	Francois Malherbe	BARADAL	M	40	5	19	46	28	24	23	6	21 15 55	French
Desmond Hampton	Kitty Hampton	PANICKER	M	40	5	29	27	26	26	24	7	22 07 14	British
David Dillistone	Ben Dillistone	ROMTEC	M	42	4	21	34	32	28	25	3	22 19 35	British
Granville Davis	Ramon Page	TIGO V	M	40	5	36	31	29	29	26	8	22 21 43	British
Wolfgang Quix	Dieter Kowalewski	JEANTEX III	M	40	5	46	37	30	31	27	9	22 22 08	German
Michael Pocock	Pat Pocock	BLACKJACK	M	38	5	38	35	31	30	28	10	22 22 12	British
Bent Lyman	Ulla-Britt Lyman	GHOSTER	M	57	2	42	32	27	27	29	8	22 22 16	Danish
Nigel Rowe	Anthony Rowe	TSUNAMI	M	40	5	43	36	34	32	30	11	23 02 09	British
Kai Granholm	Tapio Lehtinen	MOBIRA	M	40	5	48	38	33	33	31	12	23 02 52P	Finnish
Brian Wells	Barry Sanders	ASSASIN	M	38	5	44	40	38	36	32	13	23 13 06	British
Richard Trafford	James Trafford	HUMBERTS	M	25	7	34	33	35	35	33	3	23 15 59	British
Alan Thomas	John Mansell	JEMIMA NICHOLAS	M	40	5	40	43	39	37	34	14	23 19 26	British
Peter Foot	Robert Wingate	ALIEN II	C	35	6	37	25	40	38	35	4	24 14 00	British
Garry Griffon	Peter Woolland	MY GOODNESS	M	43	4	49	42	36	39	36	4	25 04 55	British
William Ker	Guy Chilver-Stainer	ASSENT	M	32	6	60	55	41	40	37	5	26 05 13	British
Mary Falk	Ann Fraser	QUIXOTE	M	34	6	58	50	48	43	38	6	26 11 52A	British
Jocelyn Waller	Philip Mayne	SILK	M	34	6	25	29	42	41	39	7	26 13 08	British
Meo Vroon	Neils Svendsen	ZEEHAAS	M	37	5	45	41	49	46	40	15	26 14 58	Neth'lds
Richard Everdij	Adriaan Valen	ROBIJN	M	32	6	59	53	44	44	41	8	26 19 45	Neth'lds
Martin Copley	Mark Stubbings	BEEFEATER	M	35	6	55	51	46	42	42	9	26 21 34P	British
John Elliott	Gordon Garman	SHOKI	M	30	7	47	49	43	45	43	4	26 21 41	British
Mik Underdown	Mark Heseltine	BLEISE	M	36	5	61	56	50	49	44	16	27 19 39	British
Hugh Farrant	Angela Farrant	SPRING GOLD	M	34½	6	53	48	47	47	45	10	28 03 53	British

Skipper	Crew	Yacht	Class									Result	Nationality
Thomas Gochberg	Nicholas Bonham	MISTRAL	M	42	4	71	59	51	50	46	5	28 18 55	U.S.A.
Brian Dale	David Baker	WITCH DOCTOR	M	30	7	65	60	54	51	47	5	28 20 54	British
Nigel Wollen	Mick Bettesworth	WISH HOUND	M	33	4	63	62	53	52	48	11	31 12 27	British
Bruno Fehrenbach	Frederique Genres	INTERMEDIATE TECHNOLOGY	M	27	7	69	64	55	54	49	6	32 07 09P	French
Christine Bryan	Sally Harrison	SADLER GIRL	M	26	7	70	65	57	55	50	7	32 20 38	British
Nick Skinnard	Robert Moncur	NEWCASTLE BROWN ALE	M	25½	7	74	67	58	56	51	8	33 05 42P	British
David Flittner	Klaus Koskimies	RAUMA REPOLA	T	45	4	16	19	24	23			Dismasted	Finnish
Simon Frost	Lock Crowther	GLUCOMETER II	C	45	4	18	14	13	11			In collision with Dutch coaster	British
Michael Cozens	Nicholas Barber	GEMERVESCENCE	M	39	5	41	39	37	34			Rtd. Lymington 29/7	British
Jane Freeman	Tod Bainbridge	ABACUS	M	41½	4	62	57	52	58			Crew left on last leg	British
Sam Nelson	Bob Evans	EFG FORESTER	C	31½	6	67	63	56	53			Crew ran out of leave on last leg	British
Mike Whipp	Adrian Thompson	BCA PARAGON	T	60	2	2	1	1				Structural damage, rtd. Peterhead	British
Hywel Price	Keith Taylor-Seddon	TAAL	M	35	6	50	54	45				Dismasted	British
Alan Mitchell	Dougie Barr	SPLASH DOWN	T	30	7	23	28					Rtd. Castle Bay	British
June Clarke	Yumi Murakami	MAX FACTOR	T	40	5	35	30					Rtd. Castle Bay	British
Derick Nesbit	John Beharrell	PACESETTER	M	39	5	39	44					Rtd. Tobermory	British
Rodney Barton	Derek Shaw	LUMBERJACK UK	M	45	4	51	52					Rtd. Castle Bay	British
Ewen Southby-Tailyour	Chris Johnson	SARIE MARAIS	M	34	6	54	45					Skipper ill	British
Cyril Simpson	Frederick Brown	PHANTOM LADY	M	42	4	56	47					Rtd. Tobermory	British
George Jepps	Robert Hinton	ELAN	M	41	4	64	61					Rtd. Tobermory	British
David Searle	David Edmonds	RUINED BRUIN II	M	30	7	66	58					Rtd. Castle Bay	British
Max Ekholm	Johan Willebrand	GEFION	M	30	7	72	66					Rtd. Castle Bay	Finnish
Lothar Kohler	Gert Kohler	HELMSMAN-INTEROCEAN	M		3	20						Rtd. 12/7	German
Jacques Bouchacourt	Herve de Willencourt	BUTTERFLY	C	32	6	31						Structural damage rtd. Donegal	French
Peter Philips	Bob Fisher	NOVELL NETWORK	C	80	1	32						Rigging problems	British
Christopher Shaw	Chris Cannon-Brookes	MICRO METALSMITHS	M	56	2	52						Strained shroud plate	British
Alexander Smith	Douglas Ellis	TUMBLEHOME II	M	32	6	57						Dismasted	British
Colin Ford	Robin Atkinson	TRIFFID	T	36	5	68						Leaking centreplate box	British
John Boyd	Geoffrey Dean	FOREIGN EXCHANGE	M	34	6	73						Rtd. Castle Townsend – rigging failure	British

\# Elapsed time includes time spent in stop-over ports.

Penalties (P against time)

	% of Elapsed Time	Time Penalty
BRITISH AIRWAYS I	0.4	58 mins
FESTIVAL DE LORIENT	0.4	59 mins
THURSDAY'S CHILD	0.8	2 hours 9 mins
MOBIRA	0.1	22 mins
BEEFEATER	0.35	1 hour 35 mins
INTERMEDIATE TECHNOLOGY	0.7	2 hours 3 mins
NEWCASTLE BROWN ALE	0.05	18 mins

ALLOWANCE (A against time)

QUIXOTE   4 hours 26 mins   for standing by another competitor.

1986 PLYMOUTH – NEWPORT

STARTERS 49
FINISHERS 35

STARTED 8 June

CLASSES

I	Over 60 to 85 feet
II	Over 50 to 60 feet
III	Over 45 to 50 feet
IV	Over 40 to 45 feet
V	Over 35 to 40 feet
VI	Over 30 to 35 feet

Pos'n o/a	Class Pos'n	Yacht	Skipper	Co-skipper	Type	LOA	Class	Elapsed Time	Nation
1	1	ROYALE	Loic Caradec	Olivier Despaigne	C	85	I	*13 06 32	French
2	2	FORMULE TAG	Mike Birch	Olivier Moussy	C	80	I	#13 26 50	Canadian/French
3	1	APRICOT	Tony Bullimore	Walter Greene	T	60	II	15 06 44	British/U.S.A.
4	2	BRITISH AIRWAYS I	Robin Knox-Johnston	Bernard Gallay	C	60	II	17 05 42	British/French
5	3	ALCATEL	Olivier Dardel	Richard le Joly	C	60	II	17 06 45	French
6	4	TUNA MARINE VOORTREKKER	John Martin	Robert Sharp	M	60	II	17 13 52	South African
7	5	BISCUITS LU	Guy Bernadin	Steve Callahan	M	60	II	&17 23 16	French/U.S.A.
8	6	COLT	Markku Wiikeri	Antoro Kairamo	M	60	II	19 04 45	Finnish
9	1	INTERNATIONAL	Joe Colpitt	Joseph Culbert	M	35	VI	20 03 13	U.S.A.
10	7	TRANSIENT	Robert Nickerson	Jeffrey Taylor	M	60	II	20 11 17	British
		CHERRY VALLEY			T	35	VI		
		SUPERDUCK			M	60	II		
11	1	BELMONT	Harry Harkimo	Michaela Koskull	M	50	III	22 01 09	Finnish
12	1	HETAERA	Gerry Hannaford	Michael Moody	M	45	IV	22 07 34	British
13	1	BULCON STAR	Tenev Svetlozar	Vasil Poov	M	38	V	22 09 12	Bulgarian
14	2	WRECKLESS	Mark Schwab	Dean Doman	M	47	III	22 12 00	U.S.A.
15	2	SILK	Jocelyn Waller	Roderick Stuart	M	34	VI	22 22 59	British
16	2	SONY HANDYCAM	Kitty Hampton	Mary Falk	M	40	V	23 04 01	British
17	3	TIGO V	Granville Davis	Ramon Page	M	40	V	23 11 57	British
18	4	BLACKJACK	Michael Pocock	Patricia Pocock	M	38	V	23 23 32	British
19	5	MOBIRA	Kai Granholm	Tapio Lehtinen	M	40	V	24 01 12	Finnish
20	6	CURLEW	Edward Brainard II	William Saltonstall Jr	M	38	V	24 09 22	U.S.A.
21	3	SARIE MARAIS	Chris Johnson	Peter Goss	M	34	VI	+25 04 06	British
22	7	JEANTEX III	Wolfgang Quix	Herbert Weingartner	M	40	V	25 12 11	German
23	8	OLLE-P	Hans van Hest	Ferdi Steger	M	40	V	26 09 00	Dutch
24	9	HANSA LADY	Robert Moncur	Nick Skinnard	M	36	V	27 01 24	British
25	4	SNOWBALL	Dieter Kowalewski	Ralf Steinhardt	M	33	VI	27 14 24	German
26	5	ASSENT	William Ker	Alan Perkes	M	32	VI	27 21 50	British
27	10	CARTE BLANCHE	Jeremy Tetley	Maureen Tetley	M	36	V	28 07 15	British
28	2	DOUBLE MAXIM	Joseph Kayll	David Kayll	M	42½	IV	29 05 41	British
29	6	STAAL BANKIERS	Anton Jongbloed	Albert Vesink	M	35	VI	30 03 45	Dutch
30	11	MOTHER GOOSE	Ann Melrose	Eric Vischer	M	40	V	31 08 03	British
31	7	WEST END GIRL	Anthony Blofeld	Ian Hutchings	M	34	VI	31 11 42	British
32	12	SIFO	Michael Petrovsky	Lloyd Hircock	M	40	V	32 05 05	British/U.S.A.
33	13	GIBBS III	Stewart Whiting	Robert Davies	M	36	V	33 14 00	British
34	8	GOLLYWOBBLER	Ann Fraser	Nancy Copplestone	M	32	VI	34 04 55	British
35	9	JENNY WREN	Alan Taylor	Martin Thomas	M	31	VI	34 05 09	British

* Includes 19 mins penalty
\# Includes 4½ hour penalty
& Includes 1 hr 57 min penalty
\+ Includes 9 min penalty

Skipper	Crew	Boat				Notes	Nationality
Edvard Hambro	Richard Blindheim	SASHA X	M	37	V	Finished outside time limit on 14 July	Norwegian
Peter Phillips	Richard Gomes	NOVANET I	C	80		Blew out mainsail, returned to Plymouth	British
Philip Walwyn	Frances Walwyn	SPIRIT of ST KITTS	C	75½		Both hulls damaged, leaking. Retired to St Kitts	Kittitian
Richard Tolkien	David Bartlett	STOCKLEY PARK CHALLENGE	T	53		Float holed, retired to Exmouth	British
John Dean	Richard Reddyhoff	HYTHE MARINA VILLAGE	M	50		Working jib blown out retired to Southampton	British
David von Flittner	Kari Miettinen	YES SIR BOSTON	T	50		Electrical problems returned to Plymouth	British
Laurel Holland	Joan Greene	SEBAGO	C	45		Broke forestay, retired to St John's, Newfoundland.	Finnish
Wojciech Kaliski	Joanna Pajkowska	ALMATUR III	C	45		Dismasted, retired to Plymouth	U.S.A.
Desmond Hampton	Giles Chichester	PANICKER	M	40		Dismasted, retired to Plymouth	Polish
Jaakko Makikyla	Leo Lukjanov	INDEPENDENT	M	40		Put in to Azores for repairs, left there 2nd July for Newport	British
Vladamir Christov	Svetoslav Georgiev	AQUARIUS	M	33		Put into Azores with rudder problem, finished outside time limit, 29th July	Finnish
Peter Hopps	Vivien Cherry	TRIPLE FANTASY	T	35		Broke boom, retired to Plymouth	Bulgarian
David La Roche	David Ryan	NEAR HORIZONS	M	35		Sails blown out, retired to Falmouth	British
Beppe Panada	Roberto Kramar	BERLUCCHI	M	60		Found floating, capsized with keel missing, crew never found.	U.S.A.
							Italy

177

1988 PLYMOUTH – NEWPORT

STARTERS 95 FINISHERS 73 STARTED 5 June

CLASSES
I	Over	
II	50 ft	to 60 ft
III	45 ft	to 50 ft
IV	40 ft	to 45 ft
V	35 ft	to 40 ft
VI	30 ft	to 35 ft
	25 ft	to 30 ft

Skipper	Yacht	Type	LOA	Class	Elapsed Time	Penalty/ Allowance	Corrected Time	Pos'n O/A	Pos'n Class	Nation
Philippe Poupon	FLEURY MICHON	T	60	I	10 09 15		10 09 15	1	1	France
Olivier Moussy	LAITERIE Mt St MICHEL	T	60	I	11 04 17		11 04 17	2	2	France
Loick Peyron	LADA POCH II	T	60	I	11 09 02		11 09 02	3	3	France
Philip Steggall	SEBAGO	C	60	I	11 09 55		11 09 55	4	4	U.S.A.
Bruno Peyron	VSD	C	60	I	12 23 20		12 23 20	5	5	France
Halvard Mabire	GERARD HENON	T	60	I	13 06 51		13 06 51	6	6	France
Florence Arthaud	GROUP PIERRE 1er	T	60	I	13 10 58		13 10 58	7	7	France
Jean Maurel	ELF AQUITAINE III	T	60	I	14 10 02		14 10 02	8	8	France
Pierre Sicouri	LA NUOVA SARDEGNA	T	60	I	15 17 34		15 17 34	9	9	Italy
Tony Bullimore	SPIRIT OF APRICOT	T	60	I	14 20 40	+ 32h 06m	16 04 46	10	10	Britain
Pascall Herold	DUPON DUPAN	T	60	I	16 12 39		16 12 39	11	11	France
Nic Bailey	MTC	T	40	IV	16 17 03		16 17 03	12	1	Britain
Jean Yves Terlain	UAP 1992	M	60	I	17 04 05		17 04 05	13	12	France
John Martin	ALLIED BANK	M	60	I	17 08 18		17 08 18	14	13	S. Africa
Jose Ugarte	CASTROL SOLO	M	60	I	18 04 47	– 07h	17 21 47	15	14	Spain
Mark Rudiger	HOLSTEN OCEAN SURFER	M	40	IV	18 06 28		18 06 28	16	2	U.S.A.
Titouan Lamazou	ECUREUIL D'AQUITAINE	M	60	I	18 07 00		18 07 00	17	15	France
Michael Reppy	DAMIANA	T	42	IV	18 08 28		18 08 28	18	3	U.S.A.
Didier Caquet	TRANSPORTS GRIMAUD	C	40	IV	19 08 28		19 08 28	19	4	France
Stephen Black	EAGLE PREMIER	T	40	IV	19 10 24		19 10 24	20	5	U.S.A.
Courtney Hazelton	MARIKO	M	45	III	21 00 03		21 00 03	21	1	U.S.A.
Nigel Burgess	DOGWATCH A	M	50	II	21 05 44		21 05 44	22	1	Monaco
Roderick Stuart	CALEDONIA	M	30	VI	21 05 46		21 05 46	23	1	Britain
Bertie Reed	INVERTEX VOORTREKKER	M	49	III	21 06 16		21 06 16	24	2	S. Africa
Simon van Hagen	ROC	M	40	IV	21 10 53		21 10 53	25	6	Netherlands
Sennett Duttonhofer	MAN-O-WAR	T	40	IV	21 11 42		21 11 42	26	7	U.S.A.
Richard Wilson	CURTANA	M	35	V	21 14 37		21 14 37	27	1	U.S.A.
Jack Boye	LEGEND SECURITIES	M	50	II	21 17 17		21 17 17	28	2	U.S.A.
Robin Davie	GLOBAL EXPOSURE	M	40	IV	21 22 37		21 22 37	29	8	Britain
Herve Cleris	EMBALLAGE POLSEITE	T	40	IV	22 03 12		22 03 12	30	9	France
Gerry Hannaford	HETAERA OF GRIMSBY	M	45	III	22 07 47		22 07 47	31	3	Britain
Steve Pettengill	FREEDOM	M	40	IV	22 09 08		22 09 08	32	10	U.S.A.
Wolfgang Quix	JEANTEX T 3000	M	40	IV	22 12 11		22 12 11	33	11	W. Germany
Roy Hart	MOON BOOTS	M	45	III	22 12 58		22 12 58	34	4	Britain
Peter Goss	CORNISH MEADOW	C	26		23 03 53		23 03 53	35	1	Britain
Francis Stokes	SPARROW	M	35	V	23 05 04		23 05 04	36	2	U.S.A.
Jim Gardiner	CELOX	M	39	V	23 05 17		23 05 17	37	3	U.S.A.
Gerard Montariol	GAULOISE IV	T	45	III	23 09 39	+ 27H 51m	24 08 56	38	5	France
Morris Propp	HETAERA SAILOR'S GAME	M	43	IV	24 03 26		24 03 26	39	12	U.S.A.
Rupert Kidd	OCEAN WORLD	T	35	V	24 05 09		24 05 09	40	4	Britain
Paul Vinck	GENERALE BANK	M	50	II	24 05 30		24 05 30	41	3	Belgium
Vivien Cherry	PANICKER	M	40	IV	24 06 30		24 06 30	42	13	Britain
Jeremy Heal	ALICE'S MIRROR	M	30	VI	24 23 58		24 23 58	43	2	Britain
Peter Phillips	CHAFFOTEAUX CHALLENGER	M	56	II	25 07 43		25 07 43	44	4	Britain
Jan van Donselaar	RUTH/LESS	M	35	V	25 12 07		25 12 07	45	5	Netherlands
Olivier Dardel	ALCATEL	M	38	V	25 21 15		25 21 15	46	6	France
Vincenzo Fontana	MOANA BIP BIP	M	45	III	26 11 38		26 11 38	47	6	Italy
Are Wiig	SOREN SOPHIE	M	30	VI	26 12 13		26 12 13	48	3	Norway
Cees de Gruyter	RIGHT MEASURE	M	33	VI	26 14 07		26 14 07	49	4	Netherlands
Nigel Rowe	PIPER RISING	M	39	V	27 13 24		27 13 24	50	7	Britain
Peter Hopps	TRIPLE FANTASY	T	35	V	27 16 18		27 16 18	51	8	Britain

Skipper	Yacht	Type	Size	Class	Elapsed	Allowance	Corrected	Overall	Class pos	Nationality
Mary Falk	QUIXOTE	M	34	V	27 16 39		27 16 39	52	7	Britain
Thierry Caroni	ATHOM LE REBELLE	C	56	I	27 17 22		27 17 22	53	17	France
Roland Treinzen	STELLA POLARE	M	40	IV	27 21 30		27 21 30	54	15	W. Germany
James Hatfield	BRITISH HEART III	M	30	VI	28 00 48		28 00 48	55	5	Britain
John Melling	BURAN	M	33	V	28 05 16		28 05 16	56	8	Britain
Peter Keig	ZEAL	M	38	V	28 08 05		28 08 05	57	9	Britain
Anthony Rowe	DREAM WEAVER	M	26	VI	28 22 38		28 22 38	58	6	Britain
Josh Hall	SPIRIT OF IPSWICH	M	34	V	29 23 35		29 23 35	59	10	Britain
Henk van de Weg	PATACHE	M	30	VI	30 11 00		30 11 00	60	7	Netherlands
Jens Anderson	DIVINA	M	30	VI	31 01 45		31 01 45	61	8	Denmark
Michael Petrovsky	AMNESTY INTERNATIONAL	M	29	VI	32 04 48		32 04 48	62	9	Britain
David Rice	TEMARAIRE	M	30	VI	32 13 12	− 3h 30m	32 09 42	63	10	Britain
Clive Shelter	MACCABI	M	32	V	32 16 10		32 16 10	64	11	Israel
John Passmore	LARGO	M	32	V	32 21 40		32 21 40	65	12	Britain
Franco Malingri	MOANA 39	M	39	IV	31 08 27	+ 42h 08m	33 02 35	66	16	Italy
Bertus Buys	SEA BERYL	M	35	VI	33 05 10		33 05 10	67	13	Netherlands
Peter Connole	FREE BIRD	M	30	VI	34 00 16	− 45m	33 23 31	68	11	U.S.A.
Peter Crowther	GALWAY BLAZER OF DART	M	42	III	33 20 07	+ 5h	34 01 07	69	8	Britain
Edward McConnaughey / Denise St Aubyn	ESPRIT	M	30	VI	34 07 20		34 07 20	70	12	U.S.A.
Hubbard	FLYING LIGHT	M	42	III	34 10 00		34 10 00	71	9	Britain
Mike Golding	GAZELLE	T	30	VI	41 14 44		41 14 44	72	13	Britain
Nicholas Barham	WATER BEAR	M	31	V	47 18 30		47 18 30	73	14	Britain

PENALTIES:

SPIRIT OF APRICOT	−	Late qualifying
GAULOISE		Late inspection
MOANA 39		Late inspection
GALWAY BLAZER		Communications shortcomings

ALLOWANCES:

CASTROL SOLO	Standing by TRITON SIFO
FREE BIRD	Investigating distress flare
TEMARAIRE	Diversion to assist in casualty situation 9/6

Skipper	Yacht	Type	Size	Comment	Nationality
Lionel Pean	HITACHI III	T	60	One float detaching from main hull	French
Robin Oakley	STOCKWOOD	T	30	Holed in port float, abandoned yacht	British
Wijtze van der Zee	NEW MAJIC BREEZE	M	45	Hit something, injured one arm and ribs, lost rudder, towed to Cork	Netherlands
Roel Engels	DOORTJE	M	34	Sank after hitting unknown object. Rescued by fishing boat 49°54'N 12°52'W	Netherlands
Chay Blyth	NCR	T	60	Found recent injury too much of a handicap.	British
Thomas Veyron	CONSTRUCTION DORSO	T	30	Retired to France with damaged float.	French
Mike Birch	FUJICOLOUR	T	60	Hit whale, main hull flooded. Made Belle Ile under sail in 11 days, last three without food.	
Goos Terschegget	VOLHARDING	M	41	Retired to Falmouth with injury.	Canadian
John Chaundy	MITAK	M	40	Retired Camaret with rigging problem.	Netherlands
David Sellings	HYCCUP	M	30	Attacked by whales, yacht sank, rescued by ship 48°54'N, 28°45'W after sighting by Nimrod aircraft.	British
Richard Tolkien	WILLIAMS LEA	T	55	Forestay pulled out, 11th June, damaged bow, ret'd Plymouth.	British
Guy Holer-Saliou	LEMTEA	M	50	Sank. Rescued by French trawler in pos. 46°35'N, 40°54'W.	British
Jaques Vuylsteker	JEREMI V	M	35	Retired to Azores, generator problem, running out of time.	French
Arne Yttervik	CUNARD	M	39	Blew out headsails, retired to Norway.	French
Francis Bourgeois	SAFAR	M	36	Retired to Lorient, "no problems".	Norwegian
Robin Knox-Johnston	SUHAILI	M	32	Yacht making water, retired to Plymouth.	French
Alan Thomas	TRITON SIFO	T	39	Starboard float taking water. Towed to Nantucket by US Coastguards.	British
Jacque Dewez	SPERONE	T	40	Problem with yacht taking water over long period of race. Finally retired to Nantucket.	British
William Gilmore	ZAFU	M	38	Retired to Azores	French
John Groves	BEAUNE DRY	M	36	Towed to Halifax N.S. after running into shoal water.	U.S.A.
Noelle Corbett	OUTRAGEOUS	M	39	Overdue, found off Nantucket, with a number of problems. Towed to Woods Hole.	U.S.A.
Michael Richey	JESTER	M	26	Knocked down in heavy weather, lost starboard hatch cover. Boat flooded, unable to stem water flow due to damage. Skipper taken off and yacht taken in tow but later abandoned.	British

1989 ROUND BRITISH ISLES (first 20 results*)

STARTERS 60 STARTED 18 June CLASSES

I	Over 60	to 75 ft
II	" 50	to 60
III	" 45	to 50
IV	" 40	to 45
V	" 35	to 40
VI	" 30	to 35
VII	" 25	to 30

Skipper	Crew	Yacht	Type	LOA	Class	Place at stopovers				Final placing		Elapsed Time	Nation
						CR	CB	LK	LO	o/a	Class		
François Boucher	Loic Lingois	SAAB TURBO	C	75	I	1	2	1	2	1	1	15 07 30	French
Richard Tolkien	Peter Foot	WILLIAMS LEA	T	54	II	2	2	3	1	2	1	16 16 48	British
Mark Gatehouse	Anthony Boalch	QUEEN ANNE'S BATTERY	C	40	V	4	4	4	3	3	1	16 18 07	British
Patrick Morvan	Loic Pochet	MARINA	M	75	I	6	5	5	5	4	2	19 05 29	French
Robert Nickerson	Niall Alexander	DIX DE LYON	M	60	II	8	6	7	4	5	1	19 08 58	British
Rupert Kidd	Alan Mitchell	PANIC MAJOR	T	35	VI	13	8	8	8	6	1	19 18 42	British
Johannes Simonis	Boudewyn Simonis	FIERY CROSS	C	59	II	9	7	6	6	7	3	19 18 43	Netherlands
Peter Hopps	James Chrismas	MINT FUTURES FUNDS	T	35	VI	14	9	9	7	8	2	19 23 48	British
Anthony Sarkies	Michel Sauget	TRIPLE FANTASY	T	40	V	19	13	10	10	9	3	21 02 32	British
A. Pridie	Chris Nickol	AYO	T	35	VI	18	12	11	9	10	3	21 05 02	British
Bob Fisher	Robin Knox-Johnston	A CAPPELLA	M	45	IV	21	14	13	11	11	3	21 11 14	British
Patrick Coulombel	Daniel Molmy	TESCO PEPSI BARRACUDA	T	38	V	10	10	12	12	12	3	21 11 19	French
Richard Trafford	James Trafford	VIDAM	M	30	VII	23	17	15	13	13	1	21 23 42	British
Josh Hall	John Parker	MODI KHOLA	M	50	III	17	18	17	15	14	1	22 12 19	British
Wijte van de Zee	Henk Bezemer	NEW SPIRIT OF IPSWICH	M	45	IV	15	16	14	14	15	2	22 12 53	Netherlands
Simon van Hagen	Jan Willem Kesteloo	NEW MAJIC BREEZE	M	40	V	27	19	18	16	16	4	22 15 07	Netherlands
John Chaundy	Cees de Gruyter	RoC	M	40	V	24	20	21	17	17	5	22 16 57	British
Wolfgang Quix	Herbert Weingaertner	MITAK	M	40	V	32	26	19	18	18	6	22 20 21	German
Robin Ould	Richard Harding	JEANTEX III	M*	40	V	28	25	24	21	19	7	22 23 01	British
Peter Goss	James Getgood	CORNISH COVE	M	35	VI	36	32	28	20	20	3	23 03 40	British
—	—	BENETEAU MARINES											

* At the time of going to press the 1989 Round Britain and Ireland Race was still in progress. The results for the first 20 yachts home are shown here and all participants, both crews and yachts, are listed in the index.

Abbreviations and Glossary

ARGOS	A satellite tracking system
BST	British summer time
CABLE	Nautical measurement of distance about 200 yards ($\frac{1}{10}$th of a nautical mile)
CSTAR	Carlsberg Single-handed Transatlantic Race
DF	Direction finding
DECCA	A navigational radio position fixing system off north west Europe
DOT	Department of Trade
DR	Dead reckoning position arrived at by plotting course and speed
ELT	Electronic Location Transmitter synonymous with EPIRB
EPIRB	Emergency Position Indicating Radio Beacon
GMT	Greenwich Mean Time
IMCO	Inter-governmental Maritime Consultative Organization
IMO	Replaced the title IMCO, above
IYRU	International Yacht racing Union (World authority for yacht racing)
LOA	Length overall
LORAN	Ocean radio navigational system
LWL	Load waterline (Waterline length)
MRSC	Maritime Rescue Sub-Centre
NIMROD	Royal Air Force fixed wing aircraft used in maritime search and rescue operations
OSTAR	Observer Single-handed Transatlantic Race
RAF	Royal Air Force
RBR	Round Britain Race
RCC	Rescue Co-ordination Centre
RDF	Radio direction finder
RFA	Royal Fleet Auxiliary
RORC	Royal Ocean Racing Club, London
RWYC	Royal Western Yacht Club of England, Plymouth
RYA	Royal Yachting Association (British national authority)
SAR	Search and Rescue
SEA KING	Type of helicopter used by the Royal Navy and Royal Air Force
TWOSTAR	Short title for Two-handed Transatlantic Race
WESSEX	Type of helicopter use by the Royal Navy and Royal Air Force
Z	Suffix used to indicate Greenwich Mean Time

Index